THE MYSTERIOUS STRANGER

Universitas Press
Montreal

www.universitaspress.com

Canadian Classics Series Editor: Cristina Artenie

Editorial matter: Dragos Moraru

First published in February 2023

Library and Archives Canada Cataloguing in Publication

Title: The mysterious stranger / Walter Bates.
Names: Bates, Walter, 1760-1842, author.
Identifiers: Canadiana 20230161340 |
ISBN 9781988963433 (softcover) | ISBN 9781988963426 (hardcover)
Subjects: LCSH: Smith, Henry More, active 1812-1836. | LCSH: Criminals—Canada—Biography. | LCGFT:
Biographies. | LCGFT: True crime stories.
Classification: LCC HV6248.S6 B34 2023 | DDC 364.1092—dc23

Walter Bates

THE MYSTERIOUS STRANGER

Edited with an introduction by Cristina Artenie

Universitas Press
Montreal

TABLE OF CONTENTS

INTRODUCTION

by Cristina Artenie

"On the second day of August, 1814, in the afternoon" (the first words of this memoir, first published in 1817), Walter Bates, sheriff of King's County, New Brunswick, received in custody a stranger who had been accused of horse theft. It is through this beginning *in medias res* that Bates's memoir succeeds, even today, to capture the reader's attention. The stranger becomes more and more "mysterious," his actions more and more unexpected, but the narrator remains (or appears to remain) objective. His memoir consists of three parts: a report covering the first three months; a diary of the following ten months; and an account of his research into the stranger's life before and after his imprisonment in Kingston, New Brunswick. It is an example of the true-crime genre, which was quite popular at the turn of the 19th century in both Britain and North America, but it really stands out because, unlike all the other productions of the time, it has two main characters, the criminal and the lawman, and the story is told from the point of view of the latter. Its interest as a piece of literary nonfiction comes precisely from the immediacy of his diary entries; he actually tells the reader, in the beginning, that "The facts stated are not conjured up from memory, having been registered in a journal, kept from day to day, containing the most interesting particulars of [the stranger's] conduct." The style of a diary means, for example, that the first-person pronoun is often absent: "On going into the gaol, found his irons on whole and safe; and to prevent him from using his hands so freely, locked a chain from his fetters to his handcuffs, and left him." Bates also includes letters from magistrates, brief notes from the gaoler, and often employs a shorthand style, jotting down the stranger's ramblings. Literary nonfiction is what 19th-century Canadian authors really excel at; and it is time to assign Bates's memoir the place it deserves for its uniqueness and for its truly compelling story.

WALTER BATES

Walter Bates was born on 14 March 1760 in what was then the eastern part of the township of Stamford, Connecticut (which has grown today into the town of Darien), as the fourth son (and fifth child) of John Bates and Sarah Bostwick. His paternal great-great-grandfather, Robert Bates, was one of the earliest settlers in Connecticut, possibly present as early as 1634 when the town of Wetherfield was founded, and certainly one of the founders of Stamford, in 1641.[1] He died in 1675 in Stamford, Connecticut, and his descendants lived there for another century. When hostilities began in April 1775 between the British army and the American militia, the Connecticut loyalists (known simply as Tories at the time) were a small minority, perhaps ten percent, but they were particularly strong in Fairfield County, in towns like Stamford, Redding, or Norwalk. The young Walter followed in the footsteps of his father and older brothers and remained loyal to the King and Church of England. He was barely fifteen when he was captured by the "rebels," whipped, tortured, and threatened to be hanged or drowned. He told the story of his ordeal many years later (see Appendix II.1. in this volume), together with the story of the last few years of the Revolutionary War, when the Loyalists took refuge on Long Island and then to the western part of what was then Nova Scotia, but was soon renamed New Brunswick.

He came to the new land on the *Union*, a ship that landed in Saint John harbour in May 1783. Most of the people on that ship became the founders of Kingston and of Kings County, where Bates lived the remainder of his life. On 7 October 1784, the first marriage in the settlement of Kingston took place, that between Walter Bates and Abigail Lyon (1764-1820), another passenger on the *Union*, who had arrived with her family. She was the daughter of John Lyon from Redding, Connecticut, a captain in the Prince of Wales' American Regiment, a volunteer unit of Connecticut loyalists, raised by Montford Browne in 1776-1777. The Lyons had settled in Kingston as farmers, but they also managed an inn. For the next twenty-five years, Walter and Abigail farmed their lot on the bank of Kingston Creek (then called Portage Cove), an inlet created by the versatile Saint John River, and raised nine children (five of whom reached adulthood). Then, with a change of generations, Bates was appointed Sheriff of Kings County in 1808 and, one year later, coroner and town clerk. During the first few years as sheriff, the most suspicious people he had to pay attention to, and occasionally arrest, were dissenting ministers (especially Baptist), who were allowed to preach but not to perform marriages (see Hebb 75-76 and Bell 355-366). In 1814, however, his life changed dramatically after he took charge of a "mysterious stranger," brought to the Kingston Gaol all the way from Pictou, Nova Scotia.

The event was a major one: it was "the first instance of horse-stealing" in New Brunswick, as the owner of the horse explained in a letter to Bates (see Epilogue II. 2. in the present volume). For Bates, however, a more important event occurred on Saturday, 24

[1] For his presence in Stamford, see Huntington (especially 28). For his earlier presence in Wetherfield, see Stiles 99 and Chapin 42. Wetherfield was only the second European settlement in Connecticut, after Windsor, in 1633.

September 1814, when the stranger, who called himself Henry More Smith, duped his keepers and escaped. Aware that both he and the jailer might be charged with negligence, Bates decided to prepare for the possibility by writing a report on the stranger's seven-week stay in his town's jail. During the chase that followed, in which he took part and which he supervised, by sending various individuals and posses on the track of the fugitive, Bates also started keeping a diary. He continued his diary after the stranger was captured and brought back to him, filling it with observations on the stranger's behaviour, which became more and more unusual, before, during, and even after his trial. News of the odd behaviour of Bates's prisoner spread throughout the province, and in July 1815, Bates's letter to the Attorney General Thomas Wetmore, reporting on the stranger's doings, was published in the *New Brunswick Royal Gazette* and reprinted in other newspapers. This was the beginning of Bates's career as an author. He retold the story to relatives in his native region and at least one other letter (see Epilogue I. 1 in the present volume) was published by a Connecticut newspaper and reprinted along the east coast of the United States. By September 1816, Bates had an understanding with Arthur Shirley, the editor of the *Portland Gazette*, to publish his memoir in Maine. Being, however, diverted to New York and New Haven, where he visited the two prisons (Bridewell and Newgate) where Smith had been held, he accepted a proposal from Thomas G. Woodward, a prominent printer and publisher in Connecticut, to publish it there. Both Bates's preface and Woodward's deposit of the title in conformity with the Copyright Act of 1790 are dated December 1816. *The Mysterious Stranger* appeared in New Haven in early 1817. In the summer of the same year, a second edition was published, enlarged with the letter from the owner of the horse and a report from the keeper of Newgate.

Bates's book was also published in Halifax the same year and, in two editions towards the end of 1817, in London. Nevertheless, his life went back to normal soon after this and he did not publish anything for the next two decades (though an 1826 contract between Bates and a Saint John printer has survived, suggesting his intention of publishing a volume of religious essays). His youngest daughter Fanny died in 1818; his wife, Abigail, on 6 July 1820. Two other daughters were married in 1821 and 1823. In 1826, Bates himself got remarried to Lucy Smith, widow of Nathan Smith, a physician from Saint John. Ten years later, at the age of seventy-six, Bates was trying to publish a third, enlarged edition of his book, including all the information he had been able to tease out about Henry More Smith, alias William Newman (as he was known during his confinement in Newgate) during the two decades since the publication of the first and second editions. The printer John McMillan of Saint John placed an ad, looking for subscribers. Nothing seems to have come out of this, but Bates's manuscript probably circulated among the connoisseurs. William Cunnabell, a young publisher from Halifax, had the book printed in 1837, then William L. Avery of Saint John published it, with a new preface by Bates, in 1840. Bates had also prepared a kind of personal history of North America and published a prospectus in 1839, again looking for subscribers. Part of this work appeared in 1889 (edited by W. O. Raymond); another part, only in 1984 (edited by D. G. Bell). Bates died on 11 February 1842, in Kingston. *The Mysterious Stranger* continued to be reprinted in New Brunswick, Nova Scotia, and Prince Edward Island during the second half of the 1800s and the first 10-15 years of the following century. He may have had "little interest in literature" (Cogswell 124), as we understand it today, but he clearly had enough interest in writing. He was a teacher in his youth (during the exile on Long Island), when he also wrote bits of poetry; a lay reader in his church; and a member of the influential Society for Promoting Christian Knowledge in London, after 1816.[2]

THE STRANGER

There is no reason to believe any bit of information provided by Henry More Smith about himself. He used many names and all of them are likely to have been aliases. He usually claimed to have been born in England or Scotland, when he did not claim to be a Frenchman. In the beginning of the third edition of his memoir, Bates writes that, when Smith showed up in 1812 in Windsor, Nova Scotia, looking for employment, he "*pretended* to have emigrated lately from England." It is the only time he (finally) expresses his doubt about Smith's origins. He also adds that, "Although an entire stranger, he seemed to be acquainted with every part of the Province." Indeed, Smith can easily find his way around New Brunswick and Nova Scotia; he accurately names the officers of the 99th and 100th Regiments, stationed there; he even has no trouble travelling, by land, river, or sea, down the east coast of the United States. He states that his age is 22 in 1814, but he may have been older. On the one hand, because, in 1836, when he was confined to the Toronto Jail (if Bates is right in identifying him), he gave his age as 55, which would make him about a decade older; on the other hand, because his many various skills would take time to master. He also tells everybody that he came to Nova Scotia "on account of the war." Nobody seems to question this,

[2] One can still wonder to what extent Bates's manuscript of *The Mysterious Stranger* was improved by his editor(s), a question that was reinforced by Bell's publication of the unadulterated version of the manuscript of Bates's historical work. However, Bates, who was 80 at the time, complained of "age and other infirmities" (5) and very possibly dictated the text to somebody else.

though it is not at all clear what he means by that. The only story he tells about himself that might be considered more reliable is the one reported by Washburn (in the second edition of Bates's memoir), because he told it to fellow convicts: while in England, he would have accidentally killed a woman with an overdose of laudanum, while trying to rob a house with a couple of accomplices. This story, too, however, may very well be fabricated.

Some things that we know about Smith are, however, facts. He was employed by John Bond, a former Loyalist soldier from Rawdon, Nova Scotia, between 1812 and 1813, when he eloped with Bond's daughter, Elizabeth. They got married and had at least one daughter, but Elizabeth was later granted a divorce, probably on grounds of abandonment. He spoke at least two foreign languages: French, which he uses when pretending to be a Frenchman; and German, which he spoke with Abraham Gesner's father (see Epilogue II. 3). We know that finding one's way through the forests of New Brunswick was not one of Smith's many skills. He needed a First Nations man to "pilot" him and, when the latter quitted, he had to go back to the beaten track. We have Bates's description of Smith, which was several times reprinted by newspapers. Even after his release from Newgate, a caution to the public and a description of the prisoner, lifted directly from Bates's book, was announced in the *Hartford Courant* (on Tuesday, 16 February 1819). Barbara Grantmyre, writing in 1963, quotes "an old lady, whose grandfather had known Henry at Windsor," and who tells her that Smith looked "foxy" (17). Asked to explain the adjective, the old lady simply says that Smith looked "like a wild fox" (18). Two more things could be said about Smith from the distance of two centuries after Bates put pen to paper. First, the fact that, despite his many robberies and his life of deceit, the death sentence that Smith received in New Brunswick seems exaggerated. However, British criminal code (also followed in British North America) was at the time "the harshest in Europe" (Banner 7) and included over two hundred capital offenses, most of them involving crimes against property. It was, however, quite common to commute such sentences to transportation. This was hardly applicable in British North America (see Girard, Phillips and Brown 286); instead, it was replaced by banishment (which is what happened in Smith's case). Second, Bates expresses plenty of admiration towards Smith; he even confesses that "I am aware that I shall incur the imputation of weakness for narrating many parts of these memoirs;" this admiration survives today, especially in New Brunswick, where "the Lunar Rogue" (as Smith, alias Moon, is better known there) is remembered in museums and on stage.[3]

[3] A play entitled *The Lunar Rogue* was most recently staged in New Brunswick in February 2023.

NEW BRUNSWICK

The people and the landscapes of New Brunswick play an important role, no matter how obscured they may be by the showdown between the sheriff and the fugitive. There are, however, three different versions of New Brunswick that Bates's narrative manages to capture. First, the New Brunswick of 1814-1815 appears to be a result of the very concentrated immigration process of the early 1780s. Loyalists from the same county in New England boarded the same ship and founded new settlements together. In each parish, and even in each county in New Brunswick, the inhabitants knew one another and, quite often, they were related to each other by blood or marriage. With the passage of thirty years, despite some influx of newcomers and some movements within the province, as well as from and to Nova Scotia and the US District of Maine, people were even more related to each other. This created closeknit communities in the countryside, where everybody (including ministers, sheriffs, and justices of the peace) was a farmer; everybody was Anglican; and everybody obeyed the law. The community leaders were mature men, in their 40s and 50s, whether they had an official title or not. They thought they had rebuilt Connecticut in southern and central New Brunswick. They supervised the education of the young and the affairs of the church. They were in charge of the courthouse and they organised posses in pursuit of suspicious individuals or fugitives. This is the most obvious version of New Brunswick in Bates's memoir: Smith is confronted by a community of simple, law-abiding farmers. One of his escape attempts is discovered by Mr. Dibblee, the "gaoler," who is rather old, "infirm" (i.e., sick), and a teacher by vocation. Another attempt is discovered by Mrs. Perkins, the wife of a farmer living nearby. Bates himself was 54 years old when he met Smith, who once calls him "old man."

The second version of New Brunswick is simply a (limited) view of the "world out there," beyond the rural counties. It is a New Brunswick of bustling cities and ports, of merchants who own sloops and schooners, who sell timber and plaster down the Saint John River. It is a New Brunswick ruled by elites who, like Edward Winslow, in a letter to Ward Chipman (the presiding judge at Smith's trial) from 7 July 1783, hoped to create a colony that would be "the most Gentlemanlike one on earth" (qtd. in Conrad and Hiller 106).[4] This version of the province is much more aware of the elites of Fredericton, who come down to Kingston and even threaten to charge the local sheriff with negligence; of the neighbouring Nova Scotia, from where unexpected

[4] The letter was first published in Raymond's *Winslow Papers*, where punctuation was improved.

visitors, including horse thieves, might show up; of the fact that not all inhabitants of New Brunswick were Anglicans, not all were farmers, and not all were white. According to Fisher's *Sketches*, the Parish of Kingston had, in 1824, a population of 1,655 inhabitants, of which 1,636 were white. The same year, 7,930 people lived in King's County, and 74,176 in all of New Brunswick (Martin 254). There had been only an estimated 35,000 in 1817, so the population more than doubled in seven years. With all the newcomers, "The Loyalist mirage of compact, self-sufficient communities of well-disposed subjects had gone" (MacNutt 164).

There is, finally, a third version of New Brunswick, perhaps the least obvious in Bates's narrative, but there nonetheless, mostly hinted at from time to time: New Brunswick as a dangerous place. When Bates's memoir begins, on 2 August 1814, the War of 1812 was still raging. There are many military men whom Smith has met (and robbed) across the province, and one who comes to the Kingston Gaol trying to recruit him. Many soldiers from New Brunswick had gone to Ontario to fight the Americans, while the Maritimes had remained for a long time, for all intents and purposes, neutral. However, in 1814, British troops had occupied parts of Maine and it seemed quite clear to many that those territories would become part of New Brunswick (Bates treats them as such). However, though New Brunswick won the war of 1812, it "lost the peace" (MacNutt 160) and places like Moose Island (mentioned a couple of times in the memoir) were restored to the United States. There were plenty of deserters roaming the province (and Smith is thought to be one more than once); there was smuggling everywhere between New Brunswick and Maine; there was privateering on both sides and the harbours often received captured ships and their cargo (see Conrad and Hiller 111). This time of war encouraged confidence men like Smith; "our property is so much exposed," complained Knox, an Englishman, in a letter only published in the second edition of Bates's book. Danger came also from New Brunswick itself, from its rivers, its seasons, its forests, its fauna. In his own memoirs (see Appendix II. 2), William Cobbett mentioned being afraid of bears. In Bates's memoir, the "mysterious stranger" is too afraid to go through the forest without a First Nations guide, and has to go back, allowing himself to be captured.

THE BOOK

Deciding which edition to use as copy-text was not difficult. Only the first version, published (likely rushed) in early 1817 in New Haven preserves the immediacy of Bates's very personal style. Both the British edition and the second New Haven edition of 1817 have improved punctuation, spelling, and the division into paragraphs, which is clearly the work of local editors. The third edition makes a compelling case, since it contains Bates's last decisions. However, the bulk of the text is the same; all additions (mostly Bates's discoveries post-1817) could be (and have been here) included in epilogues and appendices or mentioned in footnotes; and, more importantly, Bates's decision to retell Smith's story in chronological order was made not on stylistic but rather on moral grounds. He was afraid, from the beginning, that a narrative emplotted around his own point of view, with those first months when he thought the stranger might be innocent and the many months that followed when he could not but admire him, would be too enticing for an unsuspecting reader. In a passage that only appeared in the second edition, he had already taken the first step towards the changes of the third with the following statement:

> If I had felt competent to add such moral reflections as the subject would naturally inspire in a serious and reflecting mind, the work would have been rendered more conducive to the propagation of good morals, and far more worthy of public notice—but conscious of my inability, I have been contented with a simple narrative of facts, which my reputation is pledged to support, and which that reputation is sufficient to substantiate wherever I am known. To expose the deformities of vice, and the consequences of a vicious life, must produce the strongest incentives to virtue—and it would be the author's greatest pride to feel the assurance that the publication of these memoirs should have deterred a single individual from falling into that unhappy course of life, which brought the subject of them to shame and disgrace, and to the verge of a painful and ignominious death. (114-115)

The danger was perceived as real by others as well. The British edition includes a preface from the editor in which "the moral utility" of the book is discussed at length (vii-ix). A review of the book, in the British *Literary Panorama*, warned that *The Mysterious Stranger* might not present "a useful guard against imposture," but that "it is more likely to prove an elementary tract, in the hands of practised villains, by which to initiate young beginners in deceit and crime." Bates realised that the form in which he had presented Smith's story had something to do with his book's moral ambiguity; he had to start with Smith's previous life of crime, so as to cast him as a villain from the beginning: "to render the Work as complete, interesting, and acceptable as possible, it begins with a short sketch of his life and character, from the time of his first appearance at Windsor, in Nova-Scotia, in the year 1812;" "As I have deemed it necessary also, to give the public a description of his person, I have chosen to give it a place in this part of the Work, that the chain of the narrative may be preserved unbroken, as much as possible." Since we are less concerned today with readers being seduced by Smith; since Bates's moral legacy is probably safe; and since the third edition, published toward Bates's life, might have been completed with the help of an amanuensis and/or an editor, the first version has been chosen here as the basis for the present edition. This does not mean that other versions have not been put to use.

In fact, five different editions have been used in the making of the present one. It would be a good idea at this point to take a look at the different versions of the text:

1. The first edition was published in early 1817 by Maltby and Goldsmith of New Haven. Woodward, the printer, claimed the copyright (only citizens and residents of the US could do it) on 27 December 1816. This version includes a preface by Bates (dated December 1816) and a letter to the editor of the *Portland Gazette* (dated September 1816), which do not appear in subsequent editions. The following is the title of the first edition:

The / Mysterious Stranger; / OR / MEMOIRS / OF / HENRY MORE SMITH; / *alias* HENRY FREDERICK MOON; / *alias* WILLIAM NEWMAN: / WHO IS NOW CONFINED IN SIMSBURY MINES, IN / CONNECTICUT, FOR THE CRIME OF BURGLARY. / Containing / *An account of his extraordinary conduct during / his confinement in the gaol of King's Coun- / ty, Province of New-Brunswick, where / he was under sentence of death: // With a statement of his succeeding conduct, be- / fore and since his confinement in Newgate.* // BY WALTER BATES, / Sheriff of King's County. / [short double rule] / NEW HAVEN: / *Published by Maltby, Goldsmith & Co* / [short rule] / T. G. Woodward, Printer. / 1817.

2. The second time Bates's text saw the light of day was in Nova Scotia. First, it was serialised in the *Acadian Recorder* from 10 May to 21 June 1817. Then, in the 7 June 1817 issue, that day's instalment was followed by this notice: "A PAMPHLET, containing the whole account of the Mysterious Character, *Henry More Smith*, during his confinement in New-Brunswick, is just published, and may be had at the Office of the Acadian Recorder—Price, 1*s.* 6*d.*" There was also an ad with similar information on the next page; the notice ran until 21 June, the ad until the 28th. While a copy of the pamphlet may never be recovered, we know that the text serialised by the *Recorder* is the same as the first New Haven edition.

3. The second New Haven edition was published in the summer of 1817 (July or later) and is clearly identified as a "second edition" on the title page. There are improvements in spelling, punctuation, and the division into paragraphs, very likely by the editor(s). Woodward's copyright notice is dated 25 January 1817, suggesting the decision to reprint it was made quite early. We know, however, that it appeared in the summer, because it includes an "Advertisement" from the editor, dated "New-Haven, Con. June 1817." This "advertisement" was placed opposite the copyright notice, at the very beginning of the book, to reassure the reader that the narrative is based on fact and on real people: "To remove every scruple on these grounds, the publishers are able to state, that Mr. BATES is well known to many of the most respectable persons in this town, and in Stamford, his native place, where his connections reside—who saw him here while the first edition of this work was progressing." An additional argument is that of the presence of tangible documents: "The original manuscript of the work, from the pen of Mr. B. is in the hands of the publishers, with other documents and papers from persons named in the narrative, who stand pledged with him to substantiate its truth—and the concurring testimony of Sheriff ROSSITER of this city, and Capt. WASHBURN, the Keeper of Newgate, affords the strongest evidence that no exaggeration was necessary in delineating the character and conduct of this Mysterious Stranger." The second New Haven edition includes many changes in punctuation, spelling, and division of paragraphs. More importantly, it includes new text: first, a letter from Wills Frederick Knox (dated 16 October 1816), which Bates probably received too late to have it inserted in the first edition; second, a report ("Further Particulars") added at the end of the book, after a blank page, which seems to be based on Washburn's report to the New Haven publishers. The "Advertisement" quoted above seems to suggest that Washburn's testimony was not requested by Bates himself. This would explain why Bates did not keep it in the third edition (and why, consequently, it has never been reproduced until now). But why did he also drop Knox's letter, which, with its extra information about Smith's early adventures, would have fit perfectly in the third edition, the way Bates had conceived it?[5] One possibility is that Bates, who, as the editor's notice quoted above suggests, was in New Haven only for the publication of the first edition, did not (or no longer) own a copy of the second when he was preparing the third in the late 1830s.

This is the title of the second New Haven edition:

[5] Bates may have disliked Knox (as Grantmyre suggests in her retelling of the book), but he does give him enough of a voice elsewhere.

[*SECOND EDITION.*] / The / Mysterious Stranger; / OR / MEMOIRS / OF / HENRY MORE SMITH; / *alias* HENRY FREDERICK MOON; / *alias* WILLIAM NEWMAN: / WHO IS NOW CONFINED IN SIMSBURY MINES, IN / CONNECTICUT, FOR THE CRIME OF BURGLARY. / Containing / *An account of his extraordinary conduct during / his confinement in the gaol of King's Coun- / ty, Province of New-Brunswick, where / he was under sentence of death: // With a statement of his succeeding conduct, be- / fore and since his confinement in Newgate.* // BY WALTER BATES, / High Sheriff of King's County, New-Brunswick. / [short double rule] / NEW HAVEN: / *Published by Maltby, Goldsmith & Co* / [short rule] / T. G. Woodward, Printer. / 1817.

4. The first British edition appeared in late 1817 (it includes a portrait of Smith dated October of that year). It also includes a preface by the editor, who confesses almost succumbing to the temptation "to make some alterations in the style of writing, and provincial phraseology, of the Author" (xi), but finally deciding that its "stamp of originality, and with it, in great measure, the pledge of veracity, would have been lost" (xii). (This is not entirely true, since the spelling and punctuation differs from that of the New Haven editions.) Moreover, he finds that "The Narrative, as it is now printed, affords, in its *manner*, an amusing specimen of the English language, as it is ordinarily spoken on the eastern coast of America, together with some striking indications of the state of local society and manners. As to the language merely, the terms and phraseology are what are usually termed *Yankee*—a mixture, first, of words properly provincial or peculiar—and secondly, of forms of speech that are merely illiterate, and that are spoken and written, though rarely *printed*, among ourselves" (xii). The same editor added footnotes clearly identified as belonging to him (others are not, which suggests they were added by somebody else, maybe even Bates) as well as a "Postscript. By the Editor" on Caraboo, a female impostor from Bristol, to whom "Smith," or rather "Moon," was being compared. A brief description of all places mentioned in Bates's narrative was also added at the beginning of the volume and it is not signed. This edition has sometimes been called "Companion for Caraboo," which is really only a superimposed tagline, not to be confused with the actual title. (The British reviewer for *The Literary Panorama*, mentioned above, was aware of this and did not include it in the title he gave Bates's book.) It is, instead, the first edition that foregrounds the name "Moon," to the detriment of "Smith," which had been preferred by the previous versions and would be preferred by the subsequent ones. Here is its title:

COMPANION FOR CARABOO. / [short rule] / A NARRATIVE OF / *THE CONDUCT AND ADVENTURES* / OF / HENRY FREDERIC MOON, / *alias* HENRY FREDERIC MORE SMITH, / *alias* WILLIAM NEWMAN, / **A Native of Brighthelmstone, Sussex,** / AND NOW UNDER SENTENCE OF IMPRISONMENT, / IN CONNECTICUT, IN NORTH AMERICA; / CONTAINING AN ACCOUNT OF / HIS UNPARALLELED ARTIFICES, IMPOSTURES, / MECHANICAL INGENUITY, &C. &C. / DISPLAYED / *During and subsequently to his Confinement in one of His Majesty's Gaols in / the Province of New Brunswick.* / [short rule] / By WALTER BATES, Esq. / HIGH SHERIFF OF KING'S COUNTY, IN NEW BRUNSWICK. / [short rule] / with / **An Introductory Description of New Brunswick**; / AND A POSTSCRIPT, / CONTAINING SOME ACCOUNT OF CARABOO, / THE LATE FEMALE IMPOSTOR, AT BRISTOL. // WITH A PORTRAIT. / [rule] / **London:** / PRINTED FOR ALLMAN AND CO. PRINCES-STREET, HANOVER- / SQUARE; / AND SOLD BY ALL OTHER BOOKSELLERS. / 1817.

5. A second edition, unchanged, of the British version appeared the same year. It is practically a second print run, evidence of the book's success.

More evidence comes from the fact that extracts of Bates's memoir (from the British edition) were included in J. Hudson's *The Chronicle of Infamy; or, Authentic Memoirs of the Most Remarkable Characters Who Have Violated the Laws of Their Country, Collected from Authentic Sources of Information* (London: W. Emans, 1820). The New Haven editions were sufficiently known in the United States and *The Mysterious Stranger* is casually mentioned in an anonymous review of John Reid's *Essays on Hypochondriacal and other Nervous Affections* dated "Philadelphia, June 12, 1817" and published in the prestigious *Analectic Magazine* (Thomas Jefferson was a subscriber). To the "many curious instances . . . of the control which our will has over the diseases of the body" (62), the reviewer adds "that of a person, who, under the name of William Newman, has given so much trouble to the sheriffs and jailors of New Brunswick and of New England. When he was first confined in gaol, he so admirably counterfeited a quick consumption, through all its stages of raising blood, and progressive debility, that the doctors in the neighbourhood were completely deceived. He was thrown into jail on the 2nd of August, 1814; but it was not till the 22nd of September, that his dissolution was threatened. Towards evening of that day, the jailor's son entered the prison and found Newman already cold to the knees. The dying man asked for a hot brick to warm them; and, while honest John (that was the name of the jailor's son) went out to get it for him, he leapt out of bed; escaped from the prison, and eluded the vigilance of all his pursuers" (63). The title of the book is quoted in a footnote, in which the reviewer explains that "No man, who has read the book, can have the least doubt, as to the authenticity of the marvellous facts which it contains. It is written by Walter Bates, the sheriff, who had the most to do with the prisoner."

Nevertheless, the book seems to have been forgotten during the two decades that followed, when two editions appeared, both of which are in contention as "third edition."

6. The first was published in Halifax, probably in 1837, with the following title:

THE / MYSTERIOUS STRANGER; / OR, / MEMOIRS OF THE NOTORIOUS / HENRY MORE SMITH. / CONTAINING / A CORRECT ACCOUNT OF HIS EXTRAORDINARY CONDUCT DURING / THE THIRTEEN MONTHS OF HIS CONFINEMENT IN THE JAIL / OF KING'S COUNTY, PROVINCE OF NEW BRUNSWICK, / WHERE HE WAS CONVICTED OF HORSE STEALING, / AND UNDER SENTENCE OF DEATH. / ALSO, / A SKETCH OF HIS LIFE AND CHARACTER, / From his first appearance at Windsor, in Nova Scotia, in the / year 1812, to the time of his apprehension and confinement. / TO WHICH IS ADDED / A HISTORY OF HIS CAREER, / UP TO THE LATEST PERIOD, / EMBRACING AN / **Account of his Imprisonments and Escapes**. / COMPILED FROM THE MOST AUTHENTIC SOURCES. / [short rule] / HALIFAX, N. S. / PRINTED BY W. CUNNABELL—37 GRANVILLE STREET.

Though the year is missing, the Cunnabell edition cannot be from 1835 (as it has sometimes been said), since it mentions in the text a letter from 18 September 1836 (also it is generally assumed that William Cunnabell did not take over the business of his brother Jacob before 1836). Cunnabell probably stepped in and published the manuscript that was being advertised by John McMillan in the spring of 1836. This version does not include a preface and the very last paragraph (a reworking of a line from Revelations) is missing.

7. The other, which will be referred to in the present volume as "the third edition," was published in 1840 by William L. Avery in Saint John, New Brunswick. The title is a little different (Smith is "noted," rather than "notorious," as he appears in the Cunnabell edition) and Bates is identified as the author of all three editions, including this one, which has been "revised, enlarged, and improved." There are hundreds are small differences in spelling and punctuation between the two competing editions. Bates prepared a special preface for Avery's (acknowledging that he wrote it for an edition published later than Cunnabell's, since "upwards of twenty years have now elapsed"), and there is an extra paragraph at the end. This is the title of Avery's edition:

THE / MYSTERIOUS STRANGER; / OR, / Memoirs of the Noted / HENRY MORE SMITH, / CONTAINING / A correct account of his extraordinary conduct during the Thir- / teen Months of his confinement in the Jail of King's Count- / ty, Province of New-Brunswick, where he was convic- / ted of horse stealing, and under sentence of death. / ALSO, / A Sketch of his Life and Character, from his first appearance at / Windsor, in Nova-Scotia, in the year 1812, to the time / of his apprehension and confinement! / *To which is added—A History of his Career up to the present time, / embracing an Account of his Imprisonments and Escapes.* / SELECTED FROM THE MOST AUTHENTIC SOURCES, BOTH PUBLIC / AND PRIVATE. / [short rule] / **THIRD EDITION**, / *Revised, Enlarged, and Improved,—by* WALTER BATES, *Author / of the First and Second Editions.* / [short double rule] / SAINT JOHN, N. B. / PRINTED AT THE BRUNSWICK PRESS, PRINCE WILLIAM STREET, / **By WILLIAM L. AVERY**, / AND SOLD BY HIM, WHOLESALE AND RETAIL. / [short rule] / 1840.

In the seven decades than followed, there were several other editions (at least seven in the 19th century and two in the early 20th), published throughout the Maritimes, reproducing either Cunnabell's (more often) or Avery's version. Avery's was the base for George W. Miller's reprint in Southampton, NB (1855), though this version does not include the information that it is the third edition. Miller's edition was later reproduced by the press of Haszard & Owen in Charlottetown. It is, however, not easy to keep track of all the reproductions and, as Gwendolyn Davies observed, "No enumerative bibliography has ever been done on Bates's book" (43n3).

8. One of the more (aptly) mysterious versions of Bates's book is what will be mentioned here as "the Barry edition." James Barry, a miller and fiddler from Nova Scotia who moonlighted as a printer and bookbinder (see Samson), used the text published by George W. Day in 1856 (based on Cunnabell). His version includes a rather perfunctory preface on Bates's reliability and, more importantly, three letters signed by witnesses from Nova Scotia, who met Smith before or at the time of his arrest in July 1814 (reproduced in this volume in Epilogue II. 3). The letters are dated 1857 and 1863, but it is not clear if Barry found them in another version of the book (published by Day after 1856 or by someone else) or if he himself collected them. His volume apparently dates from 1891, but Barry (born in 1819) could have met the three witnesses (though it is more likely he obtained them from someone else). This is the title of this (pirated) edition:

THE / MYSTERIOUS STRANGER, / OR, / MEMOIRS OF THE NOTED / HENRY MORE SMITH. / CONTAINING / *A correct account of his Extraordinary conduct during the / Thirteen Months of his Confinement in the Jail of Kings County, / Province of New Brunswick, where he was convicted of Horse- / Stealing, and under sentence of death, and finally pardoned / and set at liberty.* / ALSO, / **A Sketch of his Life and Character**. / *From his first appearance at Windsor, in Nova Scotia, in the year* / 1812, *to the time of his apprehension and Confinement.* / TO WHICH IS ADDED / A HISTORY OF HIS CAREER / Up to 1841, embracing an account of his / IMPRISONMENTS AND ESCAPES. / Selected from the most Authentic sources, both Public and private. // BY WALTER BATES, ESQUIRE. // SAINT JOHN, NEW BRUNSWICK. / ORIGINALLY PRINTED BY GEORGE W. DAY, 4, MARKET STREET. / 1856.

9. A special mention deserve 20th- and 21st-century retellings of Bates's narrative. Barbara Grantmyre's 1963 *Lunar Rogue* is a modern retelling of the story. Grantmyre used "the Hants County edition, published in 1912, seventh edition" (13), based on Bates's own third edition, which means she also retells the story beginning in 1812. She also keeps some of Bates's mistakes from this version: for example, Pearson is first called Parsons. Smith's conversations (with Bates and others) are rearranged so as to look like the dialogue of a novel. She also adds conversations with two or three old people whose grandparents had seen Smith (she prefers to call him "Moon") and a couple of old supernatural "tales, not in Bates's book, [which] are part of the folklore of the Rawdon region" (19), mostly involving Smith's taking advantage of his good relationship with the devil. The story was retold again in 2006, in "Abatos," a poem in Peter Sanger's *Aiken Drum.* Sanger showcases the poetical virtues of Bates's simple narrative by arranging them in stanzas. The first half of the 20-page poem is very literal; the second half more and more metaphorical, as Smith's most unusual sayings are re-placed in different contexts.

Of all these versions of the text, five have been used in the present volume: the first New Haven edition (the copy-text); the second New Haven edition (for Knox's letter; Washburn's report; and some minor differences); the British edition, in its two print runs (for the footnotes and the anonymous description of New Brunswick); the Avery "third edition" (for all the extra material, including Bates's preface, as well as various minor differences, which are identified in footnotes); and the so-called "Barry edition," for the letters from Nova Scotian witnesses.

Interest in Bates's book has been sparse in the last century and a half. In 1889, when his other memoir (about the Loyalists of 1783) was published, a review by Jonas Howe remarked its "great local historic value" (80). A 1927 review in the *Dalhousie Review*, signed by the American Ernest Sutherland Bates, did little more than narrate the plot of the book. Though Bates's memoir should stand out in Canadian literary history as one of the first productions by a New Brunswicker, one of the first prose works that is not a mere description of a province or a travelogue, and one of the first nonfictional works ever to introduce such a vast array of real, simple people as its characters, it has long been overlooked mainly because it did not fit into the traditional literary-historical master narrative of the "rise of the novel" (and of fiction in general). One of the most influential assessments of *The Mysterious Stranger* came six decades ago from Fred Cogswell, in the *Literary History of Canada*, where the book was discussed in a section on Maritime fiction.[6] Cogswell conceded that it "was actually designed as biography rather than as fiction, as it presents an illusion of reality much more vividly than any of the works mentioned above [i.e., 19th-century fiction from the Maritimes]. . . . Its subject, the simplicity of its style, and the seeming truth of its background make *The Mysterious Stranger* still a readable book. One feels that it achieves its modest success because its author was not sufficiently acquainted with popular British fiction to spoil it by imitation" (Cogswell 124-125).

Cogswell also compares Bates's style with Defoe's, which rings somewhat true, though Bates's language and references all belong to the early 19th century. He does have something of Defoe's journalistic intensity. However, more interesting seems the connection (also suggested by Cogswell at the end of the quotation above) with "popular British fiction." The link was taken further a few years ago by David Skene-Melvin, writing about Canadian crime writing. He calls *The Mysterious Stranger* "The earliest crime novel on the Canadian literary scene" and "Canada's contribution to what were known as 'Newgate novels'" (125). Skene-Melvin, who repeats some of Cogswell's assessments, as well as the desire to somehow turn nonfiction into fiction, is too hasty in his comparison: the so-called Newgate novels are mostly a phenomenon of the 1830s and 1840s; and Bates's memoir is clearly an example of the "true crime" genre.[7] A link could be made, on the other hand, to the often reprinted and enlarged *Newgate Calendar*, which included many stories of criminals, some centuries old. In her

[6] So little known was Bates's book 60 years ago that Cogswell initially wrote that *The Mysterious Stranger* was "published in London in 1817 and afterwards pirated several times in the United States." He removed this sentence in the second edition (1976).

[7] Skene-Melvin is also wrong in stating that Bates put together "what is purportedly Smith's true-life confession," which is why he concludes the book is Bates's "contribution to the plethora of real or invented life stories of criminals that were popular at the time." In reality, unlike those popular lives of criminals, Bates's narrative stands out because it is told from the point of view of the lawman. Any "confession" from Smith is rejected as deceitful.

accurate (but all too brief) analysis of Bates's memoir, Gwendolyn Davies refers to Daniel A. Cohen's analysis of "New England crime literature" and she is right to do so. Of course, the popularity of the genre in that particular area of the United States must have encouraged Bates's publishers in 1817 and certainly had a role in the relative success of the book. However, all the nonfictional books and pamphlets discussed by Cohen are autobiographical narratives of the criminals themselves. The true-crime genre at the turn of the 19th century belongs indeed to memoirs of criminals like those of Stephen Burroughs (1798) and Henry Tufts (1807). What Bates produced is an early example of the true-crime genre in which the story is told from the point of view of the lawman. Though it remains nonfiction and it lacks that important ingredient of detective stories which is the gradual discovery of the criminal, *The Mysterious Stranger* is a step forward in the development of detective fiction, a genre which emerged in the 1840s and which actually took its inspiration from nonfictional stories told by lawmen.

Works cited

A General Account of the Society for Promoting Christian Knowledge. London: Ann Rivington, 1816.

Banner, Stuart. *The Death Penalty: An American History.* Cambridge, Mass.: Harvard University Press, 2002.

Bates, Ernest Sutherland. "Nor Iron Bars a Cage." *Dalhousie Review* 7: 4 (January 1928), 456-465.

Bates, Walter. *Kingston and the Loyalists of 1783. With Appendix—The Diary of Sarah Frost.* Ed. W. O. Raymond. Saint John: Barnes & Co., 1889.

Bell, D[avid] G[raham], ed. "Walter Bates on the Rise of Religious Dissent." *The Newlight Baptist Journals of James Manning and James Innis.* Saint John: Acadia Divinity College, 1984. 355-366.

Chapin, Alonzo B. *Glastenbury for Two Hundred Years: A Centennial Discourse.* Hartford: Case, Tiffany, 1853.

Cogswell. "Literary Activity in the Maritime Provinces (1815-1880)." *Literary History of Canada: Canadian Literature in English.* Ed. Carl F. Klinck. Second edition [Reprinted with corrections]. Toronto: University of Toronto Press, 1977 [1976]. 1: 116-138.

Cohen, Daniel A. *Pillars of Salt, Monuments of Grace: New England Crime Literature and the Origins of American Popular Culture, 1674-1860.* Amherst: University of Massachusetts Press, 2006 [1993].

Conrad, Margaret R., and James K. Hiller. *Atlantic Canada: A History.* Don Mills, Ont.: Oxford University Press, 2015.

Davies, Gwendolyn. "Loyalist Literature in New Brunswick, 1783-1843." *New Brunswick at the Crossroads: Literary Ferment and Social Change in the East.* Ed. Tony Tremblay. Waterloo: Wilfrid Laurier University Press, 2017. 19-44.

Fisher, Peter. *Sketches of New Brunswick . . . By an Inhabitant of the Province.* Saint John: Chubb & Sears, 1825.

Girard, Philip, Jim Phillips, and R. Blake Brown. *A History of Law in Canada.* Volume One: Beginnings to 1866. Toronto: University of Toronto Press, 2018.

Grantmyre, Barbara. *Lunar Rogue.* Fredericton: Brunswick Press, 1963.

Hebb, Ross N. *The Church of England in Loyalist New Brunswick, 1783-1825.* Madison: Fairleigh Dickinson University Press, 2004.

Howe, Jonas. "Publications Received." *Canadiana. A Collection of Canadian Notes Published Monthly* I: 5 (May 1889) 79-80.

Huntington, E[lijah] B[alwin]. *History of Stamford, Connecticut.* Stamford: by the Author, 1868.

MacNutt, W[illiam]. S[tewart]. *New Brunswick: A History, 1784-1867.* Toronto: Macmillan, 1984 [1963].

Martin, R[obert] Montgomery. *The British Colonies; Their History, Extent, Condition and Resources.* British North America, Vol. II. London: J.&F. Tallis, 1850.

Raymond, W[illiam]. O[bder]., Ed. *Winslow Papers, A.D. 1776-1826.* Saint John: The Sun Printing Company, 1901.

"[Reid on Insanity]. Review of *Essays on Hypochondriacal and other Nervous Affections.* By John Reid." *The Analectic Magazine* 10 (July 1817), 61-73.

Samson, Daniel. "Is This a James Barry Edition?" *Rural Colonial Nova Scotia.* 29 August 2019. https://danieljosephsamson.com/uncategorized/is-this-a-james-barry-edition/

Skene-Melvin, David. "Canadian Crime Writing in English." *Detecting Canada: Essays on Canadian Crime Fiction, Television, and Film.* Eds. Jeannette Sloniowski and Marilyn Rose. Waterloo: Wilfrid Laurier University Press, 2014. 19-51.

Stiles, Henry R. *Families of Ancient Wethersfield, Connecticut.* Part I. Westminster, Md.: Heritage, 2007.

NOTE ON THE TEXT

For reasons expressed in the introduction, the text used here is that of the first New Haven edition of 1817. Additional text from the second New Haven edition has been used in the section entitled "Epilogue." Footnotes from the British edition of 1817 have been included among the footnotes of the present edition. Other material from that version is present here in the epilogue and the appendices. New material from the third edition (i.e., the 1840 version by Avery; see again the Introduction) has been used in the epilogue, but many minor changes have been signalled in the footnotes. Wherever changes operated in the third edition are mentioned in the footnotes, but there is no mention to the second edition, that is because the first and the second editions do not differ (punctuation changes are not signalled). Letters added to the so-called Barry edition are included in the epilogue. Texts by other authors and other productions by Walter Bates, included in the epilogue and appendices, are preceded by a brief introduction in different typeface.

The spelling, punctuation, and division into paragraphs are those of the first New Haven edition. Any significant changes operated in either the second or the third edition are mentioned in footnotes. In the epilogue and the appendices, brackets are used around the name of an author when authorship is doubtful and around the title of a text when that title has been created for the purposes of this volume.

THE

Mysterious Stranger;

OR

MEMOIRS

OF

HENRY MORE SMITH;

alias HENRY FREDERICK MOON;

alias WILLIAM NEWMAN:

WHO IS NOW CONFINED IN SIMSBURY MINES, IN CONNECTICUT, FOR THE CRIME OF BURGLARY.

Containing
An account of his extraordinary conduct during his confinement in the gaol of King's County, Province of New-Brunswick, where he was under sentence of death:

With a statement of his succeeding conduct, before and since his confinement in Newgate.

BY WALTER BATES,
Sheriff of King's County.

NEW-HAVEN:
Published by Maltby, Goldsmith & Co
T. G. Woodward, Printer.
1817.

Title page of the first edition,
published in early 1817 in New Haven, Connecticut.

The portrait of the "Mysterious Stranger"
(based, no doubt, on Bates's description of him),
from the British edition of the book.
It was also reproduced in J. Hudson's 1820 *The Chronicle of Infamy* (between pages 320 and 321), where it is identified as produced in "London. Published by H. Gray No. 2 Barbican." H. Gray was a London printer.

TO THE READER.

Having received repeated solicitations from Portland, New-York, Connecticut, and other parts of the U. States, as well as from many persons in the Provinces of New-Brunswick and Nova-Scotia, to publish the facts attending the conduct of *Henry More Smith*, while in my custody, I have complied with them, and now lay before the public the succeeding Narrative. The facts stated are not conjured up from memory, having been registered in a journal, kept from day to day, containing the most interesting particulars of his conduct. This journal was commenced from necessity; to enable the Sheriff and Gaoler to traverse the indictments found against them for suffering him to escape from prison. As it proceeded it grew interesting, and is now transformed into these memoirs.

Proposals were issued for publishing the work at Portland, and I left Kingston with the view of having it published there, but a fortuitous circumstance having brought me to New-York, and having connections in Connecticut, of which I am a native, I concluded, after identifying *William Newman* as the same person I had had in custody at Kingston, to collect the facts attending his conduct in this part of the country, and to publish the work here. This explanation will account for the address of the following letter to the Editor of the Portland Gazette.

Since my arrival here, I have been twice to Newgate[1] to see him, and have found to my own satisfaction, that he is acting a farce there, perhaps not less astonishing than his preceding conduct; by which he has already relieved himself from labour, and I have no doubt still contemplates his liberation.

W. B.

NEW-HAVEN, DEC. 1816.

[1] Today known as Old New-Gate Prison, a historical site in East Granby, Connecticut. It operated as a prison between 1773 and 1827. See also note 171.

The Guard-House and the entry to the former Simsbury Mines, turned into the Newgate prison. Though Bates never mentions it, he would have been perfectly aware that Newgate had been used as a prison for Connecticut loyalists during the American Revolutonary War.

To the Editor of the Portland Gazette.[2]

SIR,

I have received your proposals for printing memoirs of *Henry More Smith*, alias *Moon*, alias *Newman*, now supposed to be in Newgate prison, in Connecticut, requesting a correct statement of his character and conduct, while in the provinces of Nova-Scotia and New-Brunswick, to be published under the title of "*the Mysterious Stranger*."

It would be satisfactory to the public mind, no doubt, to have the life of such an uncommon character traced back to its origin; his conduct, however, while in these provinces, has been such, that no credible information can be ascertained, who he was, where he came from, or by what means he came into these provinces. He was not known to follow any particular profession, but was said to execute to perfection any branch of mechanism that came to his hand. He made no enquiries, but appeared to know every thing, and every place. He was seen in all parts of Nova-Scotia; but no one knew his business. He formed a connection by marriage in a respectable family at Rawdon,[3] in Nova-Scotia; but still remained a stranger. He was found to possess a wonderful command of his mind, his passions, and the natural powers of his body, and the art of deceiving to perfection. In short, as far as I have been able to collect his whole conduct for about three years in these provinces, was a scene of mystery and wonder.

Thirteen months he was in my custody; and experience gave me some knowledge of his character. I wish it could have fallen to a more able pen to delineate his conduct, but as I have undertaken the task, I shall confine myself wholly to a statement of facts, and, however unaccountable they may appear, *I pledge myself, and every person named in the Narrative* for the

[2] The editor of the *Portland Gazette* (established in Portland, Maine, in 1798) was, at the time, Arthur Shirley (1782-1864).

[3] Rawdon was a township in Nova Scotia, settled by United Empire Loyalists in 1782. In 1861, it became part of the municipality of East Hants.

truth of what is related of him while in my custody. Those facts derived beyond my own knowledge are from creditable sources, and are undoubtedly authentic.

I have learnt satisfactorily that *William Newman*, now confined in Newgate, in the State of Connecticut, is the same person who was in my custody, and I have no doubt that these memoirs will be interesting to the American people.

I shall, therefore, with deference to the public, begin my statement, with my first receiving him into custody, relating what took place while in my charge, including the information I have received from other parts of the British provinces, and from the United States, up to the present time. Sensible as I am of my own inability, and the imperfect state in which it must appear from my hands, I hope only that no unworthy motives will be attributed to me, by an indulgent public.

WALTER BATES,

Sheriff of King's County, New-Brunswick.

KINGSTON, Sept. 1816.

MEMOIRS
OF
HENRY MORE SMITH, alias MOON, alias WILLIAM NEWMAN.

On the second day of August, 1814, in the afternoon, I was called upon by WILLS FREDERIC KNOX, Esq. resident in the parish of Norton, Kings County, Province of New-Brunswick, son of the celebrated WILLIAM KNOX, Esq. formerly Under Secretary of State, and Agent for the Province of New-Brunswick and Prince Edward Island,[4] who requested me to take into custody and confine in the gaol of the said County of Kings, a decent looking young man by the name of HENRY MORE SMITH, who, he informed me, had been apprehended for stealing and carrying away a valuable horse from him, on the 20th of July last;[5] and that he had himself pursued him into the Province of Nova-Scotia, as far as Pictou,[6] a distance of 270 miles,[7] which the prisoner had performed in three days—That, by procuring fresh horses, he overtook him on the 24th, and had

[4] William Knox (1732-1810) had been under-secretary of state for the American colonies (1770-1782). The province of New Brunswick, as a territory where land grants could be provided to the expelled Loyalists, was created (at least in part) at his suggestion. Knox sent his youngest son, Wills Frederick (1783-1825) to occupy the family grant in the new province. Wills became a justice of the peace, churchwarden, and tavern keeper.

[5] In the diary (first published in 1993) of Azor Hoyt (1770-1842), a resident of the parish of Hampton (south of Norton), the theft ("W.F. Knox's horse stolen out of the pasture") is reported as having occurred on the 19th of July. This is confirmed by Knox's letter (see "Epilogue, Part II"): Knox discovered the theft on the 20th, but it must have occurred the night before.

[6] Pictou (pronounced "Pick-toe") is a small coastal town in Nova Scotia (with a population of a little over 3,000). In the early 19th century, however, it was a major entry point for Scottish immigrants, and an 1817 census counted 8,737 inhabitants. The population almost tripled in the following two decades.

[7] The source of this number is probably Knox's letter (see note 31), only used for the second edition. It was changed to 170 miles in the third edition. The real distance is about 200 miles.

him apprehended by John Pearson, Deputy Sheriff at Pictou,[8] and taken before the Justices, in their Court, then sitting at that place[9]—that he had recovered his horse, a watch, and fifteen guineas,[10] found with the prisoner—and obtained a warrant of conveyance[11] through the several Counties to the County of Kings, in order there to take his trial—that he had found him to be a great villain; that he assumed different names; had committed depredations on the road to Pictou—and attempted several times to make his escape from the Sheriffs—that if it had not been for his own vigilance, they would not have kept him—that he had thus brought him safe to prison—and unless he was well taken care of he would effect an escape yet. I replied, Sir, I think you deserve credit for your exertions in pursuing the thief, and recovering your horse; but if such is his character, I cannot thank you for bringing him to me; I had much rather you had left him to his fate in that Province. I fear we shall have much trouble with him, (which was verified in the extreme, as will appear in the sequel.) I shall take care, however, that he does not escape very easily.—He was then received into prison, on the warrant of conveyance, for examination, without a regular commitment.

The prisoner came on horseback—it was raining and near night. Having rode all day, he was very wet; and not having a shift of clothes, and the stove out of order in the criminals' room in the prison; I directed the gaoler to put him hand-cuffed into the debtors,[12] and give him fire, that he might dry himself, or his health would be in danger. The day following he was removed into the criminals' room, which being very strong, irons were considered unnecessary—and as he appeared to be very inoffensive, his handcuffs were taken off, and being provided with a comfortable birth,[13] with straw and blankets, he seemed

[8] John Pearson (1792-1844), a native of Truro (see note 24). In the third edition, he is mistakenly called "John Parsons." He was the son of Colonel Thomas Pearson (1757-1818).

[9] Following a long-established British tradition, local courts (called quarter sessions) sat four times a year to review cases that could not be tried by justices of the peace.

[10] Guineas (coins worth 21 shillings, i.e., one pound one shilling) remained in circulation until 1816.

[11] Not usually called a warrant, but rather a written order by the judge requiring that a prisoner be delivered to another court and/or prison.

[12] Most prisons in Canada had special rooms for debtors. Imprisonment for debt in New Brunswick was abolished in 1874.

[13] "Berth" (as it appears in the third edition) was still often spelled "birth" in the early 1800s.

reconciled to his situation. He wished for an opportunity to send for his portmanteau, which he said he had left, with some other articles, in the care of Mr. Joseph Stackhouse, near St. John,[14] and which contained his clothes. He stated that all his money had been taken from him, and that he must sell his clothes to purchase necessaries, and procure a lawyer, as he was a stranger in this country and knew nobody, and had no friends to help him—that he was young, only twenty-two years of age, and had never seen a court, or knew any thing about the law—and had not been in America more than one year and a half—that he came from England on account of the war; that he was born in Brighton;[15] that his father and mother were living there now, and that he expected them to come out to Halifax next spring, as he had lately purchased a valuable farm on the river Philip[16] and had wrote to them to come—that he had rode to Saint John on business, and saw Col. Daniels of the 99th regiment[17]—who enquired of him if he knew a horse that would span[18] with one that he drove in his carriage—he said he thought he did—the Colonel told him

[14] Saint John was the province's largest city, a commercial hub, and a major port of entry. When Bates's narrative begins, it had around 5,000 inhabitants (Acheson 5). Saint John County is contiguous to the south border of King's County. Apart from the city of Saint John, it included many different communities, which are today the city's suburbs. The most important at the time was Carleton, on the other side of the river, where Joseph Stackhouse (1747-1827), a loyalist from Philadelphia, had settled. In the third edition, Bates explains that Stackhouse's house was isolated: he "resided in a bye-place within a mile of the City."

[15] Brighton, a major seaside resort in southern England, had been officially called Brighthelmstone until 1810, and this is how it appears in the long subtitle and in the editor's preface of the British edition. However, the shortened version of the name had been in common use since the 18th century.

[16] The River Philip runs through Cumberland County, the only Nova Scotia county which borders New Brunswick. Halifax, the capital and major port of Nova Scotia, had around 10,000 inhabitants in 1814.

[17] His name was corrected to "Daniel" in the third edition. The 99th Regiment of Foot (or Prince of Wales's Tipperary), raised in Ireland in 1805, was in Nova Scotia at the time. It was renumbered 98th in 1816 and disbanded in 1818. Its nominal colonel was the Honourable Montague Mathew, brother of the Earl of Landaff. The lieutenant-colonel, according to the *Army List*, was John Daniel.

[18] The editor of the British version added an explanation for this word: "Match." The meaning was typical of New England and it came from the practice of "spanning," that is, yoking or harnessing oxen and horses two by two. They "spanned well" if they were a match in size and, by extension, in colour.

if he would bring him a horse that would span with his within a fortnight, that he would pay him two hundred dollars—he then said that he had not money enough to purchase the horse; that if he would let him have fifteen guineas[19] he would leave the mare he then rode, in pledge, until he brought the horse; as he knew there was a vessel then ready going from Saint John to Cumberland,[20] where the horse belonged—to which proposal Col. Daniels agreed; and gave him the money. Leaving the mare, he went to his lodgings, about one mile out of town: but, before he returned the vessel had gone and left him, and having no other opportunity to go by water was obliged to set out on foot; and having a long distance to travel, and short time to perform it, was obliged to travel all night, and at day break was overtaken by a stranger, with a large horse and a small mare, which he offered for sale; and being tired with walking, offered ten pounds for the mare, which he accepted—and they rode on together some time, when he began to find that the mare would not answer his purpose; that he had not money to purchase the horse he was going after—that he should not be able to sell the mare, and would thus lose his object—and as the horse was a good looking one, which he might sell for the money again, he bantered the man for a swap,[21] which he agreed to, and exchanged the horse, saddle and bridle, for the mare and 15 pounds to boot, which he paid him, and took a receipt for the money, which he produced, written in the following words:

"Received, July 20th, 1814, of Henry More Smith, fifteen pounds in swap[22] of a horse, between a small mare and a large bay horse, that I let him have, with a star, six or seven years old.

James Churman."[23]

---

[19] A British pound was officially worth $4.44, so 15 guineas (see note 10) would have been about 70 dollars. There was currency devaluation and fluctuations during the War of 1812 and each province as well as some organisations (especially the Army) gave different valuations to the different currencies, but it is quite clear that Smith was asking for one third of the money down.

[20] The community of Fort Lawrence (Cumberland County, Nova Scotia) has replaced the former township of Cumberland, located on the Isthmus of Chignecto, close to the border with New Brunswick. Smith made the journey on land, on what Peter Fisher (in his 1825 *Sketches*) called "the main road from Saint John to Cumberland" (61).

[21] The editor of the British version felt the need to explain this as "Made overtures for an exchange." The term "swap," though recorded with this meaning as early as the 17th century, was still considered a rare, slang word.

[22] The British editor again explains "in swap" as "in exchange."

[23] The name is spelled "Churnan" in the British edition.

This receipt was written and signed in two distinct hand writings. He said that he then proceeded on his journey to Cumberland, and bargained for the horse, which was the object of his pursuit; but not having money enough to pay for him, was obliged to sell the horse that he rode, and hearing that Col. Dixon of Truro[24] wanted such a horse, proceeded there in great haste; and arriving at Truro, found Col. Dixon had gone to Pictou, forty miles farther, to attend court, which was to sit at that time; and he was obliged to proceed on with all speed—The next day being Sunday, was obliged to stay until Monday, before he could sell his horse;[25] and was there overtaken by Mr. Knox, who had him apprehended and charged with stealing his horse; and taken before the Court there—and being a stranger and no one to speak for him, they had taken all his money and his watch from him; and sent him back to King County Gaol,[26] there to take his trial—and complained of being misused on his way by Mr. Knox. He shewed great anxiety about his situation, and to make enquiry after the man who sold him the horse, as he was convinced the horse was stolen, and that the thief would be out of the way unless he was taken soon; and then his case must be desperate, as he had neither money or friends, and knew nothing of the law himself.

It so happened, the day following, that I had occasion to go to the city of Saint John, in company with Doctor Adino Paddock, sen.[27] On our way had occasion to call at Mr. Nathaniel

[24] Truro (named after the city in Cornwall) is a town in Nova Scotia, in Colchester County (east of Cumberland). Lieutenant-Colonel William Dixon was in Nova Scotia between March and July 1814 with the 1st Battalion, Royal Regiment of Artillery.

[25] There would have been no sales allowed on Sunday, the Lord's Day.

[26] The jail (as it is usually spelled in the third edition) in the county (Bates spells it "Kings" and "King's" elsewhere) had been built and rebuilt before (as Acts of the Legislative Assembly of New Brunswick from 1786 and 1807 show) and was still a work in progress in 1814 (as Bates's narrative suggests). A new, more solid, structure was constructed in 1840, but it was then moved stone by stone to Hampton Parish in 1871. Exactly one century later it was closed and is now a museum.

[27] Adino Paddock (1760-1817) of Boston had studied in England. After the Revolutionary War, he settled in Saint John, New Brunswick. His son and grandson (of the same name) were also physicians. In 1812, Adino Paddock, jr. (1787-1859) had married Bates's wife's younger sister Nancy. He will be mentioned soon, first as "Paddock, jr.," then simply as "Paddock," as he was the resident doctor in Kingston since 1808.

Golden's Tavern, at the French village in Hampton;[28] and when placing our horses under his shed, I saw a man mount a horse in haste that stood at the steps of the door, and ride away toward Saint John with great speed, apparently as if in fear of being overtaken—and on enquiry who he was, we were told by Mrs. Golden, that he was a stranger who had called there once or twice before, and that she believed his name was Churman or Churnun—I replied to the Doctor, that was the name of the man that the prisoner Smith said had sold him the horse. Mrs. Golden said she could know by enquiring in the other room, which she did, and answered in the affirmative. We then made enquiries on the road as we travelled toward Saint John; but heard nothing more of the stranger by that name ever afterwards.

After my return from Saint John, I informed the prisoner, Smith, of the circumstance—he appeared extremely elated with the idea of having him taken, and said if he had money or friends, he could have him taken and brought to justice; and then be set at liberty—but if he made his escape out of the country, his own case must be miserable. He wished to apply to a lawyer for advice, and was advised to employ CHARLES I. PETERS, Esq. Attorney at St. John,[29] and told that he need not fear, but if there was any way to get him clear, that he would do it for him faithfully.

The first opportunity that offered, he wrote an order to Mr. Joseph Stackhouse at St. John, where he had lodged, for his portmanteau, and some articles left for sale, and if sold, to apply the money as a retainer to Mr. PETERS, his attorney. The return brought a genteel portmanteau and a pair of boots, leaving a small consideration in the hands of Mr. Peters, as a retainer, upon condition of his making up the remainder to the amount of five guineas before Court; with which he appeared perfectly

[28] French Village is an unincorporated community in Hampton Parish, King's County, southeast of Kingston. In later editions, the tavern keeper's name is "Golding." However, he appears in documents as both Golden and Golding.

[29] Actually, Charles Jeffery Peters (1773-1848), who was at the time the senior practising lawyer in all of New Brunswick, as well as a civil servant, occupying several positions in the government of the province. In 1828, he became Attorney General of New Brunswick (an office he fulfilled until his death). His family (who had sailed from New York and settled in Saint John in May 1783) was part of the loyalist elite of the province. The name was corrected to "Charles J. Peters" in the second and third editions.

satisfied, and said he must sell his clothes and other things out of his portmanteau, that he could spare, and make the money. He gave me his key, with which I opened his portmanteau, and found it well filled with clothes. I found two or three genteel coats, with vests and pantaloons of the first cloth and fashion, with silk stockings and gloves, a superfine over coat of the modern fashion, faced with black silk; a number of books, consisting of a neat pocket bible and prayer book, London Gazetteer, Ready Reckoner,[30] and several other useful books for a traveller—he had also a night and day spy glass of the first kind, and a small magnifying glass in a turtle shell case, and several other useful articles, without any thing suspicious, which induced us to think, at least, he had been fitted out by careful parents, and was possibly innocent of the charge. He soon commenced selling his clothes and other articles; any person who wished to speak to him, was permitted to come to the wicket door, through which he disposed of his articles, as he said, out of necessity, to raise money to retain his lawyer and to purchase necessaries; and many purchased out of compassion for his situation—Among others, a young man, who said he knew him while at Saint John, came once or twice to visit him; and some of the glass being broken, he found it convenient to talk with him through the grates at the window; and the last time took away the night and day glass, as he said, for a debt he was owing him; but I suspect left an old watch in exchange.

The prisoner continued to complain of a bad cough, and pain from the ill usage which he said he received from Mr. Knox. He appeared to employ himself in reading his bible, and behaved himself with great decency and propriety.[31]

On the 13th of August I received a letter from Mr. CHIPMAN, Clerk of the Circuit Court,[32] directing that the prisoner be

[30] A "gazetteer" was a historical and geographical atlas; the *London Gazetteer*, despite the name, covered the entire world. A "ready reckoner" was a book containing multiplication tables and other various types of calculations tailored specifically for the benefit of various trades and businesses.

[31] In the second edition, Bates inserted here a letter he had received from Wills Frederick Knox, detailing the apprehension of Smith (see "Epilogue, Part II").

[32] This is Ward Chipman Jr. (1787-1851), still at the beginning of his career (he will become Speaker of the Legislative Assembly of New Brunswick in 1824 and chief justice of the Supreme Court of New Brunswick in 1834). His father will be mentioned soon.

examined before two magistrates, and regularly committed.[33]—After proper notice, Judge PICKETT, Mr. Justice KETCHUM,[34] and Mr. KNOX, attended his examination, and the facts found were to the same effect as before related, upon which a regular commitment was made out. In the course of his examination he said his name was HENRY MORE SMITH—Being asked what occupation he had followed in this country? he answered, No one in particular. Mr. Knox hastily asked him how he had got his living then? He replied, with great firmness and composure, *By my honesty, Sir.* He was then returned to prison, and showed no anxiety about what had taken place. He complained of pain in his side, and appeared to cough very hollow, but submitted to his confinement without a murmur.

The prison was kept by Mr. WALTER DIBBLEE, a man of learning and talents,[35] who for several years had been afflicted with that painful infirmity the gravel,[36] so that for the most part of his time he was confined to the house, and frequently to his room in the County-House, where he taught a school, which, together with the fees and perquisites of the Gaol and Court-House, afforded a decent and comfortable living for his small family, which consisted of his wife, a daughter, and a son

[33] The letter is given in full in the third edition: "Dear Sir, Mr. Knox has left with me the examination, &c. relating to More Smith, the horse-stealer, now in your jail; these are all taken in the Province of Nova Scotia, before Magistrates there, and I would recommend that he be brought up before the Magistrates in your County, and examined, and the examination committed to writing. I do not know under what warrant he is in your custody; but I think it would be as well for the same Magistrates to make out a Mittimus [i.e., a warrant for someone to be taken into custody] after the examination, as it would be more according to form. I remain, dear Sir, yours, Ward Chipman."

[34] David Pickett (1743-1826) came to New Brunswick on the same ship as Walter Bates; he served as justice of the peace, presiding judge of the Kings County Court House, and treasurer of Kings County. Richard Ketchum (1773-1845) came to New Brunswick with his parents, who settled in the northern part of York County (which later split off, with his help, and became Carleton County). From 1827 to 1830, he served in the Legislative Assembly of New Brunswick.

[35] Walter Dibblee (born in 1764) was, like Bates, a native of Stamford, Connecticut. They came to New Brunswick on the same ship (the *Union*) in 1783 and, while the church was being built, Dibblee led the community in prayers. He later moved to Saint John County, was a schoolmaster in Maugerville (in the neighbouring Sunbury County), but then returned to Kingston. While serving as Kings County Gaoler, he was also the local schoolteacher.

[36]. Gravel is an old term for kidney stones.

about nineteen years old, named John Dibblee, who constantly assisted his father.[37] It is necessary to mention that Mr. Dibblee was in high estimation in the Masonic Lodge held at Kingston, of which he was a principal member.[38] Under these circumstances I had but seldom occasion to visit the prison and, as I lived at the distance of half a mile, did not visit it oftener than once a week, except on special occasions. I am therefore indebted to Mr. Dibblee for some of the particulars related in the subsequent narration.

Shortly after his commitment, Smith was visited by Lieut. A. Baxter, and officer of the New-Brunswick Fencibles,[39] then recruiting at Kingston, who proposed to him to enlist. He spurned the idea of being permitted to enlist to get out of prison—He was, however, prevailed upon to write to his attorney upon the subject, and received for answer, in very short words, that it was inadmissible, and he advised him to content himself and wait the issue of his trial. He appeared much dissatisfied with the shortness of his answer, and said he did not know what it meant; that the attorney appeared very angry, and that he could not have much to expect from such a man. He was advised to reply with confidence on Mr. Peters, and assured if any thing could be done in his favour it would not be neglected. He never after enquired for his attorney, but set out to free himself from prison by a more summary process than the law. He continued to complain of the ill usage he had received on the road when taken, particularly of a blow from Mr. Knox with a pistol in his side, (as he said) which felled him to the ground like a dead man—that when he came to, he raised blood,[40] and it was some time before he was able to

[37] John Frederick Dibblee (1794-1847). He replaced his father as teacher when Walter died in 1817.

[38] Dibblee was married to the daughter of Rev. John Beardsley (1732-1809), considered the founder of freemasonry in New Brunswick.

[39] The New Brunswick Regiment of Fencible Infantry ("fencible" is an old term for someone who served in the army strictly in defence of his homeland) was raised in 1803; in 1810 it was included in the British Army and renamed the 104th Regiment of Foot. The men served in the War of 1812, and, in early August 1814, they were involved in the Niagara campaign, taking part in the Siege of Fort Erie. Abraham Baxter (1771-1836) had been created lieutenant with temporary rank in that regiment in 1813. He was the youngest son of Simon Baxter (see Baxter 92), sometimes known as the first of the United Empire Loyalists (because he received a land grant and the right to settle in New Brunswick in 1782, one year before the arrival of the first Loyalist fleet).

[40] Old expression for "spit blood."

breathe regular—that he continued to raise blood two or three days on the road, and the pain had never left him, but now increased very fast, owing to the cold he had taken—that he believed it was gathering on the inside; that it swelled and was very painful; and he frequently raised blood when coughing. He showed the bruised place in his side, which appeared black, swelled and sore, verifying his complaints. This was about the 7th September.—Finding him so ill, we repaired the stove pipes, supplied him with fuel, and made the room comfortable. He appeared to complain as little as possible, but lost his appetite, and required light food. His health seemed gradually to decay, and his complaints regularly to increase—Pain in his head and eyes, with dizziness, and sickness at the stomach; puking and raising blood, with great complaints of the soreness in his side, and consequent debility and weakness. On the 11th Sept found him gradually falling away—Sent for a Doctor, who examined his side and other complaints, and gave him medicine.—The 12th he appeared to be something better—13th, at evening, grew worse, pains increased—14th, unable to walk, very high fever—15th, puking and raising blood—16th, the Rev. Mr. Scovil[41] visited the prisoner in the morning; found him very ill; sent him toast and wine, and other things for his comfort—At 3 P. M. the Doctor attended and gave him medicine—At 6 o'clock much the same; unable to help himself—could eat nothing—puked up every thing he took.—18th, the prisoner appeared still to grow worse—Judge Pickett, with several other neighbours, visited him; asked him if he wanted any thing that he could take; he said, nothing, unless it was an orange or a lemon.—19th, appeared sensibly to decline and very low—At 2 o'clock the Doctor attended him; said the man must be removed out of that room; that he was too ill to be kept there, and that it was of no use to give him medicine in that place.—20th, in the morning, found him no better—At 10 o'clock Mr. Thaddeus Scribner[42] and others went in to see the prisoner; examined the room and found no dampness—4 o'clock, the

[41] Elias Scovil (1771-1841), the son of James Scovil, the first rector of Trinity Church, Kingston, whom he assisted after 1803 and then replaced after his death in 1808. Elias's younger brother, Edward, was a farmer married to Bates's daughter Mary Lucretia (known as Polly).

[42] Thaddeus Scribner (1760-1837) was born in Norwalk, Connecticut and came to King's County on the same ship as Walter Bates and Walter Dibblee. A farmer, he also appears on the ship's manifest as a shoemaker.

Rev. Mr. Scovil attended him as a clergyman—Smith told him he had no hope that he should ever recover; that he was born in England; that his parents were formerly of the persuasion of the Church of England, but latterly had joined the Methodists; that he came away on account of the war, and expected his father and mother out.—21st, the Rev. Mr. Scovil and other of the neighbors visited him—found him no better, but evidently falling away, and no hopes of his recovery.—22d, the prisoner very low, and his complaints of the most fatal nature; violent fever, accompanied with agues and chills; his feet and legs cold at turns; great pain, with inflammation in his bowels; nothing but blood had come from him for two days; his weakness increasing, was not able to help himself up or down, and had but just strength enough to speak above his breath—he feared he should die for want of medical assistance, as the Doctor had refused to attend him any more in that place—He had, from his decency and the inoffensive simplicity of his manners, excited the compassion of all who visited him—At 6 o'clock the Rev. Mr. Scovil and a large number of the neighbours came in, and staid until 10; they did not think he would live till morning.—Friday, Sept. 23, went early to the gaol—found the prisoner lying naked on the floor, and in great distress—had fallen through pain and dizziness (as he said) and could not get himself up—was lifted into his bed almost expired—he continued to decline; could take no nourishment; and could speak with difficulty only to be heard, until 5 o'clock P. M. when he was supposed to be dying—all signs of life were gone long enough to go to another room for a bottle of hartshorn,[43] with which he seemed to revive—Called in the Rev. Mr. Scovil, Mr. Perkins, and Mr. G. Raymond, near neighbours, and Mr. Eddy, from St. John,[44] who happened to be there, and all supposed him dying; he, however, revived, and recovered his senses—He was told that he had had a fit—He said he was sensible of it; that it was a family infirmity; that most of his connections had died in that way, and that he could not survive another, which would probably come upon him about the same time next day; that he should

[43] Hartshorn (the antler of a hart) was used as a source of ammonia in smelling salts.

[44] Both Francis Newman Perkins (1770-1833), an innkeeper, and George Raymond (c.1790-1870) were sons of United Empire Loyalists. Raymond was a merchant and was to become Overseer of the Poor in the parish. Mr. Eddy of Saint John must be one of the several people in Saint John County named "Eddy," "Eady" or "Edy."

not recover, but God would have him; and asked Mr. Scovil to go to prayer, which he did, and prayer was attended with solemnity by all present. He had had no regular watchers, but it was thought highly improper to leave him alone this night, and John Dibblee and Charles Chambeau were appointed by the sheriff to watch with him; and the following letter was written by the sheriff, and dispatched by Mr. Raymond, to Mr. Peters, the prisoner's attorney:

"DEAR SIR,—I fear we shall be disappointed in our expectation of the trial of the prisoner, MORE SMITH, at the approaching Court, as I presume he will be removed by death before that time. He is dying in consequence of a blow that he received (as he says) from Mr. Knox, with a pistol, which he has regularly complained of since he has been in gaol, and is now thought past recovery. As it will be a matter of inquiry, and new to me, will thank you to let me know by the bearer what will be the necessary steps for me to take—and not fail, as I have but little hopes of his continuing until morning.

Yours, &c. W. BATES."

The return if the bearer brought the following answer:

"SAINT JOHN, Sept. 24.

DEAR SIR,—Your favour of yesterday I received this morning, and am sorry to hear so desponding an account of the unfortunate man in your custody. It will be your duty, I conceive, immediately to have a Coroner's inquest of the body, and then cause it to be decently interred. With respect to the charge of the cause of the death, that is a circumstance which must rest wholly on the facts. If any Physician shall attend him, let him be particular in taking down in writing what the man says in his last moments as to the circumstances—and if a Justice should be present it would not be amiss.

In haste, Yours sincerely,

C. J. PETERS.

W. Bates, Esq."

Saturday, Sept. 24th, the watchers reported that he had passed a very restless night, and but just survived the morning. The following note was then sent to the physician who had attended him:

"KINGSTON, Sept. 24, 1814.

DEAR DOCTOR,—Smith, the prisoner, says that he is suffering for want of medical assistance, and that you will not attend him unless he can be removed into another room, which cannot be permitted, but he must take his fate, and if he dies in gaol an inquiry will take place which may prove to your disadvantage. I must therefore request your attention.

I am truly yours, &c, W. B.

Dr. A. PADDOCK, Jun."

At this time the compassion of the whole neighbourhood was very strongly excited, especially that of the family of Mr. Scovil, who sent him any thing he wanted for his comfort, as did also Mr. Perkins' and Mr. Raymond's families, who were near. Mr. Perkins visited him about 10 o'clock, and kindly offered to watch with him that night, for which he appeared very thankful. About 5 o'clock the Doctor attended him, and gave him some medicine—found him so weak that he was obliged to have him lifted up to give him his medicine, and to all human appearance he was unable to help himself in the least; but the Doctor said he did not think him so near his end as to die before morning, unless he went off in a fit. He was then left to himself, with a probable expectation that he would shortly be taken with another fit, and would undoubtedly expire.[45] About 6 o'clock in the evening the Rev. Mr. Scovil observed to his family that it was about the time that Smith had his fit yesterday, that he thought it probably he would die suddenly, and that he would walk over to Mr. Dibblee, at the gaol, and be ready there at the time, as it would be unpleasant to him to be alone. This so much raised the sensibility of Madam Scovil, she could not bear the reflection that a child, perhaps, of respectable parents, should lie so near to her, in a strange country, and die upon a bed of straw—so calling her wench *Amy*, here, said she, take this feather bed and carry it to the gaol, and tell your master I have sent it for Smith to die on. Mr. Scovil had not been in the house and set down with Mr. Dibblee but a few minutes, when a noise was heard from Smith in the gaol—John Dibblee,

[45] Two details were added here in the third edition. First, that the prisoner made his will: "*All his clothes*, at his death, he willed to John Dibblee; and his money, about three pounds, which he always kept by him in his *berth*, he bequeathed to the Jailer for his kind attention to him in his *sickness*. The money Mr. Dibblee proposed to take charge of; but Smith said it was safe where it was for the present." Second, that a local named W.H. Lyon spread the rumour that Smith was already dead that evening, because, while walking through the village, he had seen his ghost "pass by him a short distance off, without touching the ground." William Henry Lyon (1782-1854) was one of the brothers of Bates's wife, Abigail, and an uncle to Henry Lyon who will take part in the pursuit (see note 73).

who constantly attended him, ran in haste, unlocked the prison door, and found Smith expiring, his feet and legs cold to his knees, and in great pain—He begged of John to run and heat a brick that was near, to give one moment's relief while he was dying. John, of course, ran in haste from the gaol, round the stairway, through a passage that led to the kitchen, where was a large fire of coals, into which he put the brick, waited no more than three minutes, and returned with it warmed, but to his indescribable astonishment FOUND NO ONE IN THE BED. He ran with the tidings to his father and the Rev. Mr. Scovil, (who were sitting in a room by which he must have passed to go out) who could not believe the report, until they had examined and found that *not only the man was gone, but every thing he had in the room was taken away with him.*—On going out and looking round the house for him, Mr. Scovil met Amy with the feather bed, who said to him, Misses send the bed for Smith—Her master told her to take it home, and tell her mistress Smith was gone. Amy ran home and told her mistress, Massa say Smit gone; he no want em bed—Ah! exclaimed her mistress, poor man! is he dead! Well, Amy, then you may run and carry over a shirt and a winding sheet to lay Smith out in. Amy ran over and told her master accordingly—You may take them back, said he, *Smith is gone*—Where he gone, massa? I don't know, said he, without the devil has taken him off—So great was his astonishment at the deception. In the mean time the alarm spread in the neighbourhood, and a Mr. Yandle,[46] who happened to be passing, was sent with the tidings to the Sheriff, whom he meet on his way to the gaol, to see the last moments of Smith. Being told that Smith was gone—Poor fellow! said he, I expected it; what time did he die?—But he is *gone off clear!*—It is impossible he can be far out of bed. Why, said Mr. Yandle, on passing, I saw them all out about the gaol looking for him, and no one could tell which way he had gone. Unparalleled and abominable deception!—How did he get out of gaol? He believed John Dibblee left the door open, and while he was gone to heat a brick, Smith made his escape. This was our first introduction to the true character of Henry More Smith; and it is impossible to express, or even to conceive, with what wonderful plausibility he imposed a feigned illness upon all who saw him as a profound reality.

[46] Probably William Yandell or Yandall (c.1782-1861), who had move recently near Belleisle Bay. His name was replaced by "a messenger" in the third edition.

In order to explain his further progress the reader should have some knowledge of the country.

KINGSTON is situated on a neck or tongue of land, formed by the long reach of the river St. John and Bellisle Bay, running north east and south west, on the east side[47]—and by the river Kennebeccacis running the same course on the west side, and emptying into the Grand Bay of the river St. John, about five miles from its mouth[48]—leaving a tract of land between the two rivers, of about five miles in width, and upwards of thirty miles in length. The winter road by ice, from Frederickton (the seat of government)[49] to the city of St. John, crosses the land to the Kenebeccacis, and is inhabited on both sides. This road is intersected in the centre by another, running north east, about seven miles, and thence branching easterly, crossing the Kennebecasis at the distance of thirty miles, leading through the county of Westmoreland, heading the bay of Fundy at Cumberland;[50] and leading from thence, by different roads, to Halifax, Pictou and every part of Nova-Scotia. The western branch of said road running northerly to the head of Belisle Bay, thence to the Washadamoac lake;[51] crossing the ferry, from thence to the Jemsag Creek,[52] and thence to Frederickton

[47] What is sometimes called the "Kingston Peninsula" is created, on its western side (Bates was confused here, but he corrected it in the third edition) by the Saint John River, which flows north-south to a place opposite the community of Kingston but suddenly turns south-west (the new direction is known as the Long Reach), and by Belleisle Bay, a fjord-like branch of the river, which shoots off in the opposite direction (north-east) for about ten miles; and, on its eastern side, by a major tributary of the Saint John, the Kennebecasis.

[48] The Kennebecasis River (which is spelled three different ways in this paragraph) joins the Saint River in the Grand Bay, south of which lies the City of Saint John.

[49] Fredericton, settled by loyalists in 1783, was chosen as capital of New Brunswick in 1785 because of its position close to the centre of the province.

[50] The New Brunswick county of Westmorland and the Nova Scotia county of Cumberland (see notes 16 and 20) lie on each side of the isthmus of Chignecto, which separates the two provinces. The Bay of Fundy is delineated by the isthmus itself, the mainland (New Brunswick) and the Nova Scotia peninsula.

[51] Lake Washademoak is a long, narrow lake, entirely within the borders of Queens County, just north of Kings. It drains into the Saint John River.

[52] The short Jemseg river connects Grand Lake (also in Queens County) and the Saint John River.

by land, through Maugerville,[53] on the east side of the river St. John. At the intersection of these roads, on an eminence, stand the Church and the Court-House, (under which is the prison) fronting each other.[54] There is also a road running north west, and south east, from the Gaol, leading westerly to Bellisle Bay, crossing a ferry at a distance of five miles; thence to a short ferry at Tenant's Cove, thence to the ferry crossing the river St. John; and from thence through Gage-Town,[55] on the west side of the river, to Frederickton, distant sixty miles:—the said road leading southeasterly from the Gaol to the ferry over the Kennebecasis; and from thence on the west side of the river to the city of St. John. The house of Mr. F. Newman Perkins, standing northerly at the distance of ten rods[56] from the Gaol—at an equal distance southerly, the house of the Rev. E. Scovil, and other houses in different directions—the land all clear, and no shelter for a considerable distance, but fences.

From this situation the prisoner escaped without any track or trace of him being discovered. After searching the fences and fields, and finding nothing of him, it was concluded that he had gone either toward St. John, or on the road to Nova-Scotia, by which he came. Accordingly men were sent to the ferry, and on the road to Saint John—and I, with Mr. Moses Foster, Deputy Sheriff,[57] pursued on the road toward Nova-Scotia, with all speed; setting watchers in different places, until we were sensible we must have passed him; and arriving at a house that he could not pass without coming very near, we watched for him all night. At day-break, hearing nothing of him, I furnished Mr. Foster with money and sent him on the road, with directions to proceed on to Mr. M'Leod's tavern,[58] distant 40 miles, and if he got no intelligence there, to return; and returned to Kingston myself, where I was informed,

[53] Maugerville (pronounced Major-ville), on the way to Fredericton, was first settled by the English in 1762.

[54] In the third edition, the sentence continues as follows: "east and west, at a distance of about eight rods." One rod equals 5.5 yards (about 5 metres).

[55] Tennants Cove is a small community at the mouth of Belleisle Bay. Gagetown is a village on the west bank of the Saint John River, in Queens County.

[56] About fifty meters (see note 54).

[57] Moses Foster (c.1762-1817) was a Connecticut Loyalist and, according to Hoyt's diary, a freemason.

[58] McLeod's inn, "where the ferry landed" (Thomas 162), near (today, in) Fredericton, was built in 1791.

toward evening, that a man who answered his description, had crossed the ferry at Bellisle Bay, in great haste; said he was going express[59] to Frederickton, and must be there by ten o'clock next morning; and no doubt it was the man. It was now Sunday evening; he had twenty-four hours start, escaping for life, had got out of the County, and no hopes remained with me of apprehending him—I, however, forwarded advertisements after him, offering a reward of twenty dollars, to any one who would apprehend, and bring him back.

Monday morning, the 26th, Mr. Moses Foster returned, of course, without success;[60] and many unfavorable reports began to circulate respecting his escape—and I felt myself not a little chagrined with my situation. A Court of Oyer and Terminer and General Gaol delivery[61] having been ordered, and the Jury summoned from all parts of the County, to attend at the Court-House on Tuesday following, for the special purpose of trying the horse stealer, my whole attention was required to make the necessary preparations; and added not a little to my chagrin and disappointment—But still more when, on Tuesday morning, I was informed by Mr. E. Jones,[62] that the villain, instead of escaping for his life, and getting out of my reach in the most secret manner, had only travelled about ten or twelve miles the first night, and was seen next morning lying on some straw before the barn of Mr. Robert Bailes,[63] on the road toward Gagetown; and that he lay there until about twelve o'clock in the day—and seeing Mr. Bailes and his wife, going from home, leaving the door unlocked, and no person in the house, he went in, broke open a trunk, and carried of a silver watch, eight dollars in money, a new pair of velvet pantaloons and a pocket

[59] In the third edition, Smith went "on an express to Fredericton." In other words, he claimed he was carrying a message there (one message only, with no stops to deliver anything else).

[60] Though Foster went to Fredericton, just like Smith (according to the reports that reached Bates), he had taken the road on the east bank of the Saint John, while Smith would have taken the one on the west bank.

[61] A court with power and jurisdiction to try all matters, capital, criminal, and civil.

[62] This is likely Edward Jones (1743-1831) a loyalist from Greenwich Parish (north of Kingston), not his grandson of the same name.

[63] This settler on the road to Gagetown must be the one documented as Robert Belyea or Bulyea (perhaps pronounced like "Bayle" of "Boyle"). In the second edition (but not afterwards), his name is spelled "Boyle."

book, with other articles; that he then walked leisurely away, and stopped in at the next house, and at all the houses that were near upon the road, and did not get more than three or four miles before dark—when Mr. Bailes came home, found his house had been robbed, and by the track of the heel of his boot, thought he was the man. He alarmed his neighbours, who pursued him in great spirit, hearing of him on the road but little ahead of them, and expecting to overtake him in a few minutes; but were disappointed, as he disappeared from the road, and no track or information could be found, and after the most diligent search and pursuit as far as Gagetown, returned the next day without any intelligence, leaving advertisements at Gagetown and Fredericton, describing the man and the watch. Late on Sunday night, a man came to the house of Mr. Green, living on an island, at the mouth of the Washedemoac lake,[64] who said he was a Frenchman, going to Fredericton after land, and came in to inquire the way—Mr. Green informed him he was on an island, and he might stay till morning, and then he would put him in his way; made up a large fire, by which the man examined his pocket book, and was seen to burn several papers, and at last, threw the book into the fire and burned it up; which caused a strong suspicion in Mr. Green, it being in time of war, that he must be a bad character; and in the morning he took him in his canoe, and paddled him directly to justice Colwell, a neighboring magistrate,[65] to give account of himself—where, on examination, he appeared to answer with so much simplicity, that the justice could find nothing that would justify detaining him; and so inoffensive, that there could be no harm in him; and in consequence, let him go—that he went to an Indian Camp,[66] and hired an Indian to take him, (as he said) to Fredericton; and crossing the river, went to Mr. Nathaniel Veal's tavern, on Grimross Neck,[67] nearly opposite

[64] James Caleb Green (c.1747-1825) an old loyalist soldier or perhaps his son Willet Green (c.1776-1855). The island is probably Lower Musquash Island.

[65] John Colwell (1749-1833) was an old loyalist from New Jersey.

[66] Probably a Mi'kmaq camp north of Gagetown (see Ganong, "Historic Sites" 228).

[67] Grimross Neck is an island in the Saint John River near Gagetown. It forms a long cape at its northern end. The name of the tavern keeper appears as "Vail" in later editions. Nathaniel Vail or Veal was an old loyalist who had died soon after relocating to New Brunswick. The tavern was kept by his widow, Elizabeth, and his son Nathaniel Vail jr.

Gagetown, where Mr. Bailes, who he had robbed the day before, was getting his breakfast, and writing advertisements in pursuit of him. The wind blowing hard ahead, he called for breakfast for himself and his Indian; staid sometime; had his boots cleaned; and about eleven o'clock left there, taking with him a set of silver tea-spoons, from a bye closet in the parlor of Mrs. Veal, and nothing had been heard of him since. Four men, with my advertisements went in pursuit of him.

About eleven o'clock, Tuesday morning, the Attorney General[68] arrived from Frederickton, with very unfavorable impressions on his mind; bringing information, that the prisoner was still traversing along shore, stealing wherever he came, and not apprehended. The Jury also were collecting from different parishes in the County, and brought with them unfavorable ideas, from the reports in circulation, respecting the escape—Among which, was a report studiously circulated, that the prisoner was a Freemason, and that it was believed the Masons had contrived to let him escape, because he was one of their order.

The public mind became so prejudiced, that we could say nothing in our own justification, but the plea of his deception, which no one could believe, except those who saw it. As the prisoner escaped through the door, strong suspicion was entertained of a voluntary connivance at his escape. With such impression the Court assembled. His Honor Judge CHIPMAN presided.[69] The most favorable hope and expectation was entertained that the prisoner would be apprehended, and brought before the Court, as he was pursued in all directions. After the Grand Jury were impanelled and sworn, the Court adjourned until eleven o'clock next day, waiting the return of the prisoner—To hasten which, I despatched Mr. Benjamin Furnald,[70] with a boat, and directions to pursue him as far he could hear of him, until he brought him back—Wednesday

[68] The Attorney General of New Brunswick from 1809 to 1828 was Thomas Wetmore (1767-1828). Born in Rye, New York, he had arrived with his Loyalist family in 1783. He was also a member of the Legislative Assembly (1809-1816). He was married to Sarah, sister of Charles Jeffery Peters (see note 29).

[69] Ward Chipman (1754-1824), a Massachusetts Loyalist who came to New Brunswick in 1784, was the most prominent lawyer of the province (Peters had been one of his students) and a puisne judge of the Supreme Court. After the War of 1812, he negotiated the boundary between New Brunswick and the United States.

[70] Probably Benjamin Fernald, originally from Maine.

the Court met, and went to other business—heard nothing of the prisoner—In the afternoon, Mr. John Pearson, witness against the prisoner, arrived from Nova-Scotia, a distance of 280 miles—Toward evening, reports began to circulate that the horse stealer had evaded all his pursuers, and had disappeared.

No account could be heard from him up the river St. John, and strong suspicion was had, that he was making his way back for Nova-Scotia—and it was reported that a man had been seen crossing the Washedemoac to Bellisle Bay with an Indian; but nothing to be relied on. The Court adjourned until next morning at ten o'clock—Nothing more was heard until Thursday, early in the morning, when Mr. B. Furnald returned, and reported, that he pursued him through Maugerville; that he lodged the night before he arrived at Mr. Solomon Pearley's,[71] and stole a pair of new boots; had offered the spoons for sale to Mr. Pearley; that he then walked up as far as Mr. Bailey's tavern,[72] where he stopped some time, and from thence was seen, towards night, under a bridge, counting his money. No farther track could be discovered of him, in that part; and it was believed he had taken an Indian to pilot him, and gone by the way of the Washedemoac, and head of Bellisle, for Nova-Scotia. At ten o'clock Thursday morning, the Court met according to adjournment, to conclude the business then before them, with but little hope of seeing the horse-stealer; and of course, a gloomy appearance on our side—when about three o'clock in the afternoon, a servant of Mr. Knox came express to the Court, with information to his master, that his other horse was missing out of the pasture; that he was seen at one o'clock at night, and was gone in the morning; that a strange Indian had been seen about the place, who it was believed had piloted Smith through the woods; upon which a general alarm took place. Mr. Knox was quite outrageous, would hear nothing to the Sheriff, who doubted the report;—would bet a thousand guineas that Smith had stolen his other horse; that he knew him to be the greatest villain upon earth; and that his life was in danger, if he was suffered to go at large; and the whole Court were in consternation—His Honor the Judge observed that great remissness of duty appeared—A bench warrant was issued by the Court, directed to all the

[71] Solomon Perley (1779-1831) was the son of Israel Perley, one of the first settlers in Maugerville and a well-known farmer and surveyor. The name was corrected in the third edition.

[72] Zachariah Bailey's was a well-known roadhouse.

Sheriffs and ministers of justice throughout the province of New-Brunswick, commanding them to apprehend the said More Smith and bring him to justice—Mr. Knox, with Henry Lyon and Isaiah Smith,[73] went in pursuit of him toward Nova-Scotia; Moses Foster, deputy sheriff, and Nathan Deforest,[74] were dispatched by the head of Bellisle Bay to Frederickton, and directed to pursue on to the American settlement,[75] and as far as they could get any information of him. The Sheriff then wrote an advertisement for the public papers, offering forty dollars reward, and the Attorney General added forty more, which made the reward eighty dollars. *Indictments were prepared, and the Grand Jury soon found a bill against the Sheriff and Gaoler for negligent escape*;[76] and they were recognized to appear at the next Court of Oyer and Terminer and General Goal Delivery,[77] and traverse the indictments.

The business before the Court being nearly finished, after paying the witness, Mr. Pearson, for his travel and attendance, amounting to one hundred dollars, the Court adjourned without day.[78]

Nothing was heard of our adventurer until after the return of Mr. Knox with his party, from a fruitless pursuit of ten days, into the province of Nova-Scotia, as far as Rushabucteau.[79] The day following, Mr. Foster and Mr. Deforest returned, and reported, that they had pursued on to Frederickton without hearing any thing of him, until they past Frederickton about three miles, where they heard of a stranger having staid all night at a private house, that answered his description, and had gone

[73] Henry Lyon (1794-1864) and Isaiah Smith (1790-1818) were children of Loyalists settled in 1783.

[74] Nathan Deforest (1765-1840) had arrived with his parents on the same ship as Bates, in 1783.

[75] Better known today as Houlton, in the State of Maine, located just west of Woodstock, New Brunswick, on the USA-Canada border; at the time, it was under British occupation during the War of 1812.

[76] The editor of the British version explained in a footnote that "They entered into recognizances."

[77] One of the many inconsistencies in spelling; "goal" was, in fact, an alternate spelling of "gaol" throughout the 18th century, but it had become obsolete in the early 19th century.

[78] Legal term meaning "indefinitely."

[79] Richibucto, a town in eastern New Brunswick, at the mouth of the river of the same name. The name was corrected in the third edition.

on the road toward Woodstock,[80] and pursuing on, found he staid at Mr. Ingraham's tavern[81] the next night, slept till late next morning, being fatigued, paid his bill and went off, having previously opened a trunk that was in the room adjoining where he slept, and taken away with him, a full suit of new black clothes of Mr. Ingraham's that cost forty dollars, a silk cloak, with other articles, which he concealed so as not to be discovered. This intelligence left no doubt of his being the person they were in pursuit of. Mr. Ingraham, not missing his clothes immediately, had not pursued him.

The next day he went only as far as Mrs. Robertson's,[82] where he found a collection of young people—played the fiddle for them, and staid the next day and night. He then proceeded towards Woodstock, leaving the spoons with Mrs. R. and taking a shirt—took passage in a canoe, and happened to fall in company with another, that had been at Frederickton, in which was passenger the Rev. Mr. Dibble, missionary at Woodstock,[83] with a young man poling his canoe. The young man had seen at Frederickton the advertisement of Mr. Bailes, describing the man and the watch, which had a singular steel chain, and observed to Mr. Dibble that they both answered the appearance of the stranger. Being close along side, Mr. D. asked him the time of day—Being told, he asked him to let him look at his watch, observing that he might be mistaken. He very readily gave it him, and it was found so exactly to answer the description that he challenged it as the property of Mr. Bailes. Smith very deliberately said it was a favorite watch that he had owned a long time, but if he had heard of one like it being stolen, he had no objection to leave it with him till he returned, which would be in about two weeks. Mr. D. replied that the suspicion was so strong, by what the young man said from the

[80] Woodstock is a town in western New Brunswick, first settled in 1783 by veterans of the loyalist De Lancey's Brigade, raised on Long Island, New York.

[81] Abijah Ingraham was one of the veterans (see note 80) settled in Woodstock after 1783.

[82] Ruannah (née Cypher) Robertson, widow of Aaron Robertson. A few years later, she relocated with her children to Sullivan, Maine, where she married Thomas Ash.

[83] Rev. Frederick Dibblee (1753-1826), born in Stamford, Connecticut, was Walter Dibblee's (see note 35) uncle. He was rector of four parishes and lived in Woodstock. He is known today for his diaries, kept from 1803 to 1826. The name was corrected in the third edition, but it often appears in contemporary documents as "Dibble."

advertisement, that he thought he would detain him also, until he could hear from Frederickton. He answered that he was on important business and could not be detained; but if he would pay his expenses and make himself responsible for damages incurred by his detention, that he had no objection to stop till he could send to Frederickton—otherwise, he should be back in ten or twelve days, and by that time he might be satisfied, and he would leave the watch until his return. He appeared so indifferent and unconcerned, and talked so plausibly, without exhibiting one sign of guilt, that they let him go, but kept the watch as a pledge for his return. He continued on through the settlement of Woodstock until he came to the road that leads to the American settlement; being near night, he was asked by a man of whom he inquired the road to tarry all night, as he could not get to the settlement till late, the distance being 12 miles—He said two men had gone on before him, on their way to the United States, and he feared they would leave him in the morning, and went on. It happened, a short time after they parted, that two young men arrived there from the settlement; being asked if they met two men on the road, they said no. It was then concluded Smith was a deserter. They turned about and pursued after him to the American side, but found nothing of him. They day following, Mr. Foster and Mr. Deforest arrived at Woodstock, and went on to the American settlement, but could hear nothing of him. They informed the inhabitants of the character of Smith, described him, and offered a reward of £20. The people seemed well disposed, and promised, if he came that way, to secure him.

Messrs. F. and D. then returned to the river St. John, and again got track of the prisoner—found he had crossed the river, stopped at several houses for refreshment, and called himself BOND; enquired after a thief that had broke gaol at Kingston; said he was a notorious villain, that he would certainly be hanged, if taken, and that he was in pursuit of him. They traced him down the river to an Indian camp, where they found he had agreed with an Indian to pilot him through the woods to the U. States by the way of Ell River,[84] a rout[85] frequently travelled,

[84] Eel River (the name was corrected in the third edition) runs through the southern boundary of Woodstock Parish, in western New Brunswick (not to be confused with the Eel River in northern New Brunswick).

[85] Route was still sometimes spelled "rout" well into the 19th century (it was updated in the third edition).

and had finally escaped; upon which they thought proper to return, and make their report.

It appeared afterwards, that the Indian, after travelling a day or two on his rout through the woods, probably finding that his journey would not be very profitable, and discovering Smith to have a pistol, began to be jealous of him, refused to pilot him any further,[86] gave him back part of his money, and returned.[87] Smith, of course, was obliged to return with him, and try his chance the other way, by the American settlement, where he arrived about the 10th of October, in the morning, said he was in pursuit of a deserter, and wanted some refreshment—While his breakfast was preparing, notice was given among the inhabitants, when Dr. RICE, a principal character there,[88] caused him to be taken and secured. The clothes he had stolen from Mr. Ingraham he had on, except the pantaloons, which he had exchanged for a pistol—He said he purchased the clothes, very cheap, of a man who, he believed, was a Yankey.—He was then placed in charge of Mr. A. Putnam and a Mr. Watson of Woodstock,[89] and ordered back to Fredericton. On their way they stopped with the prisoner at the Attorney-General's, about three miles from Fredericton, and then proceeded into town, where the Supreme Court was then sitting. He was brought before the Court, and a large number of spectators. The Hon.

---

[86] The editor of the London edition added an explanatory footnote for the British readership: "'To pilot,' to guide; 'to be jealous,' to be suspicious." Bates later changed these and, in the third edition, the Indian, who "discovered that Smith carried a pistol, which he did not like very much, refused to guide him any longer."

[87] The importance of this event is emphasised in the third edition: "This materially turned the scale with our *adventurer*, and Fortune, that had hitherto smiled on his enterprize, refused, like the Indian, to conduct him much further."

[88] Dr. Samuel Rice (1784-1858) had come from New Salem, Massachusetts, to Houlton, Maine, in 1811 (see Gilman 12); as most of his patients were in Woodstock, he relocated there in the early 1820s.

[89] Aaron Putnam (1773-1849), originally from New Salem, Massachusetts, opened the first store in Woodstock in 1805 and also operated a ferry starting in 1809. Like Dr. Rice, he often moved between Woodstock and Houlton, but he eventually relocated in the latter. "A. Putnam" could be him, but it is more likely that it is his son, Amos (1794-1849). The second man who takes charge of Smith, "Mr. Watson of Woodstock," is very probably one of the many sons of Peter Watson, a settler from England, perhaps his eldest, Peter Jr. (born in 1789).

Judge SANDERS[90] asked him his name—he said, *Smith.* Are you the man that escaped from the gaol at Kingston?—*Yes.* He was then ordered to prison. Being asked how he made his escape, he said, *the gaoler opened the door, and the priest prayed him out.* The day following he was remanded to Kingston gaol—Putnam and Watson sat out with him in an Indian bark canoe, one sitting at each end—He was handcuffed, pinioned, and tied to a bar of the canoe, in the centre. They were obliged to watch him in the first night. The next day they arrived at the house of Mr. Bailes, opposite Spoon Island,[91] where he had stolen the watch, &c. It was near night, and the passage to Kingston difficult—They being strangers, Mr. Bailes told them if they would stop till morning he would pilot them down—They accordingly stopped, and having been up all the night before, Mr. B. said they had better lie down and get some rest, and he would watch the prisoner with his family. Smith enquired the way to St. John, if there were any ferries on this side the river, &c. and asked for a blanket and leave to lie down—Mrs. B. made him a bed on the floor—He then said he had occasion to go to the door—and Mr. B. awaked Watson, who got up to attend him—Smith told him, if he had any apprehensions, he had better tie a rope to his arm, which he did, above the handcuffs, and with the other end wound round his hand, they went out—In an unwary moment, Smith seized the opportunity, knocked him down with his handcuffs, and went off, leaving the rope in the hand of Watson, having slipped the other end over his hand, tied the same as it was put on.

The night being very dark, no discovery was made which way he escaped.[92] The next morning was rainy—Mr. Putnam came to the sheriff at Kingston with the report, who supplied

[90] John Saunders (1754-1834), a native of Virginia who had fought on the British side in the American Revolutionary War. After a spell in England, he came to Fredericton in 1790, being appointed a judge of the Supreme Court of New Brunswick. He was a major landowner. In 1822, he became Chief Justice of the province. His name was corrected in the third edition.

[91] Spoon Island is in the Saint John River, in the Hampstead Parish of Queens County.

[92] The third edition includes an account of Putnam and Watson's "chagrin" and their decision to wait: "To pursue him in the night, which was unusually dark, and rainy besides, was both hopeless and vain; it was therefore thought best to inform the Sheriff in the morning of what had taken place, and receive his advice as to their future proceedings."

him with money, and he went in pursuit toward St. John by the Long Reach.[93] The sheriff, with two men, proceeded to Bailes'—found he had taken the rout toward Frederickton—had crossed the Oaknabock Lake[94] the first night in haste; said he was going to purchase land, and had agreed with Putnam and Watson, who had *gone to Kingston with the thief*, to take him up in their canoe on their return, and was to meet them at the intervale above[95] early next morning. We had then no doubt he was making his way to the Oromucto,[96] the only remaining passage to the United States. Watson had gone in pursuit that way. Being informed that a canoe had been taken from the shore above where he had crossed the Lake, and was found on the shore of the Bellisle, it was again suggested that he had made his way toward Nova-Scotia on that rout, as it was thought he would not return to Frederickton, where he was known. Pursuit was made that way, but we found no trace of him.

Nothing more was heard of our adventurer until about the 26th of October, when it was found that, instead of going off, he had made his way direct to Frederickton. The first day being wet and cold, he came to a small house, in a bye place, where no one lived. An old man, named Wicks, and his son, were there at work, repairing the house and getting in some potatoes. He came in, wet, cold and hungry. Wicks told him he did not lodge there, but if he would go with him to the next house he could stay all night. He replied that he must go 8 or 10 miles further that night, and went away, as did Wicks and his son. The next morning it was found Smith had turned back and staid all night; had burnt all the wood; roasted a parcel of potatoes, and was seen at day light, travelling toward Frederickton. The next night he came to the house of a Mr. Wilmot,[97] where, it appeared, he

[93] This means he went south-west along the river (see note 47), then south towards the city.

[94] Lake Otnabog, on the west bank of the Saint John River.

[95] An "interval" or "intervale" is a section of low ground or shrubland between a river and the nearby hills. Bates gives it a definition in his "Description of New Brunswick" (see Appendix I). "Intervale" was pronounced "interval" (Ganong, "Place-Nomenclature" 210).

[96] The Oromocto River, a tributary of the Saint John River, flowing from the west.

[97] Probably John McNeil Wilmot (1775-1847), who was living in Lincoln, York County, on the west bank of the Saint John, between Fredericton and Oromocto. He was one of several sons of Captain Lemuel Wilmot (1743-1814), of New Haven, Connecticut, one of the first loyalists settled there in 1783.

went in, and finding a washing of linen clothes, just sprinkled for ironing, he made seizure of the whole, together with a coat belonging to a young man in the house, and finding them rather burdensome, took a horse, saddle and bridle, and proceeded on his journey. Within two miles of Frederickton lived Jack Patterson, a mulatto man,[98] who had a barrack or hovel full of hay—Here Smith concealed himself and his booty, giving his horse some hay, and letting him run upon the common during the day, at night catching him and riding into town in the full fruition of unrestrained liberty. Thus he continued for several days, committing frequent depredations. At length he determined to pay a visit to the Attorney-General, about three miles above, where he was acquainted, having stopt there on his way down. He arrived between 8 and 9 o'clock in the evening, and knowing the form of the house, went boldly into the hall. There being much company in at the time, his modesty would not permit him to intrude amongst them, but he paid his respects to their loose garments, the whole of which he carried off, consisting of five great-coats, three plaid cloaks, tippets, comforters, and other articles. He returned through the town to his deposit. Having made a fine booty at the Attorney General's, he gave his horse a large allowance of hay, that he might the more willingly stay by him for the next night's service; but, unfortunately for him, his generosity to his horse, led to his discovery. The negro seeing the hay lying in an unusual manner out of the window of his barrack, supposed that some person had been in to sleep; and going in, found Smith lying in the hay, with a white comforter or tippet about his neck, and seeing him a stranger, asked him where he came from; he said, from the Kennebeccasis, and was going after land, had got belated, and had slept in his hay; he hoped it was no harm—but on the negro going to the house, Smith slipped out of the window and made toward the woods—The mulatto supposing him a deserter, called for help, and soon apprehended him, as he did not appear to make much exertion to escape. It was soon discovered who he was, and he was committed to gaol at Frederickton. The mulatto not finding the tippet with him that

[98] John Patterson (c.1768-1833) came to New Brunswick in 1783 on the ship *Generous Friends*. He was then described as "15, fine boy, M[aster Charles Loosley]. Says he was born free, is now indented to Mr. Loosley" (Hodges and Brown 55). By 1814, he had fulfilled his indenture and was farming a lot outside Fredericton (see Davidson 35-46).

he saw about his neck, was induced to look in the hay for it, and thus discovered the secret deposit, which contained all the articles mentioned, and many more, which the owners had the good fortune to recover. He gave them no satisfaction; said a soldier brought them there in the night, and rode a little black horse, and left the saddle and bridle.

He was then ordered to be taken by the Sheriff of York,[99] and safely delivered to the Sheriff in the gaol of Kings County. Accordingly, the Sheriff prepared for his safe conveyance, an iron collar made of a flat bar of iron, 1 inch and a half wide, with a hinge and clasp, fastened with a padlock, which he put around his neck, with a chain about ten feet long fastened to it; put a strong pair of hand-cuffs upon his hands; and with the negro Patterson holding the chain (*after searching to see that he had no saws or other instruments,*) sat off with him on board a sloop, and the wind being favorable, arrived safe at Kingston, sixty miles distant, about 12 o'clock, on the night of the 30th October, 1814. He appeared as composed as if nothing had happened. The next morning we took him to the gaol, where he was the first man that entered, knowing perfectly the way. The room had been swept clean of every thing, and searched closely after his escape; in doing which, we found the remains of several wheels of a watch, the barrel in particular, that contained the main-spring, which convinced us that he had procured it while he was in gaol, from the young man that took away the spy-glass, and was intended to effect his escape. We also found a knife, which he had cut in two, no doubt with a saw which he had made of the main-spring, which gave us strong suspicion that he must have saws about him, probably concealed in his clothes.

Mr. Barton had searched him before he left Frederickton. However, I took off his handcuffs and ordered him to strip off his clothes, which he did without the least reluctance, to his shirt. We then searched the sleeves, wristbands and collar of his shirt, and the hair of his head, that we might be sure that he did not bring the smallest thing to effect his escape again—We then put on him other clothes, and took and carried out of the

[99] The Sheriff of York County was George Duncan Berton (1774-1828). He was born on Long Island, New York and came with his family as a nine-year-old to New Brunswick. He is an ancestor of Canadian author Pierre Berton. Bates calls him below "Barton" (and, in the third edition, "Burton"). York County contains the provincial capital Fredericton.

goal all the clothes he had on him when he came, hat, shoes, and every article that he brought with him.

The prison in which he was confined, was 22 by 16 feet, built of stone and lime, wall three feet thick on three sides; the other side being the partition wall between the two prison rooms, was timber, twelve inches thick, lathed[100] and plastered on both sides; the prison plastered with lime on every part; the floor was of timber ten inches square, on which rested the side wall; the door was of two inch plank, made double, and lined with sheet iron, hung on three iron bar hinges, three and a half inches wide, clasping over staples in the opposite post, and secured with three padlocks, with a small iron wicket door, secured also with a padlock—There was one window through the stone wall, iron grated within and without, enclosed with glass outside, so that no conveyance could be had undiscovered—The passage that leads to the door, is about twenty feet in length, and three feet in width, secured at the entrance by a padlock on the door; the outside door also so locked, that no communication could be had, without going through three doors, the keys of which were always kept by the gaoler; who, being in an infirm state of health, never left the house day or night; and having had much trouble in consequence of his escape, was now uncommonly strict: no person was permitted to speak to him. In that situation, I put on him one iron shackle on his right leg, with a chain just long enough to reach the necessary, and to take his provisions from the wicket door, stapled in the timber of the floor near the partition wall, so that he could not come to the grates by five or six feet; and allowed him a bunk with straw and blankets to sleep on—After these precautions, he was thought perfectly safe. His wrists being much swelled, took off his handcuffs; told the gaoler to look to him frequently at the wicket door, and see that he remained secure, and that I would visit him occasionally—The gaoler always found him sitting up in his birth reading, or lying down, and made no complaints. I visited once or twice a week, and to see that his fetters and chain remained secure, ordered him to come to the door, which he always did, without any reluctance. He appeared comfortable, and satisfied with his situation, without saying a word about the fate of his cause. Under these

[100] "Lathed" here refers to the operation of "lathing," i.e., building the wooden framework for the plastered partition wall out of "laths" (thin strips of wood).

circumstances, began to calculate that we should keep him safely, until a Court would be ordered for his trial, without any material difficulty. On the twelfth day, I was informed that Mr. Newman Perkins heard a strange noise in the night, which induced him to believe that Smith was at work at the grates—On enquiry, Mrs. Perkins said she had heard a noise like rubbing or filing late in the night, and by putting her head out of the window, she thought she discovered it to be at the gaol; which appeared altogether improbable, knowing the situation of the prisoner, and the impossibility of his having any thing to work with. I went immediately to the gaol—Moses Foster, George Raymond, Allen Baston,[101] Mr. Dibblee and others, were with me—it was then evening, and we had two or three candles—the gaoler opening the door, on going in, I found him lying in his birth, chained, just as I left him; and said to him, Smith, you have not got out yet—He answered No, *not quite.* I then examined every bar of the grates, as strictly as possible; as did also every one present, again and again, until we were all satisfied the alarm must be imaginary—Smith lying quiet, answering readily any question asked him. Mr. Allen Baston, however, continued searching the inner grate. There had been observed by all, a small chip lying on one of the flat bars of the outer grate, and supposed to happen there accidentally—Mr. Baston being fully satisfied in viewing the inner grates, his fancy led him to reach through and take off the chip on one of the outer grates, in doing which, he perceived it to hang a little, which led him to further examination, when he discovered the bar of the grate cut one third off, and concealed with the feather edge of the chip, which astonished all present, knowing it could not be done without first getting through the inner grates; on proving which, we soon found that he had so neatly cut one of the bars, that he could take it out and replace it, at his pleasure, and conceal it in such a way, that it could not be observed; and would undoubtedly have completed his escape in two or three nights more. I then asked him what he cut the grate with; he answered with indifference, with *this saw* and *this file;* and without any hesitation, handed to me out of birth, a case knife, steel blade, cut in fine teeth very neatly, and a common hand-saw file. I then asked him how he got to the

[101] Allen Baston (1783-1823) was born in present-day New Hampshire. He was a brickmaker who later plied his trade in Fredericton, where he died of smallpox. His name is misspelled as "Basten" in the third edition.

grates, and whether he had slipped the shackle off his foot—He said No, he had *cut the chain;* and calmly shewed me where he had cut the chain in the joint of the links, where it could not be readily discovered. I then asked him where he got his tools—he said he left them when he went away from here; and that they were all the tools he had—but we perceived from the shape of the knife, being so much thicker on the back than the edge, that the bars were never cut so nicely without some other tool; and on a strict search, we found in a broken place of the wall, near the grates, a neat watch-spring saw, with a string at one end. I asked him who gave him those tools; with great indifference he answered, you need not ask me that again, for I never will tell you. I then renewed the chain to his leg, put the iron collar about his neck, and stapled the chain to the floor, with a heavy pair of hand-cuffs, with 7-8 bolt, on his wrists, all of which he received very willingly. After searching his bed and clothes, we left him on Saturday night about eleven o'clock. Sunday, at four o'clock, I was at the gaol; the gaoler informed me he was lying in his birth, with all his irons on, had been enquiring if the Sheriff was not coming to examine his chains. About twelve o'clock the same night, I was alarmed by a man sent by the gaoler, informing me, that Smith had got loose from all his irons, had got through the inner grate, was cutting the outer grate, and had nearly escaped—that from the vigilance and attention of Mr. Dibblee, the gaoler, he was discovered to be at work, about ten o'clock at night; by silently moving towards the prison, he got to the door undiscovered, and with a candle at the end of a stick of a yard long, in an instant opened the wicket door and shoved the light into the gaol, while Smith was yet at work; the gaoler ordered him to leave every thing, and take to his birth; he very calmly complied; but returned suddenly to the grates, which were in a situation out of the sight of the gaoler, and then went quickly to the necessary, and threw something down, which the gaoler heard, and then came to his bed; the gaoler watching him until the Sheriff came. On going into the gaol, I found he had extricated himself from all his irons, had got through the inner grates with all his clothes, and in the act of cutting the outer grates, which he had cut two thirds off, and would have effected his escape before day light. I said to him, Smith, you keep at work; he said that he had done work now; and that all his tools were down the necessary—which, by letting down a candle, was strictly searched, but nothing discovered. He was then stript of every rag of clothing, except his shirt, which were searched, every hem and seam; his birth knocked all in pieces, removed out of the gaol, and searched in every joint and split, and the room swept critically, for watch-spring saws, which we suspected he had; but nothing was discovered—We then replaced all his chains with padlocks, put on him a pair of screw handcuffs, which confined his hands close together; and then left him, at four o'clock on Monday morning. On Monday, Mr. John Jarvis, blacksmith,[102] had mended the grates, and came to put them in. We found Smith lying on the floor, apparently in the same situation that we had left him; but on examining his handcuffs, found them cut in two, and that he could put them off and on when he pleased. Being asked why he destroyed his handcuffs, he said they were so stiff that nobody could wear them. No doubt then remained that he must have his saws concealed about his body. Doctor Paddock being present, was requested to examine him. He stript off his clothes without any reluctance, and on taking off his shirt, the Doctor discovered a muslin strip, tied about his thigh, close to his body, so hard that it could not be discovered by rubbing the hand over it, which concealed on the inside of his left thigh, a fine steel saw plate, two inches wide, and ten inches long, with teeth cut on both edges; no doubt of his own make. After this discovery, we put on him a light pair of handcuffs, and secured his chains with padlocks, and set four men to watch him the whole night. The next day secured the inner grate with hard bricks, filling the squares of the grates, and wedging them from behind; and filling the space between the grates solid with brick, lime and sand, leaving only one space at the upper corner, five by four inches, with a square of glass plastered with lime in the middle, and glass also in the sash without, which prevented all possible conveyance to him undiscovered—this space, through a wall three feet thick, conveyed little or no light, and left the room a complete dungeon, so that he could not be discovered from the door at any time of day without a candle; and we never after went into the gaol without two candles, and three or four men. On the 13th Nov. I addressed a letter to Judge Chipman, and received the following answer:

[102] John Jarvis (1752-1845) was born, like Bates, in Stamford, Connecticut.

"ST. JOHN, Nov. 14, 1814.

DEAR SIR—I have received your letter of yesterday's date, relating to the new attempt of H. M. Smith to escape—I have forwarded the same to Frederickton. I presume that a Court will be ordered for his trial, as soon as it may be practicable from the state of the travelling, and the necessity of procuring the witness from Nova-Scotia, though, I should suppose, probably not before the ice makes.[103] In the mean time, the utmost vigilance and precaution must be made use of to secure him; and you will be justified in any measures of severity that you may find it necessary to adopt for this purpose. I am, dear sir, very faithfully yours,

W. CHIPMAN.

W. BATES, Esq."

Wednesday, Nov. 16th—went into the gaol and found he had injured the room by beating the plaister[104] off the partition wall with his chain; had broken one of the padlocks, and appeared to have been loose; seemed very vicious; said he would burn and destroy the building; he would make it smoke before he left it, and we should see it. I then procured a pair of steel fetters, well case-hardened, about ten inches long, with a chain from the middle stapled to the floor; a chain from the neck collar to the fetters; the shackles around both his legs well riveted; and his handcuffs riveted to the chain from his neck. The whole of the irons and chains he received without showing the least reluctance or concern. The blacksmith, after he had finished riveting them, said to him, "Smith, I would advise you to be quiet after this, for if you are not you will have an iron band put round your body, and be stapled fast to the floor"—He calmly replied, *Old man, if you are not satisfied, you may put it on now—I do not regard it—if you will let me have my hands loose, you may put on as much iron as you please.* In this situation, loaded with irons, without any thing to sit or lie upon but the naked floor, he was not the least humbled, but grew exceeding noisy and vicious, seemingly very spiteful to the gaoler, who, in return, having had so much trouble with him, showed him but little favour or compassion. He soon began to roar and rave with madness, and would take little or no notice of any thing said to

[103] That is, as soon as the ice is strong and safe to travel on.

[104] Plaster (gypsum) was mined in several places in New Brunswick (see Marsden in Appendix I), including in Kings County.

him, sometimes praying and repeating texts of scripture, till at length despair seemed to combine with madness, when, with a tremendous voice, he would cry out—O thou cruel devils! thou murderers! man-slayers! thou tormentors of man! How I burn to be revenged! Help! help! help! Lord help me to be avenged of these devils! help me, that I may tear up this place! that I may turn it upside down! that there may not be one stick of it left! My hair shall not be shorn, nor my nails cut, till I grow as strong as Sampson; then will I be avenged of all my enemies! Help! help! O Lord help me to destroy these tormentors! these murderers of man! tormenting me in chains and darkness! (Hallooing and shouting) Darkness! Darkness! O darkness!—Not light to read the word of God! Not one word of comfort from any one! All is, you rogue, you thief, you villain! you deserve to be hanged! No pity—not one word of consolation! All darkness! All trouble! (Singing) Trouble, trouble, trouble, trouble—O God! help me, and have mercy on me! I fear there is no mercy for me!——Yes, there is mercy! It is in Jesus, whose arms stand open to receive me! but how shall I dare to look to him whom I have offended! Then he would call upon his parents, and deprecate his wicked life; then rave gain—Murderers! Tormentors! Consider you have souls to lose as well as I, a poor prisoner! Consider you have children that may be brought to trouble as well as me! Consider I have parents! If they knew my situation it would kill them!—My wife! Begone from my sight! why will you torment me! It is for you I suffer all my sorrow! It is for you my heart bleeds! It is for you only is all my trouble!—Not a friend comes to see me; nothing before me but pain and sorrow, chains and darkness, misery and death! O wretched me! how long am I to suffer in this place of torment! Am I to linger a life of pain and sorrow in chains and misery! No! I will cut the thread of life, and be relieved from this place of darkness, and trouble! (singing) trouble, trouble, trouble, a thousand times repeated. He continued in this strain a considerable time, and would not answer when spoken to, or take the least notice of any one present, until he grew very hoarse, and at last *he left off speaking at all, on any occasion.*

The weather growing cold, I allowed him his bunk again, and made him a comfortable bed. He made one attempt to hang himself, by making a rope out of his blankets, which were taken from him. He then attempted, for three or four days, to starve himself, but gave that over.—He lay in his bed most of the time, day and night, without committing any act of violence, until the 16th of December, when, on going into the prison, I found he had broken the iron collar from his neck, and drawn the staple from the timber, returning it slightly to its place, so that it would not be readily discovered. On the 17th, put a chain about his neck and stapled him to the floor, in a situation to prevent him from reaching either of the staples. In this situation, his wrists being galled by his previous exertions, and very much swelled and sore, he remained more quiet, hallooing occasionally, until January 15th—The weather being very cold at this season, and having no fire, he was in danger of freezing. I took off all his irons except his fetters and handcuffs, for which relief he showed not the least thankfulness or acknowledgment, but grew more noisy and troublesome, especially at night, so much so that no sleep could be had for the strange noises he would make—not like the human voice, but by such tremendous screeches and howlings as were never heard before, without uttering a word. In this manner he continued five months, committing many outrages upon himself and his chains, doing many curious and astonishing acts, as will be related, and during all which time *he could never be provoked or surprised to speak one word*, and took no notice of any person, or any thing done or said to him, any more than a dumb or senseless creature. He had the New Testament, which he kept by him, and a leaf in it was observed to be turned down; on examination it proved to be at the 3d chapter of Corinthians, beginning in these words, "*And I, brethren, could not speak unto you*," &c.[105]

The weather being extremely cold throughout the month of January, fears were entertained that he must perish without fire, presuming that no man could keep from freezing in his situation. I visited him almost every day, and examined his hands and feet, but never found him cold. He kept in his bunk night and day, and his chains always felt warm. He made no more attempts to escape until February, when the weather began to moderate a little, and he became more restless and troublesome. Early in the month he began to tear off the lime wall and lathing from the partition; broke every thing he could get hold of; a strong iron-hopped bucked, that held his drink, he broke all in small pieces; not a piece of the iron hoops was

[105] From 1 Corinthians 3: 1: "And I, brethren, could not speak unto you as unto spiritual, but as unto carnal, even as unto babes in Christ."

left more than three inches long; and when the gaoler came to the wicket door with a candle to see him, he would throw the pieces with such dexterity as to put out the light, although handcuffed. He continued, as the weather moderated, to grow more noisy and vicious. On the 10th I received the following note from the gaoler:

"DEAR SIR,—There must be something done with Smith—He is determined to let me know what he is, if no one else does—He sleeps in the day time, and when I go to tell him to keep quiet at night, he yells so as not to hear what I say. Instead of thanks for taking off his irons, he makes all the noise he can by yelling and screaming all night, and knocking very loud with some part of his irons. I wish you would come up early and advise what is best.

W. DIBBLEE."

On going into the gaol, found his irons on whole and safe; and to prevent him from using his hands so freely, locked a chain from his fetters to his handcuffs, and left him. On Sunday the 19th, two gentlemen from Nova-Scotia, who had been requested by his wife to make some enquiry after him, called upon me. I persuaded them to go with me to the gaol, to see if he would speak, or take any notice of them or any thing they might say to him from his wife. They said a great deal to him—told him his wife wished to know his situation, and if he wished her to come to him; what she should do with a colt he had left; if he would have him sold, that he would fetch 200 dollars, &c. but all made no impression on him any more than if he was a dead man, which convinced us all that if he should be hanged he would go to the gallows without speaking a word, or changing his countenance.

The week following he grew more restless and vicious, and the next Sunday, on going into the gaol with Mr. Ruloffson and Mr. Griffith from Woodstock,[106] found Smith had broken up part of his birth; had broken the chain from his handcuffs, leaving one link to the staple, the parted links secreted; torn up part of his bedding, and stopped the funnel of the necessary so

[106] The latter is certainly Benjamin Peck Griffith (1796-1875), son of an officer of the same name, one of De Lancey's veterans (see note 80) settled in Woodstock, who had died in 1809. If the former is another young man, then he is probably not Ruloff Ruloffson or Ruliffson, a former Loyalist sergeant-major who had settled in 1783 on the banks of the Kennebecasis (in Hampton Parish, as Bates specifies in the third edition), but his son William (1792-1827).

that it could not easily be cleared. It appeared also that he had been at the grates, but how he got there was a mystery, as the chains to his legs were whole, and the staple well in the timber; but he had evidently been there, as some of the boarding was broken and pieces of pine left in the bricks. We then raised the staple, and again put on the chain to the handcuffs, and drove the staple in another place, more out of his reach. The next day found he had again parted the chain from his hands, and torn off a large portion of the lathing and plastering from the middle wall, the floor covered with rubbish. I then attempted to confine him more closely, putting a chain from his feet around his neck, stapled to the floor, and his handcuffs secured to the middle of the chain.

Notwithstanding every exertion I could make to restrain him, I was still fearful that, as the weather grew warmer, he would find means to effect his escape, as he had already done things that seemed to require more than human power to execute; especially in getting the iron collar off his neck, and drawing the staple from the timber, which two yoke of oxen could not have done. The iron collar, which was made of a flat bar of iron, one and a half inch wide, the edges only rounded, he twisted the same as if a piece of leather, and broke it in two. We very often found him bloody, and his wrists swelled and sore by his exertions, but he never complained, or took any notice of what he had done, or exhibited any regard for his situation or comfort.

March 1st—on going into the gaol at evening found him out of his bed walking, and exhibiting a remarkable effigy, representing his wife, standing in gaol, supported by the wall, as large as life, apparently visiting him in his miserable confinement; himself walking before her in chains and fetters, as far as they would admit. By the light of candles this scene exhibited a most striking picture of misery and distress—A wife, visiting her wretched and disconsolate husband in a dungeon, in a most dejected posture, overcome and speechless—The husband moving restless and silently before her, despair pictured on his countenance, agitated, every muscle of his frame exhibiting marks of acutest anguish. Truly, I must say, this scene shocked the feelings of humanity; its effect can hardly be effaced from my mind. Every one present was awed and astonished at the sight—and I am fully persuaded the like never was, and never can be again produced, with equal ingenuity and effect. The effigy was formed of his bedding, and the shirt and clothes he had destroyed, with the assistance of a trough, three or four feet long, used for keeping water in the gaol for him to drink.

He continued noisy and troublesome until the 5th of March, when I took off his irons and gave him a clean shirt—let him wash himself and comb his hair, which had not been cut, nor his beard shaved, since he had been in gaol—gave him some soap, a part of which he eat,[107] and used the rest. The blacksmith again put on his irons and chains, which he received the same as an ox would his yoke, or a horse his harness.

March 6th—our Court of Common Pleas coming on it required all my attention, and Mr. Dibblee, the gaoler, having received a flattering invitation to take charge of the Academy at Sussex-Vale,[108] had engaged to remove there as soon as the Court was over, and accordingly, on the 11th of March, he removed, leaving the prisoner without a keeper, and me in an unpleasant and anxious situation. The conduct of Smith had been and continued so bad that I could find no one willing to take charge of him. The next day, however, with much persuasion, I prevailed upon Mr. James Reid,[109] a Scotchman, a man in whom I could place the utmost confidence, to undertake the task, and the day following he moved into the house with his family.

Smith appeared of a better countenance, and rather more quiet, until the 24th of March, when I was called upon by the gaoler, and informed that he was about something; that he had broken open the hole through the partition, that led the stove pipes into the debtors room, and no doubt was loose. On going into the gaol, found him loose from all his irons; his neck chain was broken in three pieces; his screw handcuffs in four pieces, and all hanging on nails on the partition wall—his great coat torn in two through the back, and stripped in pieces, one strip about his shoulders for a belt, with a wooden sword hanging in it; and with it he shewed all the exercise of the small sword, which he appeared to understand well—His chains from his legs were loose from the staples, and tied with a strip of his

[107] In the early 19th century, "eat" was still in use as the past form of the verb "to eat."

[108] The "Indian Academy" at Sussex Vale was inaugurated in 1787. Walter Dibblee took charge of it in 1815, but he died in 1817 and he was replaced briefly by his son John.

[109] James Reid (1782-1860) was born in Aberdeen. He had moved to New Brunswick in 1809.

great coat; his hands, face and clothes bloody. In this situation, he exhibited an astonishing figure. During the time he was loose, he had taken off every inch of the plastering from the partition wall; stripped off all the lathing, and the boarding over the grates; broken some of the bricks—had gathered all the fragments together, and stacking them up in a round stack, with the broken lath fenced it round with a worm fence;[110] piled all the long lath close to the wall under the grates, out of sight from the wicket door; then swept the floor clean; so that returning to his birth and tying his leg chain to the staple, on looking in with a candle, nothing could be seen out of place. In this situation I found him—Daniel Micheau, Esq., Moses Foster, George Raymond, Walker Tisdale,[111] the gaoler, and other present. I then raised the staple, secured him by the leg chain, put on a pair of strong stiff handcuffs, added a strong chain to his neck stapled to the floor, and left him. He remained in that situation until the 28th—I was then called again by the gaoler, who said he believed he was loose, and was about some mischief—I went into gaol and found him loose; his chain from his neck separated into three pieces, and had bruised the plastering from the stone wall, with his chains, about three feet long—We were obliged to leave him—While we were getting his chains mended, he swept the room clean. At night I added another chain from his fetters to his neck, and stapled him to the floor, with about four feet chain; secured his handcuffs to the chain between his neck and feet, so that when standing, he could not reach in any direction, and then left him. He remained easy, singing and hallooing occasionally, until the 31st. I was then called again, by the gaoler, who said he was certainly loose again; that opening the door to see what he was doing, he found a piece of the chain from his neck hanging on the inside of the wicket door—I went immediately to the gaol; found he

[110] A fence made of rails interlocking in a zigzag; also known as "snake fence," "split-rail fence," or "Virginia fence." The British edition includes a footnote (possibly by Bates) explaining it as "A fence, the form of which is peculiar to the settlements in America."

[111] Daniel Micheau (1761-1818) was a Loyalist born in Staten Island, New York, who came to New Brunswick in 1783. He was appointed deputy land surveyor of the province. He lived in Hampton, where he married a daughter of Rev. James Scovil's (see note 41) and became a justice of the Inferior Court of Common Pleas for Kings County. Walker Tisdale (1783-1857) was born on board one of the ships bringing loyalists to New Brunswick. He was a merchant in the City of Saint John. For the others, see notes 44 and 57.

had broken all his chains; had tied his foot chain to the staple again, long enough to reach the wicket door; was lying in bed as unconcerned as if nothing had happened, with the piece of chain about his neck. We then took his bunk bedstead from him, and every thing within his reach, and never let him have it any more; but could not discover by what means he separated his chains. No links of the chains appeared twisted, nor were any broken links to be seen. The manner in which he was chained, as well as the strength of the chains, left it beyond doubt, that he must have means to cut the links, as it was thought beyond human strength, in his situation, to break them—to ascertain which we let a candle down the necessary, by which we could see the bottom clearly; and with an iron hook prepared for the purpose, we brought up a bunch of *broken* links of his chains, which he had tied up in a piece of his shirt, and thrown down, together with a piece of his neck chain, about a foot long; which convinced us that he could have no further means of *cutting* his chains, and that he must do it by some mysterious art or power. I was then determined to break the enchantment, if strength of chain would do it; and added to his fetters a large timber chain, which was used for bunk chain of a bob sled,[112] by which four and five logs were hauled to the mill at once. (I have seen the chain made use of at the gaol in New-Haven;[113] and this chain was at least one third, if not one half larger, and twice as strong.) We then left him—April 1st, found his neck chain parted again; got it mended, and replaced it. April 6th, found his neck chain again parted—I then replaced his neck chain, with a strong ox chain, a size larger than that used in the prison at New-Haven, about seven feet long; the whole of his irons in good order, and equally strong; which, being weighed by the gaoler after they were taken off, amounted to forty-six pounds. Left him that night; next morning the gaoler informed me, that from the unaccountable noise he had made through the night, he was persuaded he must be loose from some of his chains—I then concluded he must have broken his

[112] This appears as "bob-sledge" in the British edition, where a footnote (possibly by Bates) explains it as "a kind of sledge, used for moving timber."

[113] Spelled "New Haven" in the third edition (the parenthesis here was obviously added to the diary after Bates's trip to Connecticut). The British edition (possibly Bates) explains it as "In Connecticut, one of the United States." Both the parenthesis and the April 1st entry are absent in the third edition.

steel fetters, as it was impossible for human strength to break either of the ox chains—But to my surprize, found the chain to his neck parted, and tied with a string to the staple, two feet long; handcuffs, fetters and log chain whole—secured his neck chain again—After this he remained more quiet; his wrists being much galled, and otherwise bruised and sore from his exertions.[114]

He did not commit any further outrages for some time, but busied himself in brading[115] straws, with which he made a place on the side wall to put his bread in; sometimes making an image or likeness of a man or woman, and placing them in very striking situations, discovering great art and ingenuity, and seemed to amuse himself without breaking his irons, but made much noise, hallooing and beating his chains most of the night. On the 29th, on going into the Gaol, discovered the likeness of a woman, representing his wife, sitting at the head of his bed, with the New Testament open before her, as though reading to him, and he sitting in a posture as tho' listening to her with great attention. I was induced to look into the book, and found it opened to the 13th chapter of St. Luke, the title of which was, "*Jesus teacheth Repentance*," with a leaf turned down directing to the last verse of the 12th Chapter—Appearing as though she had rebuked him for his conduct, bringing to the mind his several escapes, whilst he appeared to justify himself with that text of Scripture, which says:—"*When thou goest with thine adversary to the magistrate, as thou art on the way, give diligence that thou mayest be delivered from him, lest he hale thee to the Judge, and the Judge deliver thee to the officer, and the officer cast thee into prison.*"[116] S. Scribner, T. Scribner, and Mr. Reid were present with me.[117]

[114] In the third edition, Bates added here a letter from Ward Chipman, Jr.: "*St. John, March* 15th. Dear Sir, – At length I enclose you the *precept* for summoning a Court of *Oyer* and *Terminer* and Gaol Delivery in your County, on Thursday the 20th April, for the trial of the horse stealer. – I also enclose a letter from Major King for his saddle stolen from him at the same time. Yours,&c." For Major King, see "Epilogue. Part II."

[115] Alternate spelling of "braiding." It was corrected in the third edition.

[116] Luke 12: 58 (the entire verse). The title added above the 13th chapter ("Jesus teacheth repentance") suggests it was a New Testament published by the British and Foreign Bible Society (or reproducing that version).

[117] For Reid, see note 109. For Thaddeus Scribner, see note 42. "S." is probably one of Thaddeus's nephews, either Samuel or Seth.

He produced many more of the like representations, that discovered an uncommon genius and wonderful ingenuity, more than I am able to describe.

A Special Court of Oyer and Terminer, and general Gaol delivery had been summoned, to be held at Kingston, on the 28th day of April, for the trial of the horse stealer, but was put off and re-summoned to be held on the 4th of May, occasioned by the ice remaining unusually late in the river St. John, as will appear from the following letters:

"ST. JOHN, April 5th, 1815.

DEAR SIR,—I have received your letter of detailing the very extraordinary conduct of the culprit in your custody. There is certainly a mystery in this man's means and character which is unfathomable, and I fear there will be considerable difficulty with him at the trial. Your vigilance and exertions of course must not be relaxed. As the best thing to be done, I dispatched your letter without delay to the Attorney General, that they might adopt at Head-Quarters, any such measures as they might think expedient, for the further safeguard and security of the prisoner.

Very respectfully yours,

W. CHIPMAN.

W. BATES, Esq."

"SUNDAY, 16th April, 1815.[118]

DEAR SIR,—I have just received by an express from Fredericton, a letter from the Attorney General, stating, that from the state of the river, it will be impracticable for him to be at Kingston by the 20th; and as he has hitherto taken the whole burthen of the prosecution upon himself, the trial cannot well go on without him. From this circumstance therefore, and as the present state of the travelling would probably render it dangerous to my father's health, (who is not now very well,) to hold the Court this week, he has determined to put it of till *Thursday, the 4th of May*, for which day he wishes you to summon your Juries, and to proclaim the holding of the Court. He regrets much giving you this additional trouble, but it must be attributed to the extraordinary backwardness of the season, which was probably not foreseen when it was recommended to

[118] The original text has "1816," an obvious mistake. It was corrected in the third edition (and here, in order to avoid confusion).

hold the Court on the 20th April. I have not time to forward a new precept[119] by this conveyance, but I will forward one in time, or the one you have may be altered. This can easily be arranged when we go up to the Court.

Yours, truly, W. CHIPMAN, Jr.

W. BATES, Esq."[120]

On the 30th day of April I informed him that Thursday next, the fourth day of May, he must have his trial before the Court for his life, and that Mr. Pearson, from Pictou, had come to witness against him. He paid no attention, any more than if I had not spoken to him. May 2d, Mr. Pearson came to see him—told him that his wife was coming to see him, but he took no more notice of him than if he could not either see or hear, or had no sense. The third day found he had been at work at the wall; his face bruised and bloody; told him that the next day he would be brought before the Court for his trial. He paid no attention, ate hastily, patted his hands, hallooed, appeared very lively, sang much, and acted the lunatic or fool to perfection—sang and beat the floor with his chains most of the night.

The fourth of May, the day appointed for the trial of this mysterious character, being now arrived, the Court began to assemble at Kingston, with numerous spectators from the distant parts of the country,—early in the morning. About 11 o'clock his Honor Judge SANDERS, and the Attorney General, arrived at my house from Frederickton; the attorneys and officers of Court having previously arrived. About one o'clock, the whole came to the Court-House in procession. After opening the Court in the usual form, the prisoner was called to the bar, and placed in the criminals box; the gaoler, with four or five constables to attend him. He made no resistance, but took no notice of the Court—played a thousand monkey actions, pulled off his shoes and socks, tore his shirt, ha-ha'd a little, patting his hands, snapping his fingers as usual, and acting the fool. The Court was crowded with spectators, and every eye was fixed upon the prisoner with astonishment.—Now became a period of great expectation—The Attorney General

[119] A writ; any order issued by a legal authority.

[120] Here, in the third edition, Bates included a letter from Walter Dibblee, the former gaoler, expressing his belief that Judge Chipman would not allow the Attorney General to prosecute them (Bates and Dibblee) for allowing Smith to escape.

read his Indictment—The Judge then asked him if he plead to the indictment, *Guilty*, or *Not Guilty*—He stood *mute*; took no kind of notice that could be discovered. The Judge then admonished him, that if he stood mute out of *obstinacy*, his trial would go on, and he be deprived of the opportunity of putting himself upon his country for his *defence*, and that *sentence* would be passed against him—therefore he advised him to plead *Not Guilty*. He continued *mute*, acting the fool, without discovering the least sense, or change in his countenance, that could be observed. The Judge then directed the Sheriff to impannel a Jury of twelve men, to enquire into the *cause*, whether the prisoner at the bar stood mute *wilfully* and *obstinately*, or *by the visitation of God*.[121] The Jury being impannelled and sworn, after hearing the evidence, that he had appeared in that state for three months preceding, &c.—soon returned their verdict, that *the prisoner at the bar stood mute, by the visitation of God*. The Judge then directed, that the Attorney General enter the plea of *Not Guilty*; and counsel for the prisoner was admitted. The Court was then adjourned until next morning, at ten o'clock, in order for his trial. Friday morning, 11 o'clock, the Court being assembled, and the house crowded with spectators, the prisoner was again brought to the bar, with all the constables to attend him—He took no kind of notice of any one, but sat himself quietly down in the criminals box. Every eye was fixed on him for a few minutes in perfect silence. The Judge observed that the prisoner appeared more calm this morning, and directed that the Court proceed to his trial. The Jury being sworn, and the witnesses called, the prisoner at the bar was ordered to stand up for his defence. He took no notice of what was said—The constables were then ordered to hold him up on his feet—he fought them, and jerked from them, so that they could not manage to do any thing with him. Sent for a rope and pinioned his arms, but to no purpose; lashed the rope from his arms back to the railing of the box. He continued

[121] In other words, the jury were supposed to decide whether the defendant was unable to communicate for a known or unknown reason. It mattered little, in fact, if he was "mute of malice" or "by visitation of God" (in both cases the court recommended a plea of "not guilty" be entered on his behalf). After this, the jury were supposed to decide if the defendant was able to stand trial (either because he was deaf and dumb, or because of insanity). As this did not happen in Smith's case, the judge must have considered him sane and able to follow the proceedings.

fighting, and reaching the bannisters before him, broke them out as fast as the constables could take them from him. Sent for another rope, and tied his hands together, securing them to the railing each way. He then fell to kicking the railing, and soon demolished all the bannisters and railing in front of the criminals box, in spite of all the constables could do to prevent him—Was obliged to get another strong rope and bind his feet together, securing the rope each way, to the posts of the box—It then took two or three constables to hold him.

After thus securing him, the Court proceeded on his trial. The Attorney General read his declaration, charging the prisoner at the bar, with having feloniously stolen a certain bay horse, the property of *Willis* Frederic Knox, Esq. of the value of £35; that he was taken in the *manner*,[122] and produced his witness. Mr. Knox being sworn, stated the circumstances of his pursuit after the prisoner, as far as Truro, where he employed Mr. Pearson to pursue on to Pictou; being informed that the prisoner was going to sell the horse at that place. Mr. Peters, counsel for the prisoner, asked the witness, how he wrote his christian name—*Wills* or *Willis*—to which he replied, "I was christened after my god-fathers, Lord North and the Earl of *Willsborough*[123]—and never write my name *Willis*." Mr. Peters then produced authorities to show, that one letter in a man's name had quashed an indictment; and moved that the prisoner be discharged. This was overruled by the Court, but reserved for a question.

Mr. Pearson deposed, that he pursued the whole night, and early next morning, was shown the prisoner, and took him. He seemed but little surprised; the witness told him, the owner of the horse would be there soon—He said that *he* came honestly by the horse—The witness asked him where the horse was? He said, at that house; pointing over the creek where there was but one. He then took the prisoner before a Justice, and thence to the gaol at Pictou; that he afterward took the horse, returned

[122] That is, caught in the act, in flagrante.

[123] Frederick North (1732-1792), Lord North (and Earl of Guilford during the last two years of his life), prime minister of Great Britain (1770-1782). Bates clearly misunderstood the second reference (in the third edition he even conflates the two statesmen and speaks of only one godfather, "Lord North, the Earl of Willsborough"). It should be Wills Hill, Earl of Hillsborough (1718-1793), who occupied several cabinet positions, including that of Secretary of State for the Colonies.

about ten miles, and met Mr. Knox, who knew the horse and called him Briton.[124]

The circumstances against the prisoner were, that he gave contradictory accounts how he came by the horse; at one time saying that he bought him of a pedlar; at another, of a Frenchman; again, that he swaped for him, and at Amherst[125] produced a receipt for money paid in exchange. The counsel for the prisoner, in cross-examining, asked Mr. Knox, did you ever see the prisoner in possession of the horse? No, but he acknowledged it.—Did you ever hear him acknowledge that he was in possession of the horse in any other way, than with saying he came honestly by him? No. Mr. Pearson was cross-examined in the same words, and answered the same *no*. Mr. Peters in defence of the prisoner, produced authorities to show, that by the evidence, the prisoner at the bar was not taken in the *manner*, as stated in the declaration; and that it was sufficient for him to prove in a general way, how he came in possession of the horse, which he was able to do, by a receipt which he produced for the money paid in exchange—the best general evidence that can be given, as such is the common way of dealing in horses. He acknowledged if the prisoner had been taken on the back of the horse, he would then have been taken in the *manner*, as stated by the Attorney General; and consequently bound to prove how he came in *possession*; but in the present case, he himself, or any one present, might be in this unfortunate prisoner's situation; dragged to prison, to court, and to the gallows, because he could not produce the person who had actually sold him the horse. The prosecutor had not produced any evidence of the horse ever being in the possession of the prisoner, only by his own confession; and he trusted that the Jury would not hesitate to find that the prisoner at the bar, was not taken in the *manner*,

[124] The name of the horse appears as "Brittain" in the third edition, which also adds the following passage: "That they then returned to Pictou, where the prisoner remained in jail, and on examination was found to have in his possession a watch, and about fifteen guineas in money, with a number of watch-seals and other articles, some of which it appeared he had stolen on his way as he escaped with the horse. That he was committed to the charge of a constable and Mr. Knox, to be conveyed by a warrant from Nova-Scotia to the jail at King's County, in New Brunswick. That before he was taken from the jail at Pictou he had cut the bolt of his hand-cuffs nearly through, and had artfully concealed it, which was fortunately discovered, and new handcuffs provided, otherwise he must certainly have escaped from his keepers before he arrived at Kingston."

[125] Amherst, Nova Scotia, a town on the isthmus of Chignecto.

as stated in the declaration; but would pronounce him, by their verdict, *Not Guilty*. The Judge, in his charge to the Jury, that his being taken in the *manner*, was proved by the various accounts he gave of his getting possession of the horse, thus rendering himself liable to prove how he came by him; or to stand guilty of feloniously taking him, as stated in the indictment—That they had heard the witnesses, and if, from the evidence and circumstances before them, they were fully satisfied that the prisoner at the bar had taken the horse feloniously, as stated in the indictment, they would find him *Guilty*; and if they had any doubts, that, leaning to mercy, they would find him *Not Guilty*.

While the Jury were out, I invited the Court and other gentlemen to visit the Gaol, where I shewed them his irons and chains, and the situation in which he was placed. The Judge observed, it was fortunate that he was sent to Kingston Gaol, as no other Gaol in the Province would have kept him.

The Jury, after being out about two hours, returned with their verdict—*Guilty*.

The prisoner did not show the least sign of sensibility that could be perceived while the Judge pronounced upon him the sentence of the law, *Death, without benefit of clergy*[126]—but continued shouting and hallooing. The Court asked the Counsel for the prisoner if he had any thing to offer in arrest of Judgment, or why the sentence of *Death* should not be executed upon him. Mr. Peters then rose, and produced authorities to show that the present law that took away the benefit of clergy for horse stealing, was not in force in this Colony, and that it could not be construed to be in force until decided in the Higher Court, where he hoped to have the honor to discuss it. The Judge gave his opinion against him, but admitted the plea. The prisoner was returned to Gaol, where he received his chains with willingness and apparent satisfaction, and the Court adjourned without day. The Attorney General, however, gave me to understand that he would not be executed very speedily, and requested that I would observe his behaviour, and inform him by letter the particulars of his conduct. The next morning I visited him—found him as usual, informed him he was now under sentence of *Death*, and that he would be allowed but one pound of bread, and water once a day, for the short time he had to live—that as soon as his Death Warrant was signed by

[126] The benefit of clergy was a legal provision according to which leniency could be granted to first offenders (when it was first introduced, it was granted to clergymen).

the President,[127] he would be executed, and but little time was left him to prepare for the dreadful event. He paid no attention, patted his hands, sang, and acted the fool as usual. One of the spectators being surprised at his conduct, observed to him, "Smith, it is too late for you to deceive any more; your fate is fixed now, and you had better employ your little time in making your peace with God, than to act the fool any longer,"—which occasioned the following:—On going into the Gaol, observing his book opened, and looking at it, found a leaf turned, pointing to the following passage:—"*If any man among you seemeth to be wise, let him become a fool, that he may be wise.*"[128] In this situation I kept him nine days on bread and water, once a day reminding him of his fate. He continued in the same state, and in that time had torn off every stitch of clothing, leaving himself naked. He never shewed any penitence, or any sign of hunger more than when fed with four times his allowance. I then allowed him other provisions, and his succeeding conduct is briefly stated in the following letter to the Attorney General:

From the Royal Gazette of July 11, 1815.
Copy of a Letter from the High Sheriff of King's County.

KINGSTON, June 26, 1815.

MY DEAR SIR,—Having heard nothing from you since the late Gaol Delivery at King's County, I beg leave briefly to state to you some circumstances of the conduct of the criminal HENRY MORE SMITH, since his trial and sentence. After securing him with strong chains to his neck and legs, and with handcuffs, he continued beating the floor, hallooing day and night with little intermission, making different sounds; sometimes with jinking his chains, and sometimes without, apparently in different parts of the Gaol, insomuch that the Gaoler frequently sent for me, supposing he must be loose from his chains, which I conceived, and frequently observed was *impossible*; being far beyond the power of human strength or invention, in his situation;—but on the 24th of May, going into the Gaol early in the morning, (after having examined his chains at two o'clock the day before,) I found three links of his heaviest chain separated, and lying on the floor, being part of the chain without the staple. He continued in the same way until the 2d of June, when we found

[127] The presiding judge, Ward Chipman (see note 69).

[128] The second sentence of 1 Corinthians 3: 18.

the largest chain parted about the middle and tied with a string; which clearly proves that irons and chains are no security for him. I then put on him a light chain, with which he has been ever since. I never discovered him at work at any thing, but he frequently produced effigies of likenesses, very striking, representing his wife. He now produced an effigy of a man in perfect shape, with his features painted, and joints to all his limbs, and dressed him in clothes that he had torn off himself, (being now naked) which was admired for its ingenuity. This he would put sometimes in one position and sometimes in another, and seemed to amuse himself with it, without taking the least notice of any thing else; continuing in his old way hallooing, without any alteration, until the 13th, when the Gaoler informed me that he refused to eat, and no doubt was sick—I went to see him every day—found he did not eat—all the bread and other provisions conveyed to him he gave to his effigy, strung on a string he put into his hands—He lay perfectly still day and night, and took no notice of any thing—would drink tea or milk, which I gave him twice a day for five days; he then refused to drink any thing for two days, which made seven days he had eaten nothing. *In that time he began to speak*—would ask questions, but would hold no conversation. But the most extraordinary, the most wonderful and mysterious of all is, that in this time he had prepared, *undiscovered*, and at once *exhibited* the most striking picture of genius, art, taste and invention that ever was, and I presume ever will be produced by any human being placed in his situation, in a dark room, chained and handcuffed, under sentence of death, without so much as a nail or any kind of thing to work with but his hands; and naked. The exhibition is far beyond my pen to describe. To give you some faint idea, permit me to say that it consists of ten characters, men, women, and children—all made and painted in the most expressive manner, with all the limbs and joints of the human frame—each performing different parts; their features, shape and form, all express their different offices and characters; their dress is of different fashions, and suitable to the stations in which they act. To view them in their situation they appear as perfect as though alive, with all the air and gaiety of actors on the stage. SMITH sits in his bed by the side of the Gaol—his *exhibition* begins about a foot[129] from the floor, and compasses the whole space of the

[129] It said "two feet" in the letter as it appeared in newspapers in 1815. The *Royal Gazette*, formerly of Saint John, was published in Fredericton since March 1815. Other papers reprinted the letter..

ceiling. The uppermost is a man whom he calls the Tamborine player, or sometimes Doctor Blunt, standing with all the pride and appearance of a master musician; his left hand akimbo, his right hand on his tamborine, dressed in suitable uniform. Next him, below, is a lady, genteelly dressed, gracefully sitting in a handsome swing; at her left hand stands a man neatly dressed in the character of a servant, holding the side of the swing with his right, his left hand on his hip, in an easy posture, waiting the lady's motion. On her right hand stands a man genteelly dressed, in the character of a *gallant*, in a graceful posture for dancing. Beneath these three figures sits a young man and a young girl, (apparently about 14,) in a posture of *tilting*, at each end of a board, decently dressed. Directly under these stands one whom he calls Bonaparte, or sometimes the father of his family; he stands erect; his features are prominent; his cheeks red; his teeth white, set in order; his gums and lips red; his nose shaded black, representing the nostrils; his dress is that of the Harlequin; in one hand he holds an infant, with the other he plays or beats music; before him stand two children, apparently three or four years old, holding each other by one hand in the act of playing or dancing, which, with a man dressed in fashion, who appears in the character of a steward, sometimes in one situation and sometimes in another, makes up the show, all of which you have at one view. Then commences the performance. The first operation is from the tamborine player, or master, who gives two or three single strokes on his tamborine, that may be heard in any part of the house, without moving his body. He then dances gracefully a few steps, without touching the tamborine; the lady is then swung two or three times by the steward; then the gallant takes a few steps; then the two below tilt a few times, in the most easy, pleasant manner; then the two children dance a little, holding each other by the hand; after this, SMITH begins to sing or whistle a tune, to which they are to dance, at which, the tamborine strikes, and every one dances to the tune, with motion, ease and exactness not to be described. Many have been the observations of spectators; amongst them, an old German observed, that when he was starving the seven days, he was making a league with the *Devil* and that *he helped* him. All acknowledge with me, that it exceeds every thing they ever saw or imagined. His whole conduct from the first, has been, and is, one continued scene of mystery. He has never shown any idea or knowledge of his trial or present situation; he seems happy; his irons and chains are no apparent inconvenience; contented like a dog or a monkey, broke to his chain; shows no more idea of any thing past, than if he had no recollection. He, in short, is a mysterious character, possessing a wonderful art of invention, beyond common capacity.

I am almost ashamed to forward you so long a letter upon the subject, and so unintelligible; I think, if I could have done justice in describing the exhibition, it would have been worthy a place in the Royal Gazette, and better worth the attention of the public than all the Wax-work ever exhibited in this province.

I am, with all due respect, dear Sir,

your very humble servant.

WALTER BATES.

THOMAS WETMORE, Esq. Attorney General.

P.S. Wednesday, the 28th. This morning I found he had added to his works a *drummer*, placed at the left of his tamborine player, equal in appearance, and exceeding in performance; beats the drum with either hand, or both occasionally, in concert with the Tamborine, keeping time with perfect exactness, sometimes sitting, at others standing or dancing. He had also, in a most striking manner, changed the position of his scene. The lady above described to be sitting gracefully in her swing, with so many attendants and admirers, is now represented swinging in a dejected posture, with a young infant in her arms; her gallant has left her, and is taking the young girl before described, about 14, by the hand, with an air of great gallantry, leading her and dancing to the tune with perfect exactness, representing more than can be described. On viewing this, an old Scotchman observed; "some say he is mad, others he is a fool; but I say he is the sharpest man I have ever seen; his performance exceeds all I ever met with, and I do not believe he was ever equalled by man." This evening a gentleman from Boston, having heard the above description, came to see the performance, and declared he could say, as the Queen of Sheba did, that "*the half had not been told*."[130]

[To this the Editor of the Gazette adds the following remarks—"We have given an entire copy of the above letter, which has excited our astonishment, and will, probably, that of every other person who has not seen the exhibition and

[130] In 1 King 10: 7, the Queen of Sheba says, "Howbeit I believed not the words, until I came, and mine eyes had seen *it*: and, behold, the half was not told me." In 1815, the letter continued, "and that he had been in the Museum in Boston, which contained nothing that equalled it."

performance described in it. Those who are acquainted with the Sheriff know him to be incapable of stating falsehoods, or attempting in any way to practice a deception, and will of course give credit to the statement of facts, wonderful as they may appear to be, which he has made."—PUB.][131]

July 1st, in the morning, I found him repairing his drummer. He said he had a gentleman and lady come from France; but could not put them up—and looking archly at me, said, "the *Devil* had no chain about *his* neck." I answered him, if he did not behave worse than the *Devil*, I would give him more liberty; and took his chain from his neck, and put it to his feet. He then produced a man, fashionably dressed, and in one minute had him dancing—He said he had no clothes fit for his lady to appear in company; but if he had a needle and thread, he could have them all fit for a ball in two days. To gratify the spectators present, I consented, and they soon supplied him with thread, needle, calico, ribands, and a small pair of scissars, the first thing he had had to cut with, having used his teeth. He seemed pleased, and began to sew by candle light, but laid it by and said he could work better in the dark. The next day, found him making clothes for his family—He said he had a drum-major coming out from France, who would beat two drums at once, and his wife would stand upon her head and beat three; that he must have drum-sticks, and something for drums, which was furnished. He made some of brass and some of tin, making different sounds, trimmed in elegant style, with ribbons and tassels, and would have appeared elegant in a toy-shop. As he proceeded, he was supplied with every thing that he wanted; and was very industrious in making his improvements.

The Supreme Court being about to be held at Frederickton, and feeling anxious to know the fate of the prisoner, I attended the Court, and having ascertained that the destiny of the prisoner would not be fatal, I returned. The gaoler informed me that, the first night after I left home, Smith had drawn the staple

[131] The editor's note in the *Acadian Recorder* continued with the following: "We trust we shall be able, shortly, to furnish our readers with some further particulars of the conduct of this extraordinary man, since he has been in the hand of Justice: and it would be a vey desirable thing to trace his history back to an earlier period of his Life. He is, we understand, a young man, perhaps not more than 27 years old. At the time of his trial (in May last) he appeared quite insane, but it was supposed to be feigned; and it was there stated that he had not been known to speak one word for the four preceding months."

of the chain that had been about his neck, and had concealed both the chain and the staple so that they could not be found. The glass in the wall was broken at the same time, but the chain did not go out that way, as the outside glass was whole. The room, and every thing in it, had been strictly searched without discovering it, and it could not be conceived how the glass was broke, as it was entirely out of his reach. On going into the gaol, he said to me, that the Devil told his old Drummer if he did not put that chain out of the way he would certainly get it about his neck again; that he hated it, and had murdered it, and put it under the dirt—but he feared he should have ne peace till he raised it again. I told him he must raise it, and that I would not put it on him again if he behaved well. I then took off his handcuffs, gave him water to wash himself, with a clean shirt and jacket—A young man gave him a black handkerchief, which he put about his neck, and seemed pleased—wished he had a fiddle; he would give his shirt for a fiddle, that he might play for his family to dance—he was offered a fife; he said he believed he could learn to play—he then took the fife, and would play any tune, either right or left handed. I told him if he would behave well, I would not put his handcuffs on that day—he said then he would have his family in good order; but that when he sent one hand to do any thing, the other would follow it. Gave him some materials that he wanted, and then left him. This was the 17th of July.

On the 18th, found him at work at his children, preparing for improvements. Gave him a pen and paint, and many articles for clothing, &c. He had before used coal and his own blood for colouring. He appeared thankful, and talked more coherently. To account for the broken glass, he said to me—My old Drummer cried out for more air, his family stood so thick about him—Well, said I, tell me how to get it and I will go to work at it. He told me to make a wisp of straw long enough to reach the glass and break it, which I did, and destroyed the rope that it might not be discovered.

He continued his employment, repairing and improving his family, dressing them neatly, and painting their features all new; and adding to his exhibition, until he said they were all present that were coming. With the money that he had received from spectators, he supplied himself with calico, and about the 10th of August, completed the show, which consisted of twenty four characters, men and women; six beat music in concert with the fiddle, while sixteen danced to the tune. The other two were fighters, Bonaparte with a sword, fighting an Irishman with his shillaly.[132] His musicians were dressed in uniforms; some drummers, some tamborine players, and some bell ringers. In the centre of his dancers stood his dancing-master, in a military dress, with hat and boots on, and gloves on his hands. A soldier in Scotch uniform, at an advanced station, acted as a sentry, stepping regularly one foot before the other. Smith would sit before them and play a tune on the fiddle, to which they would all dance, and beat to the music in concert, one half on the right hand to one part of the tune, and the other on the left hand to other part, then all together, dancing to the tune as regular and as natural as if alive; the dancing-master dancing with his right hand and foot with one part, and his left hand and foot with the other part, and then together with the whole, without any stop or hindrance, to any tune that he should play, and without discovering any sign or motion by which they were made to act. His fighters, if they had been alive, could not act and appear more natural. All his figures were formed of straw, curiously twisted and interwoven. The coal he used for colouring, he got from a burnt timber in the partition wall, and their first clothing was made of the pieces of his garments which he had torn up.

It is impossible for me to it justice; therefore I shall not attempt any further description, and only add, that great numbers came to see the exhibition, and to view his person, from a great distance—among whom were several physicians, and all expressed their astonishment. A gentleman from Pennsylvania, Doct. PRIOR, a man of learning, who told me he had spent his whole life travelling for foreign and literary information, and had made it a point to view all curiosities and phenomena that he could hear of; having heard that I had an extraordinary character in prison, came to beg the favor of me to let him see him; with which I complied. After viewing his person, and every part of his exhibition and performance, he was pleased to say, that he had travelled through all the Continent of America, and part of Europe, but had never met with the equal of it—that he was now writing Memoirs of his own life and travels, and that he should not fail to fill a page with a description of this wonderful performance.

With other spectators, a gentleman by the name of Doctor

[132] Shillelagh, a sort of cudgel that can also be used as a walking stick. It appears as "shillelah" in the third edition.

COUGLYN, from Ireland, who had been Surgeon in his Majesty's service, both by sea and land, a gentleman of accomplishments and learning, came to see this new and extraordinary exhibition. After having viewed the scene repeatedly for several days that he tarried at Kingston, he declared that he had travelled through Europe, had lived in England, Ireland and Scotland—that he had been in France and Holland—at Hamburgh, and other places famous for such exhibitions, but that he had never met with any thing of the kind that equalled the one before him.[133]

August 13th—when the gaoler went into the gaol, Smith said to him that he had been fishing, and had caught a large fish, and wished him to cook it for him; on looking, the gaoler saw the chain that had been missing, then lying on the floor. After this, Smith began a new scene of mystery, and commenced fortune-telling, in which, if he did not possess the power of divination, he was at least wonderfully successful. He told his fortune in his tea-cup; after looking in it some time he took the cup and kissed it, and told the gaoler that he was going away from this place, that he was going over the water, and wanted a box to put his family in; that he saw there were three papers written and sent about him; and that one was a large letter which he did not understand.—In the evening I went in to see him, and as my curiosity was greatly excited to know the origin of so extraordinary a character, and the previous events of his life, I hoped to draw some information from him, but he would not answer any questions, and took no notice of them, but when the spirit moved him, he would talk. He said that he was going away from home—that he was going among his enemies—that every body would be afraid of him, and look upon him with distrust and horror—that he was disturbed in his sleep—that once in eight or ten nights he was troubled with

[133] A third visitor was added in the third edition: "The Doctor then belonging to the Garrison at St. Andrews [in southwestern New Brunswick], having heard, while at Head Quarters, from the Attorney General, an account of this extraordinary character, took his tour from Fredericton, by way of Kingston, for the express purpose of satisfying his curiosity, by seeing for himself. When on entering the prison, Smith, seeing the Doctor in regimentals, said to him with much good humor, 'I suppose you are come here looking for deserters: there is my old drummer, I don't know but he deserted from some regiment,—all the rest are my family.' He seemed very much pleased with his new visitor, and readily exhibited every part of his performance, to the full satisfaction of the Doctor, who expressed his astonishment in the most unqualified terms, and acknowledged that it far exceeded his anticipations."

all sorts of creatures coming about him; great hogs with cloven feet, all kinds of cattle, and creeping things, snakes and adders, frogs and toads, and every ugly thing—that he would start up from his sleep and walk about the prison, then lie down, get asleep, and they would come about him again; he would get up again and sit and talk to his children, and sometimes take his fiddle and play to amuse himself, and drive away these dreary hours. He said these snakes and adders he could read very well; he knew what they all meant, and most of the rest of them—but these frogs and toads coming together he could not understand; but he knew he was going to leave this place and go on the water; that he could see as clearly as he could see me standing by him that he should find enemies, and every body would be afraid of him, but he should hurt no body; he should find trouble, have irons upon him, but they should come off again; that the crickets came, and would get upon his children, and sing amongst them; that he liked to hear them; that his mother always told him that he must not hurt them, &c.; and going on in this way, by a natural association of ideas, seemed to betray the nature of his early education. His mother (he said) always gave him good advice, but he had not always followed it—he had been a bad fellow—done that which he ought not to have done, and he had suffered for it; had been struck, and had the marks, but he forgave all his enemies; the Lord says, if you would ask forgiveness of him, forgive thy brother also—we cannot expect forgiveness, except we repent and forgive others. The word of God is plain: except ye forgive thy brother his trespasses, neither will your Heavenly Father forgive you when you ask of him. The scripture says, Repent and pray, lest ye enter into temptation. I work and pray with my family continually—and except you repent, you will also perish in your sins; you are sinner as well as I am; all men are sinners before God; consider you have work to do as well as I; you have a soul to save as well as the poor prisoner—watch therefore and pray. I watch here, and pray night and day, but I shall not stay long. He intended to go to sea as supercargo of some vessel,[134] or he could get a living with his family as a show, in any country but England, and he had never seen such a show in England, or any where else—that he dreamed of the whole of them at once, and that he must go to work and make them, and it would be better for him; if he did not it

[134] The supercargo was the person in charge of the merchandise carried on a ship.

would be bad with him; that he had worked ever since and had almost finished them, but there was a shoemaker and a tailor which had not come for want of room; that he would make room if he did not go away. He said he had been here until he was contented to stay here; and contentment was the brightest jewel in this life. He never enjoyed himself better than he did at present with his family, and he did not care for himself so that his family looked well. He would be willing to die, and should like to die now, rather than go among his enemies; but he had one friend; he believed it was old Willy; he was in England, and was always his friend, and he would go and see him; that he had one sister in England whom he wanted to see—she played well on the Piano Forte; he could play on it well himself; that she married a Lieutenant in the army, but he was a Captain now; if he could he would go to see her in England, where he had friends; that he had an uncle in Liverpool, a merchant, and looking earnestly at me, said, my name is not SMITH, my name is HENRY MOON; my father's name (I think he said) is EDWARD MOON;[135] I was educated at Cambridge College, in England, and understand English, French and Latin, well, and can speak and write five different languages; that he could write any hand, as handsome or as bad as I ever saw—but he had been a bad man, and had suffered for it, and hoped to do better. He said he had five hundred pounds in the Bank of England, which was in the care of Mr. TURNER, and wished very much to have his wife get it, as he did not know where he should go, but knew he must meet with trouble; he did not fear what man could do to him, for he could but kill him, and he should like to die now. After hearing this talk a long time, I left him.

Aug. 14th, in the morning, he looked in his cup again, and told the gaoler that those papers were coming, and would be here to day. About four o'clock I received a package from Mr. Chipman, containing his pardon, and two other letters, just as he had predicted. At evening I went to see him, found him in his bed. He got up, but said he could not eat—asked for new potatoes, and said to the gaoler's wife, you had new potatoes yesterday for dinner. Mrs. Reid asked how he should know it, as they were the first she had had. He did not appear to be in his usual humor. I then intended to communicate to him the news of his pardon, and to impress upon him, if possible, some sense of his situation—and told the gaoler and all present

[135] The presumed name of the prisoner's father does not appear in the third edition.

to leave the room, and shut the door. He had never entirely recovered from his pretended insanity, nor did he until after discharged from my custody, for similar reasons, undoubtedly, to those which first produced it, but I was in hopes to make some impression on him by promising assistance to get him out of the Province, and shewing him that compassion which humanity seemed to demand—and for that purpose, I informed him that I had received his pardon; that Mr. Knox had been down to see him and had forgiven him all the injuries he had done him; that his Attorney had been his friend, and by the petitioning the President of the Court, stating that he was a young man, and this was the first instance of horse-stealing that had been before the Court in this Province, and praying that mercy might be extended to save his life, the President and Council had been graciously pleased to extend their mercy to him, and had respited the sentence pronounced on him—and that I was now ready to release him, on his entering into recognizance to appear in the Supreme Court to plead his pardon, when called upon, reminding him at the same time, that he was not pardoned for any other crimes he might have heretofore committed. The only notice he took of what I said, was, "I wish you would bring me some potatoes when you come again."—I proceeded to say, that as soon as he was ready and would let me know where he wished to go, I would get him a passage, and help him away—that I would get him some clothing, and give him time to put his family in good order, and give him a box to put them in, as they might be the means of getting him a living any where, until he could find better employment, without being driven to the necessity of stealing. He said to me, "haven't you got boys and girls that want to see my family dance? Bring all your family to see them; I will show them as much as they please for nothing, but others shall pay me, I am determined,"—without the least notice of, or appearing to understand what I had said, keeping up the same imposing manner with which he had carried on every thing else.

I staid in gaol alone with him near an hour afterwards, without saying any more on the subject, during which time he proceeded to talk much in the way he did the evening before—and said we must watch and pray lest we enter into temptation; he prayed with his family; they could not pray for themselves—that we must be spiritually minded—that to be spiritually minded was life, but to be carnally minded was death. Those who are spiritual are in God—those who are carnal are in the world; that God was spirit, but took human nature upon him, and came down from Heaven, and dwelt amongst us in the flesh, that we might become the children of the spirit; and began to repeat large portions of the New Testament in different parts, nearly whole chapters, when he observed, you see I read the bible without any book, as well as others can with. I can read to you almost all or any chapter in the bible you will name, in the Old or New Testament, it makes not much difference, in the dark as well as in the light. My wife is a good little woman; she would read in the bible on Sundays, and say to me, "Henry, come sit down and hear me read in the bible,"—but I would laugh at her, and tell her I could read better without the book than she could with, and would go out and look to my horse, or do any thing on Sundays. I have been a bad fellow. When I was in England, I gave all my attention to reading the bible, and was a great Methodist, went to all their meetings, and could pray and exhort amongst them; and finally took up preaching. I have preached in Brighton, North-Hampton, South-Hampton,[136] and London; and great numbers came to hear me. I was sometimes astonished to see how many followed to hear me preach—but I did not follow that long, only about fifteen months, when I gave it up; the reason was, I got amongst the bad women in London, and got the bad disorder, and after that it would not do for me to preach among the good Methodists any longer, and I was obliged to come away—and that was the reason I left England. I was a bad young man—I am young now, only 23, not 24 years old yet. I did not know but I would preach again, but I am now contented where I am, and do not wish to go into the world any more. He never intended to leave this place, he was better off here than any where else, he would stay here until he died, and should like to die. When he was a preacher, he was spiritually minded, and all was peace, all was Heaven to him; but ever since he had been in the world, all was trouble and misery, and he never wished to go into the world again.

August 15th, at noon, went to the gaol, gave him a good dinner, and read his pardon to him. When I took it out of my pocket, he cried out, that looks like the paper I dreamed of about a month ago—I saw that paper, with two angels and a ship on it, and something that looked like snakes—I wish you would give it me; I knew it was a coming. When reading it he

[136] Northampton (in the Midlands) and Southampton (a port city in southern England).

paid no attention to the nature of it, but asked questions as foreign to the subject as possible. I told him as soon as I could get him some clothes, I would give him the paper, in order to take it with him, and that I would help him away with his show, that he might not be driven to the necessity of stealing.

August 16th, at evening, went with a tailor to take measure of him for a coat. When he saw the tailor with his measure, he said, I wish you would give me that ribbon in your hand—It is no ribbon, said the tailor, but a measure to measure you for a coat; come, stand up—What! said he, do you think you are tailor enough to make me a coat?—Yes. But you don't look like it—Let me look at your hands and fingers—which he did—You are no tailor, said he, you look more like a blacksmith—you shall never make a coat for me; I can make it better myself; and would not be measured.

August 17th—we found he had improved his Scotch sentry by giving him a carved wooden head, very complete, with the national features of an old Highlander. This was the first of his carved work. At evening he had also much improved his fighters—Bonaparte, by some unlucky stroke, had killed the Irishman, taken off his head, and hung it up at his right hand; a brawny old Scotchman had taken his place, and gave Bona a hard time, knocking him down as fast he could get up. I told him he must get his family ready to move, and left him.

August 18th, at noon, went to see him; he was fiddling remarkably well, and singing merrily; but when I went in he was busily at work carving a head, which he said was to take Bonaparte's place, as the old Scotchman would overpower him soon. He said carving was a trade in England; that he did not think he could do so well at it till he tried, and remarked that a man did not know what he could do until he set himself about it; that he never undertook any thing but he accomplished it; except that he was stopped in this place; and he had been so long here he had rather stay here than any where, and never enjoyed himself better. He wished I would give him a candle to work by; and he would make himself a waistcoat; said I need not be afraid he should do any harm with it; he would set it in the middle of the floor, and take care that his straw and chips did not get fire and burn up his family, which he could not do without, as he could not labour for a living; beside, said he, if I was disposed, I could burn up the house without a candle, for I can make fire in one hour any time. When I was a boy, said he, every body took notice of me, and I had a license for shooting when I was fifteen. One day I was out shooting, and killed a rabbit upon a farmer's land where I had no right. The old fellow came after me, and I told him if he came near me I would knock him down; but he caught me, and tied me fast to a large stack of faggots, and went off; whilst he was gone, I made a fire and burnt up the whole, and went off; but the old farmer never knew how his faggots took fire. You don't use faggots in this country, said he; they are little sticks, tied up and sold in bunches, to boil tea-kettle with. If I would give him a candle, he would find fire to light it.[137]

I am aware that I shall incur the imputation of weakness for narrating many parts of these memoirs, but as every part of his conduct appeared to me equally astonishing, I shall relate the simple facts as they occurred, with the fullest consciousness that I am neither obstinately blind nor wilfully deceived.

He said he had told his fortune in his tea-cup, and it came always alike. He could tell a great deal by dreams—The devil helped fortune-telling, but dreams were the inspiration of God. When the hogs came to see him he could tell a great deal by them. He could tell me any thing that had happened within a year past, or that would happen in a year to come. My neighbour, he said, had a black sow that had pigs, some all black and some all white, and one with red spots before and behind, and by them he learnt a great deal. I knew that Mr. Perkins had a black sow with young pigs, and when I went away I had the curiosity to look a them, but they did not answer his description, and I thought no more about it.

August 19th, at evening, many people came to see him and his performance, and when they were gone out, he said to me that he had carved a new figure of Bonaparte—that the first he made was after his own image, for he was a man after his own heart, but he had fallen—God made man out of the dust of the earth, but *he* made men out of the wood of the earth—God made Adam, but he soon fell, and did nothing very bad neither. He intended to carve out our Saviour on the cross, with the two

[137] Here, the editor of the British edition inserted a very long footnote about this skill, "well worth the learning," quoting almost the entirety of an article which had appeared anonymously as "A Winter's Night in the Woods. A Canadian Adventure" in *The Colonial Journal* in 1816. It was in fact a reprint from an article entitled "The Lost Traveller," which had first appeared in 1814 in *The Analectic Magazine* of Philadelphia.

thieves; one of the thieves was penitent, asked pardon, and was forgiven; so one Apostle says—the others contradict it. Three Apostles wrote, but they do not agree throughout. We cannot believe every thing; but we must believe, or we cannot be saved. The scripture says, he that believeth shall be saved, but he that believeth not is condemned already.

As I was going out, he said to me (without a word having passed relative to my examining the pigs) the pigs I told you of are not those young pigs; they are some months old. I made no reply, knowing that Mr. Scovil had a sow and pigs that answered his description in every particular.

Sunday, Aug. 20th, the gaoler carried him his breakfast, with tea. He told the gaoler he could tell him any thing past or to come; and being asked to tell any circumstance that had happened, he said, some time since you rode a great way on my account, and carried letters and papers about me, and about others too—Again, you went after a man, and you had to go on the water before you found him, and I am not sure but you found him on the water—while you was after him you saw a man at work in the mud, and enquired of him for the man you wanted, he told you what you asked of him; you was dry, and asked him if there was any water near that you could drink; he told you there was a place where he had drank, and you went to it, but found the water so bad you could not drink it. You then went after the man you was in pursuit of, found him and brought him with you, and kept him in gaol two or three days, when his friends came and took him out. The gaoler was astonished, knowing the facts to be true, in every particular, and had no recollection of ever mentioning the circumstances to any living being. Perhaps all this was but the imagery of his fancy; but how could his fancy picture out a tale so true? He often predicted things beyond the power of human foresight, which, repeated here, would seem absurd, but to my positive knowledge proved correct. The mystery is, how he could know them; that he predicted them is undeniable.[138]

[138] Here, in the second edition, Bates added two other predictions made by Smith: he foretold that "an English gentleman" with "white top boots" would visit him (that was Knox); and then that Perkins's (see note 44) son would come from his sea travels to see his show. This happened that very night and Smith refused to do his performance for him. Only the second prediction was kept in the third edition, where it was moved a few paragraphs above.

He had now been in my custody more than a year, and almost every day had produced some new feature of his character or effort of his genius. I had had much trouble with him; yet I had compassion for him, and could not turn him out of jail, naked and destitute, without friends, the terror of the neighborhood, and in such a situation that he must either starve or steal—thus rendering his pardon, instead of an act of mercy, a curse to himself and the community. Every one knew he was indicted in York County, and no one could assist him to escape.—Under these circumstances, having him in my charge, humanity dictated that I should try to get him out of the Province. I represented all these things to him, and told him I would furnish him with decent clothing, and get him a passage either to Nova-Scotia or the U. States, gave him a box to put his family in, and told him he must be ready to set off on Tuesday.—He took no notice of what I said, but asked some frivolous questions, talked about Mohawks and snakes, and played the fool, till I found I should have as much trouble to get rid of him as I had had to keep him before his trial.

On the 28th of August, Judge Pickett and Judge Micheau[139] attended at the Court-House in order to take the recognizance required, his own security in fifty pounds, to plead his pardon when called for. After liberating him from his chains, and supplying him with decent clothing, it was with difficulty I prevailed on him to leave the gaol. He took one of his children in one hand and a pair of scissars in the other, and went out; after much exertion I got him up to the Jury room, where Judge Micheau read his pardon to him, and explained the circumstances which produced it; to which he paid not the smallest attention, but looked about and talked of something else. Judge Pickett then required his recognizance, and informed him that unless he immediately left the Province he would be taken and tried on two indictments pending against him in the County of York. He took no notice of what he said; talked and danced, told the Judge he looked like a tailor, and asked him to give him his shoestrings. His pardon lying on the table, he caught hold of it, and before it could be taken from him clipped off the seal with his scissars; he wanted the ship on it[140] to carry

[139] David Pickett and Daniel Micheau have been mentioned before without being identified as judges (but see notes 34 and 111).

[140] The Great Seal of New Brunswick (approved in 1784) had a ship sailing up a river, with pine trees on each side, and the motto "Spem Reduxit" (Hope Restored).

him away with his family; tore off the cape of his coat, and cut it in pieces, as he did also his shoes. Finding we could do nothing with him, I returned him again to prison, where he said, for using him so kindly, for one shilling he would show us his whole performance. Judge Micheau handed him a half dollar piece, and said give me a quarter dollar in change, and you will have more than a shilling left.[141] He took it, said it was a nice piece of money, and put it in his pocket; but the Judge could by no means make him understand the meaning of change. He then performed his exhibition. When we were going, he seemed out of humour, and told Judge Pickett he had thrown stones at him, and he would burn his house; and threatened that this place should be in flames before morning; he could make fire in half an hour, and wanted a light, and would have one.

The Great Seal of New Brunswick in the early 19th century.

August 29th, early in the morning, I went to the gaol to prepare for his removal, but to my great vexation and surprize found it actually on fire. I opened the door immediately, and with a bucket of water extinguished it—Found him smoking his pipe, as unconcerned as ever. He had broken up the necessary, and with that and the chips of his carved work he had kindled a fire. He said fire was very comfortable, and he had not seen any before in a long time; that he made it with his own hands, and would make it again in ten minutes, as he could not do without some light. I shut him up in a suffocating smoke, which did not seem to give him the least inconvenience, and called in some of

[141] One British shilling, equal to one-twentieth of a pound, was officially worth 22 cents (see note 19); so, 50 cents meant, indeed, more than two shillings.

the neighbours to assist me, and ordered him to put his show into the box; he took no notice of it; I took down one and laid it in the box, when he seemed pleased, said he would put them all in that box immediately, and began very actively to take them down; wanted no assistance from any one; but leave him the light and he would be all ready in half an hour. We left him the candle and went out. When I returned he was walking the gaol, with every thing put up in the neatest manner; it was a curiosity to see with what skill he had packed them: gave him a pair of shoes, and with his box on his shoulder, he marched off to the boat I had prepared for his departure, and with three men to assist me we set off for St. John. He prayed and preached and sang Methodist hymns with a most inimitable tone, all the way, at the same time acting his crazy capers, tearing his clothes, &c. We made no stop on the passage, and arrived at St. John at 8 o'clock in the evening.[142] He said he must have a hot supper with tea, and wished to be locked up in a strong room, for he must see all his family to night, for they would die in the box. When we arrived at the gaol I found all the rooms of the prison occupied, or undergoing repairs, and had no place to confine him. I immediately called on the Sheriff, who had no means to assist me, as he could not receive him into custody, nor suffer him to be put with other prisoners in the gaol; and to add to my trouble, I learnt that there was no vessel to sail for several days. I returned to the gaol, and found Smith at his supper. When he had drank his tea, he looked in his cup, and immediately said he must not disturb his family to night, for he saw the ship then at the wharf that was to take him to his wife, and *there* would be crying.—The gaoler cleared out a small room in the house, with a grated window, where we secured him for the night. I had determined to send him to Nova-Scotia,[143] and going out early next morning, I met a friend of mine,[144] who informed me that his schooner, then lying at the wharf, would sail for Nova-Scotia in half an hour, and I persuaded him to take him on board. I had him brought down immediately, and at high water she

[142] The following sentence was added here in the third edition: "On his perceiving the moon as she made her appearance between two clouds, he observed that here was a *relation* of his that he was glad to see; that he had not seen one of *his name* for a long time."

[143] In the third edition, Bates explains this decision: "there was no vessel that would sail for the States before some days."

[144] The friend is identified in the third edition as Daniel Scovil (1776-1861), a merchant in Saint John, and one of the brothers of Rev. Elias Scovil of Kingston (see note 41).

hauled off and got under way with him, to the great satisfaction of all behind.—When the vessel arrived on the opposite shore, he left her without taking any thing with him, was seen in the street a short time, and then suddenly disappeared.

The first information I have of this extraordinary person is as follows: In September, 1812, he came to Windsor, in Nova-Scotia, where he was meet by Mr. BOND, a respectable farmer, of the town of Rawdon.[145] He wanted to get employment in the country, and said he would do any thing. After some conversation, Mr. Bond agreed with him to assist him on his farm, for one month, upon trial; and he proved to be extremely steady, careful and industrious, and gained the confidence of the old gentleman, while at the same time, he won the affection of his daughter. He called himself HENRY FREDERICK MOON.

Mr. Bond being a religious man, he conformed strictly to his principles;[146] was always punctual at evening and morning prayer, and seemed very devout and serious. In this way he continued for some time, when the attachment between him and the daughter was too close to be unobserved. He asked her hand in marriage, but it did not suit the old gentleman's views, and he would not give his consent. All the persuasions of her friends were used in vain to wean her from him, but her affections were so strongly fixed, that she left her father's house, and married him on the 12th of March, 1813. Her name was ELIZABETH P. BOND.[147]

---

[145] Both Rawdon and Windsor are former communities in Hants County, Nova Scotia, which have today been amalgamated into the municipalities of East Hants and West Hants, respectively. The county is located on the coast of the Minas Basin, an inlet of the Bay of Fundy (see note 50). In the third edition, Bates corrected the month, from September to July, 1812.

[146] Two things were aptly changed in this and the previous line in the third edition: the stranger did not use the name "Moon" in Rawdon, but called himself "More;" and Mr. Bond was "of the Baptist persuasion." John Bond (1758-1814), a former Loyalist soldier, was a founder, surveyor, and organiser of Rawdon after his relocation there in 1783. He died on 20 January 1814, before the arrest of his son-in-law (see Troxler for an account of his life).

[147] Her name was Elizabeth Pammeletta Bond (1793-1884). She had a daughter with Smith (Eleanor Charlotte, born in 1814). She appears in documents as late as 1819 as "Elizabeth More" or "Moor," but in December 1821 she married William Custance, an Englishman settled in Rawdon, which suggests a divorce had been granted on grounds of abandonment. She had three children born after 1821, but also two children (born in 1817 and 1820) who received the surname "Smith" and were adopted by Custance.

He continued in Rawdon, and professed to be a Tailor, but pursued no regular business. A letter from a gentleman in that town speaks of him as follows: "He could sew completely, and cut out clothes very well, but in fact could do any thing he turned his hand to. He would frequently set out for Halifax in the afternoon, and be home in the morning, always bringing with him a quantity of goods, and once was known to bring £30 in gold. He told Mr. Bond he was born in Scotland, but had lived mostly in England. No person here knows more of him, except that he always appeared decently dressed, very affable, obliging and inoffensive. He was never known to be intoxicated, never used bad language, and appeared to be addicted to no bad habits of any kind. Being asked how he procured the articles that he brought from Halifax, he said he had a friend there by the name of Wilson, who furnished him with every thing he wanted. At length some suspicions were entertained against him, and a warrant was got out to apprehend him, and getting information on it, in July 1814, he left Rawdon, and made his escape."

During his confinement, the following letter was received from his wife:

"RAWDON, May 26th, 1815.

MY DEAR HUSBAND,—I received your letter, dated October 23d, on the 24th May. You say you have wrote several letters to me; if you have I never received them. You wish me to come and see you, which I would have done had I got the letter in time, but did not know whether you was at Kingston or not. My dear, do not think hard that I do not come to see you; if you write back to me I shall come immediately, if my child is so that I can leave home; she is very sick, and I am not in a good state of health myself. My dear, as soon as you receive this letter, pray send me your answer, that I may know what to do—so no more at present; but I remain your loving and affectionate wife until death.

ELIZABETH P. M. S.

Mr. H. F. M. S. Kingston.

P.S.—I enclose this letter to Mr. Levi Lockhart,[148] and have requested him to give it to yourself. You can give your answer to him and I shall get it safe."

[148] Levi Lockhart (1783-1845) was from Newport, close to Rawdon, Nova Scotia, but had relocated to Saint John, New Brunswick. In October 1815, he joined the Saint John's Lodge (Bunting 267) and soon became its secretary. Lockhart's role in the story was left out in the third edition.

Mr. Levi Lockhart faithfully delivered the above letter to Smith, but could not make him understand any thing, or look at the writing, but twisted it up and threw it away without giving the least countenance to it.

Not long after his discharge, I heard of him at Moose Island,[149] and after that, a gentleman who knew him while in prison, saw him in the street at Portland.[150] From thence he proceeded to Boston, and on the 7th of November, he arrived at New-Haven, in the Boston stage, by the way of New-London,[151] with a large trunk full of clothing, a small portable desk, and money in his pockets. He was dressed in a genteel frock coat, with breeches and fair-top boots,[152] and remained several days.[153] After his departure, the following paragraph appeared in the Connecticut Journal, dated November 13th:

"*Another Phenomenon.*—On Thursday morning last, after the departure of the Steam-Boat[154] for New-York, the servants of

[149] A footnote in the British version (possibly Bates's) locates it "In the Bay of Passamaquady, in New Brunswick." However, after being occupied by the British in 1814, Moose Island (on which most of the small city of Eastport, Maine, is located) was relinquished to the United States in 1817.

[150] A footnote in the British version (possibly by Bates) locates in "In the District of Maine, in the United States." Portland is the largest city in Maine, which remained a district of Massachusetts until 1820.

[151] A footnote in the British version (possibly by Bates) explains that "Newhaven [sic] and New London are in the state of Connecticut." New Haven, where the first edition of this book was published, had a population of a little over 6,000. New London (about 47 miles east of New Haven) had about 3,300 inhabitants. The stagecoach line between Boston and New Haven had been founded in 1783 by Levi Pease. His was still in service, as were those of his many competitors: 40 lines were listed officially, but the number was probably higher (see Holmes 37).

[152] Boots with tops of light-coloured (bleached) leather.

[153] In the second edition, the sentence has a few more words: "at Mr. H. Butler's inn;" then, one long sentence which was subsequently left out of the third edition: "Thus in little more than two months from the time he was discharged from my custody, pennyless and almost naked, amongst strangers and without friends, and in a time of war, he finds his way from one country's territory to another, appears in the character of a gentleman—and with his neck just slipped from the halter, still struggles in the chace with 'lame-legged Justice.'"

[154] The *Fulton*, mentioned later (see note 164). The name of the captain (Bunker) is already mentioned here in the third edition.

Mr. H. Butler's hotel[155] discovered that his whole stock of silver spoons, &c. which had been carefully deposited in a sideboard[156] the night previous, had suddenly decamped, and were not to be found in the premises—and on further search by Mr. B. it was discovered that several other articles had sympathetically moved off with the spoons. This phenomenon, though not so astonishing as that of the moving stones,[157] excited suspicion that they had not departed without some physical agency, which was supposed to proceed from a person who lodged in the house, and who seemed to possess some magical appearance, and had taken himself off in the Steam-Boat. Mr. B. immediately started express[158] for New-York—arrived before the boat—found the fellow on board—seized his trunk and searched it—and though unfortunately he did not succeed in recovering his property, he nevertheless found sufficient evidence that the fellow was a villain,[159] had him arraigned, and secured in Bridewell.[160]—He called his name NEWMAN, and from the stolen property found with him it is supposed he can unravel the mystery of many phenomena of this nature."[161]

---

[155] Butler's establishment (in what was better known as "Hoadley's building") was a hotel only briefly, but it was considered "the best hotel in New Haven" (Elliot 26), famed for its dinners. His given name is spelled out in the third edition as "Henry."

[156] The sideboard, which was originally a table on which one kept everything necessary for serving dinner, had evolved into a large piece of furniture, with plenty of storage space.

[157] A reference to the story, much repeated in the fall of 1815 by American newspapers, of stones that had been seen to rise a few feet from the ground, then move away for a distance of thirty to sixty feet, in a field near Marbletown, New York. The story gained traction after it was repeated in *Niles' Weekly Register* of Baltimore, the most widely read national magazine at the time. The editor of the British version inserted here the following footnote: "A story, of stones that had been 'seen to move,' had been current in Connecticut just before."

[158] Butler hired a stagecoach to take him directly to New York (see also note 56). The increasingly popular steamboat made the first trip in March 1815 "in eleven and a half hours" (Beckford 30), but around the same time the stage trip was also done "in eleven and a half hours" (Hale 24), probably faster without any stops.

[159] In the third edition, the reader is told that Butler found "a small *ear-ring*," reported missing by one of his lodgers, and Smith was arrested "upon the evidence of this single ear-ring."

[160] Bridewell was the main prison in New York City between 1768 and 1838, when it was replaced by the Tombs. In Britain, the term "bridewell" was often used for any prison in general.

[161] This newspaper article was left out of the third edition.

On the 17th of October, 1816, I left Kingston, with the intention of proceeding to Portland, where I intended to publish these memoirs; and took passage on board the sloop Wellington, with the expectation of being landed there; but the wind coming out from the westward, when at George River,[162] obliged her to proceed to New-York, where she arrived on the 1st of November. I called on Mr. Nehemiah Allen, the keeper of Bridewell, in that city,[163] and enquired the conduct of WILLIAM NEWMAN while in his custody. He said he appeared very decent and behaved well—that he offered him a book to read, but he said he was ignorant, and could not read or write a word—and began to complain of being sick. The doctor attended him, but could not tell what was the matter with him. He raised blood, and was so ill that he was helped up by the prisoner confined with him, who thought he would die.

THE OLD BRIDEWELL.
Which formerly stood in the Park, between the City Hall and Broadway

He was removed from Bridewell to New-Haven, there to take his trial for burglary, at the Supreme Court to be held in January—but he kept up the farce of being sick, so that they lifted him out and in, and carried him to and from the Steam Boat upon a cart. He remained in prison until the 12th of January, and on the 13th the following article appeared in the Connecticut Journal:

[162] Saint George River, in Maine (the reference is clearly to its estuary).

[163] Nehemiah Allen, who served as a keeper at Bridewell, was a minor civil servant and an abolitionist in New York. In the third edition, his given name appears as "Archimial."

"*Beware of a Villain.*—One of the most accomplished villains that disgraces our country broke from the jail in this city on Friday evening last, between the hours of five and six, and succeeded in making his escape. This fellow calls himself *William Newman*, and was bound over for trial at the next sitting of the Supreme Court, on the charge of burglary, having robbed the house of Mr. H. Butler of plate, money, &c. He is supposed to be an Englishman, and is undoubtedly a most profound adept in the arts of knavery and deception. He speaks the English and several foreign languages fluently, and can play off the air of a genteel Frenchman with the most imposing gravity. He is of middling stature, slender and active, and appears to possess an astonishing versatility of genius. He is sick or well, grave or gay, silent or loquacious, and can fence, box, fight, run, sing, dance, play, whistle or talk, as occasion suits. He amused himself while in prison by making and managing a poppet-show, which he performed apparently with such scanty means as to excite the wonder of the credulous, showing the piece of an old horse shoe, whetted on the wall of his dungeon, as the only instrument of his mechanism, and complaining only of the scarcity of *timber* to complete the group. He had the address, by an irresistable flow of good humour and cheerfulness, to make some believe he was quite an innocent and harmless man, and excited sympathy enough in those who had the curiosity to see him to obtain several gratifications which prisoners do not usually enjoy. Yet the deepness of his cunning was evinced in accomplishing the means of his escape, which he effected by sawing a hole in his prison door, which is several inches thick, so neatly that the block could be taken out and replaced without showing any mark of violence. Through this hole he could thrust his arm, and by shoving back the bolts and wrenching off a strong padlock, found, at the hour of supper, when the person who waited on the prisoners was giving them their food, a free passage to the hall of the county-house, and thence to the street. The saw is supposed to be one used on board the Steam-Boat Fulton[164] for cutting iron, which he stole on his transportation from New-York (where he was apprehended) to this place, and so artfully did he conceal it that, though repeatedly searched before his confinement, and afterwards, at the suggestion of Capt. Bunker, to discover this very instrument, he was enabled

[164] The *Fulton*, with Captain Elihu S. Bunker, had its maiden trip from New York (Long Island Sound) to New Haven on 21 March 1815, soon after the British blockade was lifted.

to retain and use it for his purposes."[165]

At this time Mr. Butler happened to be in N. York, and on his return by land, a few miles from the city, met Mr. *William Newman*, travelling leisurely on the road, who passed him with as much *sang froid* as though he had nothing to apprehend. Mr. B. immediately pursued him, but he seemed to mock his exertions to take him. Coming to where assistance could be obtained, however, he took to the woods. Mr. B. hired a party of men, with dogs and guns, to ferret him out, but he eluded their vigilance. The next day he was discovered and taken,[166] again committed to Bridewell in New-York, and again returned to the gaol in New-Haven.

On his arrival at the County-House, Sheriff ROSSITER[167] had him searched, to see that he had no instrument with which he could effect his escape, and then confined him in the criminal's room, with a shackle about one of his legs, to which was attached a strong iron chain, firmly stapled to the floor. In this situation he was left at evening. In the morning he had not only raised the staple which confined him, but he had raised the floor also, which is of stout plank, secured upon the sleepers[168] with strong spikes. With the plank he had taken

[165] This was followed by a short paragraph in the second edition, which was not preserved in subsequent versions of the book: "On his escape Newman adopted the same policy he had pursued when he escaped from the gaol of King's County – He stopped a few miles from the city, in one of the adjacent towns, and made no haste to elude his pursuers – and not being personally known, his apparent unconcern rendered him less liable to suspicion."

[166] He was apprehended in a public house, where he asked for some breakfast (according to the second edition); or in someone's house, where he sat down at the family breakfast, "without invitation or ceremony," and began to eat (as stated in the third edition). The progression of subsequent events is best rendered in the second edition: "he was taken before a Justice, where he gave such an account of himself that the Justice could not commit him – not having any evidence of the facts alledged. He, however, ordered him to be taken to Bridewell, where he might be identified and properly secured – On his arrival there, Mr. Allen, the keeper, happened to be absent, and no one could recognize him – After detaining him some time, they were on the point of discharging him, when fortunately Mr. Allen returned, recognized him, and had him again committed. In a few days he was returned to the gaol in New-Haven,"

[167] Nathaniel Rossiter (1762-1835), a native of Guilford, Connecticut; he graduated Yale in 1785; he was a representative in the Connecticut General Assembly (1795-1804) and sheriff of New Haven County (1804-1819). His name is omitted in the third edition.

[168] Heavy beams laid horizontally on the ground.

up he barricaded the door, so that no one could enter—made a fire, and carrying the chain from his foot upon his shoulder, walked the room, smoking his pipe. Being ordered to open the door, he said this was his castle, and no one should enter it without his leave.[169] Sheriff Rossiter finding him determined not to open the door, and having in vain endeavoured to get in by other means, sent for a mason, and ordered him to make a hole in the brick partition which divided the lower rooms, large enough for him to enter, and the mason began the work, when Newman concluded to open the door, and the Sheriff went in and secured him. After this he was more closely confined, with irons and chains; when he renewed his old scheme or yelling and screaming all night, which he kept up until his trial, which a few days after took place.

I have obtained no particulars of trial; but have learnt, generally, that he was convicted of burglary, on the evidence of having entered a chamber in the house of Mr. H. Butler, where a young lady was sleeping, and stole one of her ear-rings which lay upon the candle-stand by the side of her bed;[170] for which offence he was sentenced to be confined in Newgate, (Simsbury Mines)[171] for three years.

In order to identify the person of *William Newman* as that of *Henry More Smith*, I came to New-Haven, where I obtained these particulars respecting him. I had a curiosity to see him, and to know how he conducted in Newgate, and proceeded there for that purpose. I was treated, by Captain Washburn,[172] the keeper, with politeness and attention. I inquired the conduct of *William Newman*. Captain Washburn said he behaved very well;

---

[169] In the third edition, Bates added that Smith was in the same cell with "two negro boys." Sheriff Rossiter asked them to help open the door, but Smith threatened to kill them.

[170] According to the third edition, "Newman obtained counsel to plead his case; but not being satisfied with the manner in which the trial was conducted, he plead his own case, in which he maintained that the ear-ring did not belong to the lady, but to his own wife."

[171] See also note 1. The prison was established inside an abandoned copper mine from the early 18th century, opened on the west side of Talcott Mountain, from the town of Simsbury, about 10 miles south of East Granby. Here, the editor of the British version inserted the following note: "A deserted copper-mine is used as a prison for convicts, for the state of Connecticut."

[172] Charles Washburn (c.1769-1821), a native of Hartford, Connecticut, was keeper of Newgate until 1817.

that when he was brought here, he was told he was a bad fellow, but he found he had so many worse ones, he did not think any thing of Newman. I asked what occupation he had given him; he said he was a tailor if any thing, but he had not been put to work much, as he was subject to fits, and unable to labour; that his fits were frightful; that in his distress he would whirl round on his head and shoulders like a top; that he had galled and bruised himself with his irons, and in his convulsive agonies had broken the shackles on his legs, so that they now only put a shackle on one leg. This information was as convincing to me as sight. On seeing him, I recognized him instantly. I asked him if he had ever seen me before—He did not know but he had, *at New-Haven.* Where did you come from?—*Canada.*[173] What countryman are you? *A Frenchman, born in France.* Was you ever in England? He had been at London and Liverpool, but never at Brighton. Was you ever at Kingston or St. John, New-Brunswick? He answered, *No, he did not know where that was!* with a countenance as firm and steady as if it had really been true. He appeared rather more fleshy than when at Kingston, but still the same subtle and mysterious being. He is the first I believe that has succeeded to relieve himself from labour in that prison, by any pretence or deception. He keeps himself clean and decent as usual, and amongst the wretched victims, fifty-seven in number, daily disgorged from the horrid pit in which they are immured, and put to their daily labour in chains and fetters, *William Newman* appears like a distinguished character.

I have been impelled both by duty and inclination to publish these memoirs, because the facts are both curious and astonishing; and because, with the knowledge of them, I thought it my duty to society to expose them to the world, that all might be better enabled to guard against the insidious approaches of an artful and designing villain.[174] The following is a description of his person.

He is about five feet nine inches high; his limbs strait and well proportioned; appears rather slender, but is large boned, close and well jointed; his wrists large, and his fingers uncommonly long; complexion light, but his skin a little of

[173] At the time, this meant either Lower (Quebec) or Upper (Ontario) Canada, but most likely Lower Canada.

[174] There is a lengthy moral excursus added here in the second edition. It is quoted entirely in our Introduction.

a sallow cast; his hair dark brown, handsomely grown, and curls naturally in front; his eyes light gray, quick, brilliant and piercing; his nose rather more prominent than ordinary, his visage thin; has a scar on the left side of his chin, and a small scar on his right cheek, near his ear;[175] always neat in his dress, and astonishingly quick and active in his motion; (would catch mice with his handcuffs on;)[176] fond of smoking; sings well, and whistles remarkably, and can play on almost any instrument of music: he is a blacksmith, a shipwright, a tailor, and a farmer; in fact any thing, for he has the strength of a lion, and the subtlety of the devil.

THE END.

[175] Here, the British version has a footnote (possibly by Bates) inviting the reader to "See the portrait prefixed to these pages." This portrait is included here before the text of the memoir.

[176] A long footnote inserted here in the British version (probably by Bates himself) is included in Appendix II (as "The Light-Fingered Gentry").

Illustration placed at the beginning of the second New Haven edition from 1817 and never used later. The original is very dark.
The caption quotes (inaccurately) one of Smith's lines:
"Leave me my hands and you may put on as much iron as you please."

EPILOGUE

PART I. AFTER 1815

I. 1. Walter Bates, [Newman, the Sorcerer]

[This is Bates's first attempt to give an account of the last months of Smith's imprisonment. When he wrote this letter, on 27 October 1815, he knew nothing of Smith's peregrinations after 30 August 1815, the day when he had put him on Daniel Scovil's schooner bound for Nova Scotia. In fact, when the letter was written, Smith was probably already in Boston or on his way there. It was first published in the *Bridgeport (Connecticut) Farmer*; this version is reproduced from the *Maryland Gazette and Political Intelligencer* 74: 26, 27 June 1816, p.1]

Some months since, we published a letter from WALTER BATES, High Sheriff of Kingston, giving an account of the conduct of an extraordinary character, by the name of *Henry More Smith*, then in his custody; but as many disbelieved the account, it may not be improper to publish the following extract of a letter from Mr. Bates to his sister. The account, it is believed, will not be uninteresting, as it not only confirms the former statement, but gives further particulars of his mysterious conduct. There is but little doubt that the person now confined in Newgate, in this State, by the name of WILLIAM NEWMAN, is the same—of whom much has been said, in consequence of his extraordinary conduct, while confined in the gaol at New Haven.

Extract of a letter from WALTER BATES, Esq. to his sister in Norwalk, Conn. dated Kingston, U. Canada,[177] October 27, 1815.

You informed me in your last, that you had seen a letter, published in your papers, from me to the Attorney General,

[177] Obvious mistake, undoubtedly because Kingston, Ontario was better known than Kingston, New Brunswick. The sister might be Elizabeth (1766-1846), who may have been in Norwalk at the time, unless the newspaper was wrong and the letter was addressed to a cousin.

giving an account of the conduct of a very extraordinary character that I had in charge, & that it was not credited amongst you; but that your family wished to hear from me to know if such a character did exist with me. To give a detailed account of all his conduct, would fill a volume: but, to give you a brief sketch, I would say, that such a mysterious stranger *did exist in my custody for more than twelve months*, as was faintly described in my letter. He was brought to me a stranger, & left me a stranger.—It was true he married a wife in Nova Scotia, and had been there about two years: but who he was, or where he came from, no one could tell, or how he lived. He was apprehended for stealing a horse, which he rode 280 miles in three days, but was overtaken the fourth, and brought with much difficulty to our prison. He was known by many names, but was committed to my charge by the name of Henry More Smith. He complained of sickness, occasioned, he said, by a hurt in his side, and a bad cold, which increased with dangerous symptoms, until all hopes of his life were past, and he apparently dead; but being brought to, and coming to his speech, said it was a fit, and that all the family had died in that way, and that he should not survive the second, which, in all probability, would take place the next day about the same hour, at sunsetting—accordingly, he was taken—the young man who attended him, found him, as he said, drawing his last gasp, and ran for help—on his return, in three minutes, he found to his astonishment that he had disappeared; and, upon the strictest search & inquiry the whole night, nothing could be heard of him. About four weeks afterwards, he was apprehended at the New Settlement, in the United States, above Woodstock, about 150 miles, and brought within 10 miles of the gaol; when he, in the night, being in irons, handcuffed, with a rope tied about his arms, above his irons, and a man hold of the other end of the rope, made his escape, and disappeared, leaving the rope in the hands of the man, with the knot tied in the same, as he had put it on. About three weeks after, he was apprehended, and put on board a sloop, with a chain and iron about his neck, and a black man hold of the chain, which he never let go until the sheriff had delivered him into my custody, in gaol; where I, by watching, kept him until he had his trial: in which time he cut the grates, cut and broke more than 30 feet of chain in short pieces, broke a number of handcuffs, and I could not find a chain that could hold him. He did not speak for 5 months.

At his trial it took five constables to hold him, being tied hand and foot. He paid no more regard to the court, than if no one was present: he was however found guilty, and sentence of death passed upon him, without his giving the least attention to it, or being at all concerned, or ever speaking a word.

He lay in prison about three months after sentence, in which time he performed every thing that was stated in my letter to the Attorney General, without the smallest assistance. About that time, the Supreme Court sat at Frederick-town; and taking into consideration his age and situation, and it being the first instance of horse-stealing in this county, the president was pleased to grant him his pardon. After this time, I permitted him to have thread and needles, calico, and cloth, with a pair of scissors, to see what improvements he could make; and truly, it was astonishing. I shall not attempt to describe—only say that he had, before he left the gaol, 24 characters, all dressed in the neatest manner; among which were six musicians; and he would sit and play the fiddle or fife, and every one of them acted their part as well as if they were really alive; keeping time with music. He never would converse, or answer any question; he would not accept his pardon, or understand any thing about it—he said he did not wish to leave the gaol, and it was with difficulty I got rid of him. He would tell any thing that happened abroad, or any thing happened to any one for some time past or would happen in a short time to come. He appeared to know every thing: said he could talk French or Latin, as well as English—that he knew enough, and never asked any questions.

At length, by good luck, I got him on board a vessel, as he himself had predicted, and sent him to Windsor, where he went on shore, and was seen there in the street about an hour, and then disappeared, which is the last I have heard from him. He probably will appear next with you.

I. 2. Walter Bates, [From Saint John to Boston]

[This passage was added in the third edition; the story begins on Daniel Scovil's schooner, travelling from Saint John, New Brunswick, to Windsor, Nova Scotia, on 30 August 1815. The largest part involves a story, which Bates qualifies as "ludicrous," featuring Smith no longer in the character of a trickster, but rather as a gothic villain, and which would have occurred in Eastport, Maine, on Moose Island. Bates was aware that, on his way to Portland, Smith would have travelled through Easport; consequently, he chose to report the story.]

While the vessel was getting under weigh, Smith was in the cabin alone, and seeing a great number of *chain traces* lying on the cabin floor, he took them up and *threw them all out of the cabin window!* "Because," said he, "they would get about my neck again." During the passage, he appeared very active: he played on his fife, and was quite an agreeable passenger. But on the vessel's arrival at Windsor, he left her immediately without any ceremony; and notwithstanding the very strong regard which he had always possessed for his family, as he called them, he left *them also*, and every thing else that he had brought with him. He was seen only a very short time in Windsor before he entirely disappeared, and never was known to be there afterwards, but was seen at some distance from Windsor, in several other places, and recognized by many, but always carefully evaded being spoken to.

After having made his appearance in different parts of Nova-Scotia, he called at a certain house, one morning, on a bye road, and ordered breakfast, and asked for a towel also, and a piece of soap that he might wash at a small brook that was near the house. The woman of the house, and a maid were the only persons in the house at the time; and Smith left a large bundle, which he carried, on a chest which was standing in the room, and went out to wash. The bundle presented rather a singular appearance, and attracted the young woman's notice, so that she said to the other, "I wonder what he has in that bundle; if you will keep watch at the window, while he is washing at the brook, I will open it and see what is in it." They did so, and found a great number of watches, of which they counted fifteen, with many other valuable articles. She tied up the bundle again, and placed it where he had left it, and said, "this man has stolen these watches." When he came in, he handed the towel to the young woman, and said, "there were just fifteen watches, were there," and with such expression of countenance, that she could not refrain from answering "Yes." "But," said he, "you were mistaken about my stealing them, for I came honestly by them." Upon which the young woman instantly recognized him to be Henry More Smith; and concluded that he was collecting his *hidden treasure*, which he had deposited while he was in RODEN.[178]

This information I received from Mrs. Beckwith, a respectable lady from Nova-Scotia, who resided at the time in that neighborhood,[179] who also said it was not known that he had ever seen his wife at that time, from the time of his release from confinement. The next account I heard of him stated that he had been seen on board of a plaster vessel at Eastport;[180] but he was not known to have been ashore during the time she remained there. He employed himself while on board engraving a number of small articles, some of which he made presents of to young ladies who chanced to come on board.

He was next seen at Portland, by a gentleman who had known him at Kingston; nothing, however, transpired there concerning him, only that he was travelling with considerable weight of baggage, through the State of Maine, which gave rise to the following ludicrous story, which I saw published at Eastport, of [a] *Mysterious Stranger*, travelling in a stage. One cold and stormy night, the bar-room of a hotel was filled with sturdy farmers surrounding a cheerful fire, and discussing the affairs of State over a mug of *flip*.[181] The night having been tremendously stormy and wet, the wind whistling all round the house, and making every door and window rattle, the landlord expressed much fear for the safety of the stage-coach; but suddenly the sound of a distant stage horn announced the approach of the coach and removed the landlord's anxieties. He replenished the fire, that the approaching travellers might have as warm a retreat as possible from the unusual inclemency of the night. Some time passed, and yet the expected coach did not come up. The landlord's fears got up anew, and with

[178] Rawdon, where Smith lived in 1812-1813 (see notes 3 and 145).

[179] There were several Beckwith families, all in the Cornwallis area, about 30 miles west of Windsor.

[180] Eastport is on Moose Island (see note 149).

[181] A sailor's drink, a hot cocktail mixing ale, rum, sugar, nutmeg, and egg.

an expression of concern, put the question around, "Did not some of you hear a horn?" and added, "I have expected the stage a long time, and I thought that a few minutes ago, I heard the horn near at hand; but I fear that something has happened in the gale that has caused it to be thus belated." "I thought I heard the stage-horn some time ago," answered the young arch farmer Hopkins; "but then you must know that ghosts and witches are very busy on such nights as this, and what kind of pranks they may cut up we cannot tell. You know the old adage, *Busy as the devil in a gale of wind.* Now who knows but they may have?"—Here he was interrupted by the sudden opening of the door, accompanied by a violent gust of wind and the dashing of rain, when in rushed, from the fury of the storm, drenched with wet from head to foot, *a tall stranger*, dressed in a fur cap and shaggy great coat. From an impulse of politeness and respect, *not unmingled with fear*, all arose on his entrance,—the expression "*The devil in a gale of wind*," rushing upon their mind with a signification to which a profound silence gave expressive utterance. The stranger noticed their reserved, yet voluntary respect with a slight nod, and proceeded to disencumber himself of his wet clothes and warm his fingers by the fire. By this time the driver entered, bearing the baggage of his passenger. "The worst storm I was ever troubled with, blowing right in my teeth, and I *guess* the gentleman there found it the same." Here a low whisper ensued between the driver and the landlord, from which an unconnected word or phrase dropped upon the ear of the inmates. "*Don't know,—came in the,—as rich as a mine*," &c. Upon this information the landlord immediately took his wet garments and hung them carefully before the fire. "I hope that your wetting will not injure your health, sir." "I hardly think it will, my good friend; I am no child to catch cold from a ducking." "Shall I show you a room, sir?" said the landlord: "we can let you have as good a room and as comfortable a supper as any in the country." The stranger was immediately conducted into a handsome parlour in which blazed a cheerful fire; and, in a short time, a smoking supper was placed on the board. After supper was over he called the landlord into his room, and sent for his trunk. "I like your accommodations," accosting the landlord, "and if you like my proposals equally well, I shall be your guest for some time, though I know not how long. Nay, I shall stay at any price you please—but remember I must have my rooms to myself, and they must not be entered without my leave: and whatever I do, no questions to be asked. Do you consent to these my terms?" "I do sir," replied the landlord, "and you shall not have cause to complain of your treatment." "Very well," rejoined the stranger, "then the agreement is completed, you may go now." "Yes, sir," returned the landlord, "but what may I call your name, sir?" "Beware, you have broken the bargain already," replied the stranger, "I forgive you for this once only, my name is Maitland, now ask no more questions, or you will certainly drive me from your house." After this, the landlord returned to his bar-room, from which the merry farmers had not yet withdrawn, but were endeavoring to penetrate the mystery that hung around the stranger. "Well, landlord," said the arch Hopkins, "what do you make him out to be?" "That is a question I dare hardly answer. He is a gentleman, for he does not grudge his money." "I would not think he should," replied Hopkins, shaking his head mysteriously. "And why not," exclaimed several of the company: "Ay, just as I thought," returned Hopkins, with another shake of the head and significant look at the landlord. "What in the name of all that is silly, is the matter with you, Hopkins," exclaimed the landlord.—"What upon earth can you know?" "I know what I know," was his reply. "Rather doubtful, that," rejoined the landlord. "You doubt it," returned Hopkins, rather warmly: "then I will tell you what I think him to be, he is nothing more or less than a *Pirate*, and you will all be murdered in your beds, Smith, (which was the landlord's name,) you and your whole family, before morning. Now what think you of your guest?" All the company stood aghast, and stared at each other in silence for some time, until the landlord again ventured to interrupt the silence again, by asking Hopkins, "How do you know all that?" Hopkins answered, in rather a silly manner, "*I guessed at it*;" which did away with the effect produced by his previous assertions; and the landlord, dismissing his fears, exclaimed, "As long as he pays well, be he man or devil, he shall stay here." "*A praiseworthy conclusion*," proceeded from a voice at the back part of the room, and at that instant the *mysterious stranger* stood before them. All started to their feet, seized their hats, and waited to ask no questions, nor make additional comments, but went home and told their wives of Smith's guest, and Hopkins' opinion of his character. Every woman fastened her door that night with suspicious care, and the mysterious stranger, and the delineation of his real character, by Hopkins, became a subject of general conversation and comment, throughout the village, and gradually became the received opinion among all the settlers; so that they set down the *mysterious stranger* for what Hopkins *guessed* him to be, and concluded that the articles which composed his baggage could not have been obtained honestly.

The stranger finding how the conversation turned upon him, did not think it prudent to protract his stay in this place, and proceeding to Boston in the coach, was never known from that time by the name of Maitland. He reached Boston about the 1st of November, where it was supposed he must have, in some way, disposed of much of his treasures.

I. 3. Walter Bates, [Escape from Newgate]

[This passage from the third edition is a development of a brief mention in the first edition, in which Bates only mentions the fact that Smith had escaped and inserts a newspaper article; this is the first time he provides information about the manner in which Smith had escaped. Instead, the third edition did not keep the newspaper article. After his arrest in New York for robbing the guests in Butler's hotel in New Haven, Smith was first confined in Bridewell, then moved to the Newgate prison in Connecticut.]

He soon began to complain of being *sick* from confinement, *raised blood*, and seemed so ill that a doctor attended him, but could not tell what was the matter with him. However, he kept up the farce of being ill until he was removed from Bridewell to New Haven, there to take his trial at the Supreme Court in January.

His change of situation had the effect, as it would seem, of restoring his health, which brought along with it that display of his ingenuity which the peculiarity of his new situation seemed to call forth. During the period of his confinement at New Haven, he amused himself by carving two images—one representing himself, and the other Butler, in the attitude of fighting. And so mechanically had he adjusted this production of his genius, that he would actually cause them to fight, and make the image representing himself knock down that of Butler, to the wonder and amusement of many that came to see him. By his insinuating manner and captivating address, he not only drew forth the sympathies of those who came to visit him, but even gained so far upon their credulity as to induce a belief that he was innocent of the crime with which he was charged.

The lapse of a few days, however, made impressions of a different nature; the January Court term drew nigh, at which our *prisoner* was to receive his trial; but on the very eve of his trial, and after the Court had been summoned, he, by the power of a mind which seldom failed him in the hour of emergency, contrived and effected his escape in the following curious and singular manner. And here it will be necessary to give some description of the prison, with the situation of the apartments, which the writer was himself, by the politeness of the *Keeper*, permitted to survey. There was a wide hall leading from the front of the County House, and from this hall, two separate prisons were entered by their respective doors: between these doors, a timber partition crossed the hall, having in it a door also, to allow an entrance to the inner prison. The object in having this partition, was to prevent any intercourse between the two prison doors, and it was so placed as to leave a distance of about two feet on each side, between it and the prison doors respectively. Newman, (for this, it will be remembered, is the name by which our prisoner is now known,) was confined in the inner prison. The doors of the prison opened by shoving inwards, and when shut were secured by two strong bolts, which entered into stone posts, with clasps lapped over a staple, to which were fixed strong padlocks. These padlocks, our prisoner, by some means, managed to open or remove, so that he could open the door at pleasure, and fix the padlocks again in so ingeniously, that it could not be detected from their appearance. On the night of the 12th of January, at the usual time of feeding the prisoners, Newman availing himself of these adjustments, opened his door, came out, and replacing the locks, took his stand behind the door of the partition, which, when open, would conceal him from observation. The prisoners in the other apartment received their supply first, and the instant when the servant was proceeding from the door to go and bring Newman's supper, he stepped through the partition door, which had been first opened and not shut again, and followed the servant softly through the hall to the front door, and walked away undiscovered! When the servant returned with his supper to the wicket, she called him, but receiving no answer, placed his supper inside of the wicket, saying "you may take it or leave it; I am not going to wait here all night." She then secured the outer door, and so the matter rested till the morning.

The next morning, finding that the prisoner had not taken his supper, the servant observed to the keeper, that she feared *Newman was dead*, for he had not taken his supper; and she called him, but could not hear or see anything of him. Upon this, the keeper came with his keys to unlock the door, and to his utter astonishment, found both locks broken and the prison empty.

I. 4. [Walter Bates], Further Particulars of the Conduct and Character of William Newman, since His Confinement in Newgate, Obtained from the Keeper of the Prison

[This is an epilogue to the second edition, published in the summer of 1817, by Maltby, Goldmith & Co., of New Haven, Connecticut, pp. 121-127. It was never reprinted in subsequent editions, even though it offers great insight into Smith's character and into his methods, provided by other prisoners, acting as spies for the prison warden. It is possible that some or all of the text came from Charles Washburn, at the request of the publishers, and that is why Bates, who always preferred to use his own experience, his research and his sources, decided not to keep this account in later versions of the book. Apart from some other hints in the text, the presence of a quote from Shakespeare is another indication that Bates did not author it.]

Since the confinement of WILLIAM NEWMAN in Newgate prison, Capt. WASHBURN, the Keeper, has made several attempts to discover his true character and to draw from him the history of his early life, but his exertions have not succeeded in obtaining, directly, any facts not disclosed in the foregoing narrative. In answering Capt. W's. enquiries, he has always avoided every thing that would throw any light upon his origin, except that he was born of respectable parents, at Brighton, in England—that he was religiously educated—declaring his innocence of any crime, until he was convicted in New-Haven of stealing an ear-ring, and for which he was sentenced to three years confinement in Newgate.—But he has been more communicative to his fellow prisoners, and less guarded in revealing his character and his crimes. He has often amused their solitary hours with the recital of his youthful follies and the rapid steps with which he advanced to the deliberate crime of murder. This last fact he communicated in confidence to his bed-fellow—who is said to be, in turpitude and cunning, but little inferior to Newman himself.

When Newman was first committed to Newgate, he attempted to pursue the same course of deception that he had before so successfully put in practice. He was at first put to do the drudgery of the prison, cutting and piling wood, carrying water, &c. but he was desirous of living entirely at his ease, and in order to procure the indulgence of the Keeper, he feigned illness, and became subject to fits, of a most violent and alarming nature, which, until his character became more fully developed, succeeded so far as to relieve him from the block, and the application to any sedentary or regular employment.

After the publication of the foregoing memoirs, no doubt remaining of the identity of his person, it was suspected that he was imposing on the credulity of his keepers, and means were adopted to detect him. Several experiments were tried during the period of his attacks to bring him to his senses; but with a determination so resolute, and an effect so imposing did he carry on his plan, that it was hard to believe human nature capable of such agonizing mockery. The evidence of his former conduct spoke strongly against him, but the evidence of his own sufferings almost spoke conviction.

His fits were of that kind denominated falling sickness,[182] and in addition to convulsions, frothing at the mouth, &c. he raised blood and complained of soreness in his lungs and a weak stomach—his pale and sallow countenance added to these symptoms of disease, an almost irresistible evidence of its reality. After he had carried on the farce for some time, he disclosed the deception to one of the prisoners, who was employed by the Keeper to endeavour to draw from him such facts as might lead to his detection in case he designed to escape, who, being furnished with ink and paper, communicated to Capt. Washburn, the substance of his communications with Newman.

The facts communicated through this source are briefly as follows:—That Newman is an Englishman; born in Brighton, where his parents reside; his name he has never disclosed; his parents gave him a good education, and brought him up in a style of life which, when he came to maturer years, he found himself unable to support. He was fond of sports and amusements, and passed all the rounds of dissipation and pleasure, till his resources failed him, when, in concert with some of his gay companions, he began to resort to unlawful means to replenish

[182] Old term for epilepsy.

his dissipated store. He had committed several robberies, undetected, and had ceased to experience those "compunctious visitings"[183] which the young offender cannot avoid, when an opportunity for plunder offered, so tempting to his cupidity that the enormity of the offence presented no barrier to its commission. A gentleman of property, in the vicinity of Brighton, had gone on business to London; leaving only a young lady as housekeeper until his return. Newman, and two of his companions, resolved to plunder the house; being inmates of the family,[184] they contrived to administer laudanum to the lady, in the course of an evening's entertainment, which throwing her into a profound apathy, they plundered the house of money and plate to the amount of twenty two hundred pounds, and departed. The young lady was afterwards found dead, and a reward of one thousand pounds sterling was offered for the detection of the perpetrators of this nefarious deed. His two companions fled, and fearful himself that some clue might be found to lead to his discovery and bring him to justice, he left England for America and arrived at Halifax. The history of his progress in this country, up to his confinement in Newgate is given in the narrative of Mr. Bates. The communications of Newman to his fellow prisoners, (none of whom have been permitted to see these memoirs,) fully confirm every thing that has been stated—He has personally related the same facts, and boasted of the means by which he accomplished his deceptions.

In one of the communications of his fellow prisoner, after stating the nature of his first attempts in falling sickness, the writer says:—"In addition to the former he succeeded in his last tumbling match. He thinks two more grand tragedies will seal the deception. The first is to take place when the Doctor is here, and he wishes me to give him notice when he comes into the gate, that he may take the opportunity without any apparent knowledge of his presence. If he succeeds in deceiving the Doctor, the next exhibition is to take place in the Chapel on the Sabbath, that he may have the audience of the town[185] to

[183] From Shakespeare's *Macbeth* (Act I, scene i, line 43). In the play, Lady Macbeth asks the spirits that no "compunctious visitings of [womanly] nature" interfere with her "fell purpose."

[184] The obsolete meaning of "inmates" is that of people residing in the same building as others.

[185] A footnote in the original text explains that "Divine service is performed every Sabbath at the prison, in a room in the guard house, neatly fitted up, where the inhabitants of the vicinity usually attend."

witness his experiments in the juggling art, in expectation that they will commiserate his unfortunate situation, and he thinks by that time he will be quite relieved from being put to the block, which is his aim and full determination at present. He declares if he is put to a block he will leave his hammer in a fit and kill some one, if he cannot shun it in any other way. He says he did not think of having fits until after he came here—that Horton (one of the prisoners) suggested it to him, and said that he had succeeded in relieving himself from labour by that means.

He has found an entire new way of raising blood, which is by pounding brick to a powder, putting it in a small rag, and chewing it in his mouth—Sometimes he pricks his gums, or sucks the blood from his teeth. He contrives to vary his pulse by pounding his elbows, and other means of violence, and thus succeeds in deceiving a physician. He tells me he can take the flesh off himself in ten days, and has experimental knowledge of the means—It is by sucking a copper cent in his mouth all night, and swallowing the saliva, which destroys the juices of the body, and produces premature decay. He is still apprehensive that he shall have to answer for the crime of murder—the reward of a thousand pounds (he says) stands good against him now if he should be taken on that ground after his discharge from prison, and he is calculating to be crazy during the last six months of his confinement, to avoid justice. He says if he is taken back to England he is sure to be hanged."

According to the information given in this communication, when the Doctor visited the prison again Newman fell in a violent fit. Capt. Washburn ordered a pail of water to be brought, and with a pitcher he poured a small and continued stream of water upon his nostrils, which prevented respiration, and obliged him to turn his head to procure breath, which he would not have done had the fits been real. The discovery, however, was not made known to Newman, and he continued to flatter himself that he was on "the full tide of successful experiment." A suitable opportunity soon offered to exhibit himself in the chapel, and accordingly just as the blessing was pronouncing by the officiating clergyman at the conclusion of the service, he fell into a fit. The sergeant of the guard, who was prepared for the event, instantly stepped upon his breast, and ordered others to confined his legs and arms, by stepping upon them, which placed the unhappy patient in a most unpleasant predicament—and not liking the prescription, he was soon restored to his senses, without producing any other effect than frightening the audience, and hastening them away with a little more precipitancy than they would otherwise have gone.

After these circumstances had transpired, Newman was put into the workshop and confined to the block in common with the other prisoners, where he has continued ever since, conducting himself well towards those whose duty it has been to watch him. He continues, however, to have fits occasionally, but always pays dear for his temerity. He has never made any attempt to escape, and it is believed he has given up any project of that kind, though he declared on being committed, that he would not remain there three months.

Capt. Washburn, in reply to a letter addressed by the publishers to him, after touching the foregoing particulars, observes: "There cannot exist a doubt that he is the man of whom Mr. Bates, the Sheriff of King's County, has written—There are many circumstances which tend to corroborate his narrative. He acknowledges that he was in Canada. He has likewise made many puppets since he came to this place, much like those described by Mr. Bates—In short, the title he has given him, viz: *the Mysterious Stranger*, could hardly be so well suited to another. Should any thing hereafter come to my knowledge respecting him, worth the attention of the public, I will, with pleasure, give you the earliest information.

I am, respectfully, yours, &c.

CHARLES WASHBURN,

Prison Keeper."

I. 5. Anonymous, [The Stranger Set Free]

[This public announcement was originally published in the *Connecticut Courant*. The writer was clearly well acquainted with Bates's book and quotes Smith's description provided there. The *Courant* was published weekly in Hartford (in fact, it is still published today as the *Hartford Courant*; it became a daily in 1837). The following is from a reprint in the *Alexandria Gazette & Daily Advertiser* 19: 5474, 1 March 1819. According to this story, Smith had been released on Monday, 22 February 1819.]

CAUTION TO THE PUBLIC

The notorious William Newman, who was committed to Newgate three years since, on the charge of burglary, having robbed the house of Mr. H. Butler of New Haven, of plate, money, &c. was liberated on Monday last from the state prison, his term of confinement having expired. This William Newman is the same person who in the memoirs which have been before the public is called the "Mysterious Stranger"—and whose extraordinary conduct during his confinement in New Brunswick when he was under sentence of death, excited so much curiosity and surprise. That the public may be on their guard against this artful fellow, we subjoin the following description of him. "He is about 5 feet 9 inches high; his limbs strait and well proportioned; appears rather slender, but large boned, close and well jointed; his wrists large and his fingers uncommonly long, complexion light, but his skin of a yellow cast, his hair dark brown, and curls naturally in front, his eyes light grey, quick and piercing; his nose rather more prominent than ordinary, his visage thin, has a scar on the right cheek near his ear; is neat in his dress, and very quick in his motion, fond of smoaking, sings well, and whistles remarkably, and can play on almost any instrument of music, and can work with wonderful facility at many kinds of mechanical business."

I. 6. R. H. Phelps, [A Noted Prison-Breaker]

[The following is from Phelps's *Newgate of Connecticut; Its Origin and Early History* (Hartford, CT: American Publishing Company, 1876), 75-76. Richard Harvey Phelps (1813-1885) was a native of Granby, Connecticut. He either had read Bates's second edition or had access to documents left by Charles Washburn.]

A convict, by the name of Newman, was a noted prison-breaker. Although he perhaps could not boast of unlocking, scaling, and digging out of so many prisons as the famous Stephen Burrows,[186] yet his character, as it was written, compared very well. He escaped in various ways from several prisons in Canada and the United States, but this one, he said, "was the hardest and most secure prison he ever entered." However, he contrived several plans for escaping; once he feigned himself to be dead. He was accordingly laid out as a corpse, and preparations made for his interment; but before finding his carcass firmly under ground, he concluded it best to have his resurrection, and at length ventured to disclose to his attendants the important fact, that he would feel quite as comfortable in his long home, if he could get the breath out of his body and make his heart stop beating. He often pretended to have fits, requiring medical aid, and what was of more consequence, the aid of a little Brandy or Madeira. He pretended to raise blood from his lungs whenever he wished to draw sympathy from the guard, until it was discovered that it was a substance made to order by chewing pieces of *red brick*, or pricking his gums. He would vary his pulse by pounding his elbows and other violent means, and thus deceive the physician. He said he could reduce his flesh in ten days by sucking a copper cent in his mouth each night, and swallowing the saliva, which destroys the juices of the body, and produces premature decay. He was continually apprehensive that he would yet be taken back to England, where he said he should have to answer for the crime of murder, as a thousand pounds reward for his arrest stood against him. His chief desire was to avoid labor at the nail-block, but he was finally cured of his tricks with the threat of having the brand of rogue set on his forehead.

[186] Stephen Burroughs (1765-1840), a notorious criminal from New England. He published his *Memoirs* in 1798. He spent the last decades of his life in Lower Canada.

I. 7. Walter Bates, Preface [of 1840]

[Bates's preface was written for the edition published by A.L. Avery in Saint John, in 1840. This is made clear by the first words of the text. The preface is Bates's justification for the chronological order of events in his new version of the memoir about Smith, as well as a way of reinforcing his warning that Smith's career is anything but admirable.]

Upwards of twenty years have now elapsed since the first Edition of the "MYSTERIOUS STRANGER" was published. In the course of this time, I have had occasion to visit the United States at four different periods, which gave me frequent opportunities of enquiring after the notorious individual who forms the subject of the following narrative, and of becoming acquainted with many of the prominent features of his conduct and career, from the time of his banishment from this Province, and during his subsequent travels through Nova-Scotia, the States of Maine, Massachusetts, Connecticut, New-York, Maryland, and Upper Canada.

As I pursued my enquiries, the facts relating to his extraordinary career became increasingly interesting and astonishing, insomuch that I considered it my duty to the world to publish them, that all might, in some measure, be prepared to guard, as much as possible, against the approaches of so artful and designing a villain, who, from a life spent in the practice of depredations, thefts, and robberies, has become so accomplished in his diabolical profession as to set mankind at defiance.

My resolution to publish this THIRD Edition of his Memoirs is also in compliance with repeated solicitations from Boston, New-York, Connecticut, and various other parts of the United States, as well as from many persons in New-Brunswick, Nova-Scotia, and Upper Canada. And to render the Work as complete, interesting, and acceptable as possible, it begins with a short sketch of his life and character, from the time of his first appearance at Windsor, in Nova-Scotia, in the year 1812, to the time of his apprehension and confinement in my custody. It presents, also, a full account of his astonishing behaviour during the period of his imprisonment under my keeping in the years 1814 and '15, with his remarkable escape from prison, and his re-apprehension and commitment to confinement again; his trial, sentence of death and pardon, and his banishment from the Province.

I have traced his subsequent career throughout the United States and other parts, up to the present period; and from the best information I could obtain,—from public prints and private correspondence, and by all possible means have collected and narrated all the principal facts connected with his remarkable history for upwards of twenty years; have detailed particularly his various imprisonments and escapes, until the narrative naturally closes with the report of his confinement in the gaol of Toronto, Upper Canada.

As I have deemed it necessary also, to give the public a description of his person, I have chosen to give it a place in this part of the Work, that the chain of the narrative may be preserved unbroken, as much as possible.

At the time of his banishment from this Province, he was about twenty-two years of age: five feet, nine or ten inches high,—straight limbs, and well proportioned; large bones, and close jointed wrists,—fingers large and unusually long,—his complexion light, but a little of the sallow cast;—his hair of a dark brown, handsomely shaded, and naturally curled in front;—his eyes of a light grey, quick and piercing,—his nose rather more prominent than ordinary, and his visage thin, with a small scar on the left side of his chin, and a slight one of the right cheek near his ear, which he received, as he said, in using the small-sword: he was astonishingly quick and active in his movements, and uniformly clean and neat in his dress. To this description of his person may be added, that he was exceedingly addicted to smoking, could sing and whistle remarkably well, and play on any instrument of music. He could speak several foreign languages, and perform all kind of mechanical business or common labour, and seemed to have in his arm the strength and power of a lion, and a mind filled with subtlety, invention, and depth of Satan.

WALTER BATES.

Kingston, (New-Brunswick.)

I. 8. Walter Bates, [Sequel and Conclusion]

[These pages, added at the end of the third edition, contain most of Bates's research into Smith's career after 1817, the year when the first two editions were published, and especially after 1819, when Smith was released from Newgate. The last paragraph is absent from Cunnabell's Halifax edition and only versions reproducing Avery's edition from 1840 include it.]

It was in the city of New Haven that the author published the *First Edition of these Memoirs*, being aware that here, where his character and unprecedented actions were perfectly known throughout the country, the publication of his doings at Kingston, and his career throughout the provinces of New-Brunswick and Nova Scotia would not only be desirable and acceptable; but would also be received with less scrupulousness, when brought, as it were, in contact with facts of a similar nature publicly known and believed.

While these papers were being prepared for the press, a gentleman from Washington, Major McDaniel, on his return from Boston, boarded some time in the same house with me, that of Mr. Joseph Nichols,[187] and having heard some details from me of his unprecedented character and actions in New-Brunswick, and having also become acquainted with the facts relating to his imprisonments and escape, &c. in that place, could not repress his curiosity in going to see him, and requested me to accompany him at his own expence. He observed that it would be a high gratification to him, on his return to Washington, that he would not only have one of my books with him, but would also be able to say that he had personally seen the Sheriff from New Brunswick that had written the book, and had seen the remarkable character in the prison of New Gate that had constituted the subject of the book, and also the prison in New Haven from which he escaped. Accordingly we set out for New Gate and my friend had the satisfaction of seeing the noted Henry More Smith, now William Newman. On our leaving him, I said to him, "Now Smith, if you have any thing you wish to communicate to your wife, I will let her know it." He looked at me and said, "Sir are you going to the Jerseys?"[188] "Why, do you

[187] Joseph Nichols (1749-1826) was a distant relative of Bates's, from Waterbury, New Haven County.

[188] New Jersey, still commonly referred to as "the Jerseys," because of the time when it was divided into two parts (east and west).

think your wife is there?" "I hope so, I left her there," was his reply, and that with as much firmness and seeming earnestness as if he had never before seen my face.—After I had left him and returned to New Haven, and furnished the printer with this additional sketch, and had the Memoirs completed, one of the books was shewn to him, which he perused with much attention, and replied with seeming indifference, that there never was such a character in existence; but that some gentleman travelling in the United States had run short of money and had invented that book to defray his expences!

Immediately after he had read the *Memoirs* of his own unparalleled life and actions, and pronounced the whole a *fiction*, as if to outdo anything before related of him, or attributed to him, he added the following remarkable feat to the list, already so full, of his singular and unprecedented actions. In the presence of a number of young persons, and when there was a fine fire burning on the hearth, he affected to be suddenly seized with a violent *convulsive fit*, falling down on the floor and bounding and writhing about, as if in the most agonizing sufferings. And what constituted the *wonder* of this masterpiece of affectation was, that in his spasmodic contortions his feet came in contact with the fire, and were literally beginning to be roasted, without his appearing to feel any pain from the burning. This circumstance confirmed the belief in the bystanders, that the *fit* was a reality; and he did not miss his aim in shewing off his spasmodic attack, which was indeed done to the life. He was consequently exempted from *hard labour*, and was permitted to employ himself in any trifling application he chose, or in making Jews harps, penknives, knives of various descriptions, and rings, in the mechanism of which he manifested much original talent and characteristic ingenuity. Many persons, from mere curiosity, purchased from him several articles of his handiwork. From among the rest, may be instanced the case of two young men, who very much admired his small penknives, and proposed purchasing two of them on condition of his engraving his name on the handles of them. He immediately engraved, with perfect neatness, "*Henry More Smith*," on the one side of one of them, "*William Newman*," on the other side, and on the other knife he engraved, "*Mysterious Stranger*." Those knives were kept by their owners as a curiosity, and many persons were much gratified by seeing them. One of them was sometime after brought to Kingston, and I, myself had the gratification of seeing the name of my old *Domestic*, engraved on the handle.

Under the indulgent treatment he received in New Gate, he became perfectly reconciled to his situation, manifesting no desire to leave it. "Contentment," he said, "is the brightest jewel in this life, and I was never more contented in my life." He consequently never attempted any means of escape.

After the period of his imprisonment was up and he had received his discharge, he left with the keeper of the prison, a highly finished pocket knife, of moderate size, the handle of which contained a watch, complete in all its parts, keeping time regularly. And what excited much wonder in reference to this ingenious and singularly curious piece of mechanism, was the fact, that he had never been found at work on any part of the watch or knife, and yet there was no doubt on the minds of those who saw it, that it was in reality the *production of his own genius*, and the work of his own hands. For this information I was indebted to a gentleman named Osborne, who resided in the neighbourhood, and who stated that he had seen the watch and knife himself, and that it was regarded by all as a most wonderful piece of ingenuity.

He left Simsbury decently apparelled, and with some money in his pocket, and in possession of some articles of his own handiwork. He directed his course eastward, and was seen in Boston; but for some time, nothing particular or striking was heard of him. The first thing concerning him, that arrested public attention, was published in the *Boston Bulletin*, and which came under my own eye: "Beware of pickpockets! A stage coach destined for this city and full of passengers, a few evenings since, when one of the passengers rang the bell, and cried out to the driver to stop his horses as his pocket had been picked of a large sum of money since he entered the coach; and at the same time requested the driver would not let any of the other passengers get out of the coach, it being dark, until he, the aforesaid passenger, should bring a light, in order to have a general search. This caused a general feeling of pockets among the passengers, when another passenger cried out that his pocket book had also been stolen. The driver did as he was directed, until the gentleman who first spoke should have time to have procured a lamp; but whether he found it or not remained quite uncertain. But no doubt he found the light he intended should answer his purpose, as he had not shewn his appearance in any other light. However the passenger who really lost his pocket book, which although it did not contain but a small amount of money, thinks he shall hereafter understand what is meant when a man in a stage coach calls out *thief*, and that he will *prefer darkness rather than light*, if ever such an evil joke is offered to be played with him again."

As he was continually changing his name, as well as his place, it was impossible always to identify his person, especially as few persons in the United States were personally acquainted with him. The difficulty of recognising him was not a little increased also by the circumstances of his continually changing his external appearance; and the iniquitous means by which he could obtain money and change of apparel, always afforded him a perfect facility of assuming a different appearance. In addition to these circumstances also, as a feature of character which no less contributed to the difficulty of identifying him, must be taken into account his unequalled and inimitable ease in affecting different and various characters, and his perfect and unembarrassed composure in the most difficult and perplexing circumstances. To the identity and eccentricity therefore, of his actions, rather than to our knowledge of the identity of his person and name, we must depend, in our future attempts to trace his footsteps and mark their *characteristic prints*.

On this ground, therefore, there is not the shadow of a doubt that the robbery committed in the stage coach, and that the *originality* of the means by which he carried off his booty, pointed with unhesitating certainty to the *noted character* of our narrative. After this depredation in the coach, with which he came off successful, it would appear that he bended his course in disguise through the States of Connecticut and New York, assuming different characters and committing many robberies undiscovered and even unsuspected for a length of time, and afterwards made his appearance in UPPER CANADA, in the character of a gentleman merchant from New-Brunswick, with a large quantity of smuggled goods from New-York, which he said were coming on after him in waggons: these he said he intended to dispose of on very moderate terms, so as to suit purchasers.

Here he called upon my brother, Augustus Bates, Deputy Postmaster, at Wellington Square, head of Lake Ontario,[189] and informed the family that *he was well acquainted with Sheriff Bates, at Kingston*, and that he called to let them know that he and

[189] Augustus Bates (1764-1842) was one of Bates's younger brothers. He was one of the earliest settlers in the township of Nelson (founded in 1806) and in Wellington Square, where he was appointed its first postmaster in 1815. Both Nelson and Wellington Square (now called Burlington) are today part of the municipality of Halton, Ontario.

his family were well. He regretted very much that he had not found Mr. Bates at home, and stated that he was upon urgent and important business, and could not tarry with them for the night, but would leave a letter for him. This he accordingly did, properly addressed, and in good handwriting; but when it was opened, and its contents examined, no one in the place could make out the name of the writer, or read any part of the letter! It appeared to have been written in the characters of some foreign language, but it could not be deciphered. This was another of his characteristic eccentricities, but his intention in it could not be well understood.

He did not appear to make himself particularly known to the family, nor to cultivate any further acquaintance with them, but proceeded thence to the principal boarding house in the town, and engaged entertainment for himself and thirteen other persons, who, he said, were engaged in bringing on his waggons, loaded with his smuggled goods. Having thus fixed upon a residence for himself and his gang of waggoners, he then called upon all the principal merchants in the town, on pretence of entering into contracts for storing large packages of goods, and promising to give great bargains to purchasers on their arrival, and in some instances actually received money as *earnest* on some packages of saleable goods, for the sale of which he entered into contracts. It may be remarked, by the way, that he wrote also in an unknown and unintelligible hand, to the celebrated Capt. Brant,[190] the same as he had written to Mr. Bates, but with what view was equally mysterious and unaccountable.

Notwithstanding his genteel and respectable appearance, there was a singularity in his manner and conduct which, with all his tact and experience, he could not altogether conceal; and hence arose some suspicions as to the reality of his pretensions. These suspicions received confirmation, and were soon matured into the reality of his being a genteel imposter, from the fact that the time for the arrival of his waggons was now elapsed, and that they were not making their appearance. At this juncture, when public attention and observation were directed to the stranger to observe which way the balance would turn, an individual named Brown, who had formerly resided in New-

[190] John Brant (1794-1832), a Mohawk leader and soldier in the War of 1812, lived near Burlington Bay (today, Hamilton Harbour), not far from Augustus Bates. He was the youngest son of the famous Joseph Brant (1743-1807).

Brunswick, and moved with his family to Canada, coming into contact with the gentleman, recognized him, from a certain mark he carried on his face, to be the *far-famed* Henry More Smith, whom he had seen and known when in jail at Kingston!

This report, passing immediately into circulation, gave the *impostor* a timely signal to depart, without waiting for the arrival of his waggons and baggage, and without loss of time he took his departure from Canada, by the way of Lake Erie, through the Michigan Territory, and down the Ohio to the Southern States.—With his proceedings, during this course of his travels, we are entirely unacquainted; therefore the reader must be left to his own reflections as to his probable adventures, as he travelled through this immense tract of country. There is no reason for doubt, however, that he had by this time, and even long before, become so confirmed in his iniquitous courses, that he would let no occasion pass unimproved, that would afford him an opportunity of indulging in the predominant propensity of a mind which seemed to glory in the prosecutions of robberies and plunder, as well as in the variety of means by which he effected his unheard of and unprecedented escapes.

After his arrival in the Southern States, we are again able to glean something of his life and history. While he was yet in the gaol at King's County, it will be remembered, that he said he had been a Preacher, and that he should preach again, and would gain proselytes; and now his prediction is brought about; for under a *new name*, that of HENRY HOPKINS, he appeared in the character of a *preacher* in the Southern States! And what wonder? For Satan himself is transformed into an angel of light.—Here, even in this character, he was not without success; for he got many to follow and admire him; yet deep as his hypocrisy was, he seemed to be fully sensible of it, although his conscience had become *seared*, and was proof against any proper sense of wrong. He acknowledged that he had been shocked to see so many follow him to hear him preach, and even to be affected under his preaching. Our source of information does not furnish us with many of the particulars which marked his conduct, while itinerating through the South in his newly assumed character; yet general accounts went to say, that he had, for a length of time, so conducted himself, that he gained much popularity in his ministerial calling, and had a considerable number of adherents. However this may have been the case for a length of time, yet as the assumption of this new character could not be attributable to any supernatural impulse, but was merely another feature of a character already so singularly diversified, intended as a cloak, under which he might, with less liability to suspicion, indulge the prevailing and all-controuling propensities of his vitiated mind, it was not to be expected, with all the ingenuity he was capable of exercising, that he would long be capable of concealing his real character. Accordingly, some high misdemeanor which we have not been able to trace, at length disclosed the hypocrisy of his character, and placed him before his deluded followers in his true light.

It would appear, whatever might have been the nature of his crime, that legal means were adopted for his apprehension; and that in order to expedite his escape from the hands of justice, he had seized upon a certain gentleman's coach and horses, and was travelling in the character of a gentleman in state, when he was overtaken and apprehended in the State of Maryland. Here he was tried and convicted, and sentenced to seven years imprisonment in the state prison in Baltimore, which, from the nature of the climate, was generally believed would terminate his career. The particulars of this adventure I received in the city of New York, in 1827, where I took much pains to obtain all possible information concerning his proceedings in the Southern States, while passing under the character of a preacher.

In the year 1833, it so happened that I had occasion to visit the City of New-York again, when I renewed my enquiries concerning him, but to no effect; no sources of information to which I had access, yielded any account of him, and the most rational conjecture was, that he either terminated his course in the state prison at Baltimore, or that one day, should he outlive the period of his confinement, and be again let loose upon the peace of society, some fresh development of his character would point out the scene of his renewed depredations.

In this painful state of obscurity I was reluctantly obliged to leave the hero of our narrative, on my return from New-York.

Another year had nearly elapsed before any additional light was thrown upon his history; but in an unexpecting moment, when the supposition of his having ended his career in the prison at Baltimore was becoming fixed, I received, by the politeness of a friend, a file of the *New-York Times*,[191] one of the numbers of which contained the following article, bringing our adventurer again full into view, in his usual characteristic style:

"POLICE OFFICE—*Robbery and speedy arrest.*—A French gentleman from the South, (so represented by himself), who has, for a few weeks past, under the name of Henry Bond, been running up a *bill*, and running down the *fare*, at the Franklin House,[192] was, this afternoon, arrested at the establishment, on the ungentlemanly charge of pillaging the trunks of lodgers. Since his sojourn, a variety of articles had disappeared from the chambers of the Hotel; and amongst the rest, about two hundred dollars from the trunk of one gentleman.

No one, however, had thought of suspecting the French gentleman, who was also a lodger, until this morning, when unfortunately for him, his face was recognized by a gentleman who knew him to have been in the state prison at Baltimore. However, on searching him, which he readily complied with, not one cent of the money could be found either upon his baggage or his person; but in lieu thereof, they found him possessed of a large number of small keys, through which, no doubt, he found means of disposing of any surplusage of circulating medium; whereupon his quarters were changed to Bridewell, until the ensuing term of General Sessions."

Here he remained in confinement until the period of his trial came round; when, for want of sufficient evidence to commit him to the State Prison, he was thence discharged, and the next account we hear of him, brings him before our view under the name of Henry Preston, arrested in the act of attempting to rob the Northern Mail Coach, as will appear by the following article extracted from the *Times*:

"*Police Office, Monday, February 22d, 1835.*—Just as this office was closing on Saturday evening, a very gentlemanly looking man, decently dressed, calling himself Henry Preston, was brought up in the custody of the driver and guard of the Northern Mail Stage, who charged him with an attempt to rob the mail. The accusers testified that within a short distance of

[191] This newspaper, published from 1834 to 1837, is not related to the more famous one, founded in 1851.

[192] The Franklin House hotel stood at the corner of Broadway and Dey Street. It was demolished in 1873. Its owner was Newton Hayes (1779-1868), born in Simsbury, Connecticut.

Peekskill,[193] they discovered the prisoner about a hundred yards ahead of the stage, and on approaching nearer, they saw him jump over a fence, evidently to avoid notice. This, of course, excited their suspicion, and they kept an eye to the mail, which was deposited in the *boot.*

In the course of a short time, the guard discovered the *rat* nibbling at the *bait*, and desiring the driver not to stop the speed of his horses, he quietly let himself down, and found the prisoner actively employed, loosening the strap which confines the Mail bag! He was instantly arrested, placed in the carriage, and carried to town *free of expence.*

Having nothing to offer in extenuation of his offence, Mr. Henry Preston was committed to Bridewell until Monday, for further investigation."

"*Police Office, Monday morning*—This morning, Henry Preston, committed for attempting to rob the Northern Mail, was brought up before the sitting Magistrates, when the High Sheriff of Orange County appeared and demanded the prisoner, whose real name was *Henry Gibney*, as a fugitive from justice!

He stated, that on Friday last, the prisoner was to have been tried for *Grand Larceny*, and was lodged in the *House of Detention*, at Newburgh,[194] on Thursday, under care of two persons—that in the course of the night he contrived to elude the vigilance of his keepers, escaped from confinement, and crossed the river on the ice, and had got down as far as Peekskill, where he says he attempted to get on top of the stage, that he might get into New-York as soon as possible."

By order of the Judges, the prisoner was delivered over to the Sheriff of Orange County, to be recognized there for his trial for the offence with which he was originally charged, at the next General Session of the Supreme Court. But before the term came round, he had, as on most former occasions, contrived to effect his escape, and directed his course towards Upper Canada!

Of the particular manner of his escape, and his adventures on his way through to Canada, we can state nothing with certainty; but like all his previous movements, we may hazard

[193] Peekskill is a city in Westchester County, New York, north of the Bronx.

[194] Newburgh is a city in Orange County, New York (a county to the north-west of Westchester; see note 193).

the conjecture, that they were such as would do the usual *honour* to his *wretched profession.* Yet with all his *tact*, he could not always escape the hands of justice; and hence his course is not unfrequently interrupted, and his progress impeded by the misfortunes of the *prison.* It is owing to this circumstance, that we are enabled to keep pace with him in Upper Canada, where we find him confined in the *Jail of Toronto*, under the charge of *burglary.*

For this information, the writer is indebted to his brother, Mr. AUGUSTUS BATES, residing in Upper Canada, from whose letter, dated 4th August, 1835, we make the following extract, which will point out the circumstances which have guided us in endeavoring to follow up the history of the *Mysterious Stranger* to the present time:

"*Dear Brother,*—I now sit down to acknowledge the receipt of a number of your letters, especially your last by Mr. Samuel Nichols,[195] in which you mentioned that you were writing a new edition of 'More Smith.' I have to request that you will suspend the publication until you hear from me again. There is a man now confined in Toronto jail, who bears the description of More Smith, and is supposed to be the same. Many things are told of him which no other person could perform. I will not attempt to repeat them, as I cannot vouch for their truth.

From current reports I was induced to write to the Sheriff who had him in charge, requesting him to give me a correct account of him. I have not heard from the Sheriff since I wrote: perhaps he is waiting to see in what manner he is to be disposed of. Report says that the man is condemned to be executed for shop-breaking—he wishes the Sheriff to do his duty; that he had much rather be hanged than sent to the Penitentiary. Many are the curious stories told of him, which, as I said before, I will not vouch for.—Should the Sheriff write to me, his information may be relied on."

Several communications from Upper Canada have reached us between the date of the letter from which the above extract is made, and the present time; but none of them contained the desired information as to the particular fate of the prisoner, and the manner in which he was disposed of, until the 18th of September last, (1836).

[195] Samuel Nichols (1773-1857) was a farmer in the Long Reach area of Kingston, who had come on the same boat as Bates, with his mother Ruth (a war widow) and his brother.

By a letter from Mr. Augustus Bates, bearing this date, it would appear that the prisoner had not been *executed*, but had been sentenced to *one year's confinement* in the Penitentiary. We make the following extract:—

"I give you all the information I can obtain respecting the prisoner enquired after. The Jailer, who is also the Deputy Sheriff, that had him in charge, says he could learn nothing from him,—said he called his name Smith,—that he was fifty-five years old, but denies that he ever was in Kingston, New-Brunswick. The jailer had one of your books, and showed it to him, but he denied any knowledge of it, and would not give any satisfaction to the enquiries he made of him.

The Sheriff says he believes the person to be the same *Mysterious Stranger*: that he was condemned and sentenced to the Penitentiary for one year: his crime was *burglary*."

It would have afforded the writer of these Memoirs great satisfaction, and no doubt an equal satisfaction to the reader, had it been in his power to have paid a visit to Upper Canada, that he might be able to state from his own certain and personal knowledge of the prisoner in Toronto, that he was, indeed, the self-same *noted individual* that was in his custody twenty-two years ago; and whom he had the gratification of seeing and recognizing subsequently, at the *Simsbury Mines*, where he played off his *affected fits* with such art and consequent advantage.

But although it is not in the writer's power to close up his Memoirs with so important and valuable a discovery—yet, keeping in view the characteristic features of the man—his professed ignorance of *Kingston*, in New-Brunswick—his denial of ever having seen the first edition of the Memoirs, and the care which he took to keep himself enveloped in mystery, by utterly declining to give any satisfactory information concerning himself: all these circumstances united, form a combination of *features* so marked, as to carry conviction to the mind of the reader who has traced him through this narrative, that he is no other than the same mysterious Henry More Smith.

There is another feature in the prisoner at Toronto, that seems strangely corroborative of what we are desirous properly to establish; that is, *his age*. He acknowledges to be *fifty-five* years of age; and although this would make him somewhat older than his real age, yet it fixes this point—that the prisoner at Toronto is well advanced in years, and so must the *subject* of our *Memoirs* be also.

With respect to his calling himself by the name of *Smith*, we could not come to any definite conclusion, as to the identity of the person; for he was, as the reader knows by this time, continually changing his name; and at that remote distance from Kingston, where he was known by that name, and after a lapse of twenty-two years, he might judge himself as safe under his real name as any assumed one.

The reader will remember that the Author stated in his *Preface* that the Narrative would close with the report of the prisoner's confinement in the Jail of Toronto. At the time this had gone to press, he was not aware that it would be in his power to furnish any further information as to the issue of his confinement there; but rather expected to hear at some future period, that he had made another escape in this usual and *characteristic manner*; but it seems, by the information we have obtained, that he has undergone his trial, and was committed to the Penitentiary for a year's confinement.

Whether he found any means of effecting an exemption from labour in the Penitentiary and then reconciling himself to his confinement, or whether he accomplished one of his ingenious departures, we are unable to determine. One thing, however, is highly probable—that he is again *going up and down in the earth*, in the practice of his *hoary-headed villainy*, except a Power from on High has directed the *arrow of conviction* to his heart; for no inferior impulse would be capable of giving a new direction to the life and actions of a man, whose habits of iniquity have been ripened into maturity, and obtained an immoveable ascendancy by the practice of so many successive years.

It must be acknowledged that there is an unprecedented degree of cleverness in all his adventures, which casts a kind of *illusive* and momentary covering over the real character of his actions, and would seem to engage an interest in his favour, (and this is an error to which the human mind seems remarkably predisposed when *vice* presents itself before us in all its *cleverness*), yet who can read the history of his miserable career, without feeling pained at the melancholy picture of depravity it presents? Who would have supposed that after his condemnation and sentence at Kingston, and his life, by an act of human mercy, had been given into his hands again, he would not have hastened to his wife, and with tears of compunction mingled with those of joy, cast himself upon her neck, and resolved, by a course of future rectitude and honesty, to make her as happy as his previous disgraceful and sinful career had made her miserable?

But ah! no, his release was followed by no such effects; rendered unsusceptible of every natural and tender impression, and yet under the full dominion of the *god of this world*, he abandoned the *inmate of his bosom*,[196] and set out single-handed in the fresh pursuit of crime.

There is, however, one redeeming feature which stands out among the general deformities of his character: in all the adventures which the history of his course presents to our view, we are not called upon to witness any acts of *violence* and *blood*; and it is perhaps owing to the absence of this repulsive trait of character, that we do not behold him in a more relentless light.

The writer would close up these pages by finally observing, that if these *Memoirs* should ever fall into the hands of HENRY MORE SMITH, the unhappy subject of them, and should he, from whatever motive, be induced to peruse them, he trusts that the review of a *life*, so wretchedly and miserably misspent, may be accompanied with conviction from on High, and be followed up with repentance unto life, that he who has so often been immured within the walls of an earthly prison, may not at the close of his unhappy and sinful course in this world, be finally shut up in the *prison of hell*, and bound hand and foot in the chains of eternal darkness, where shall be weeping and wailing, and gnashing of teeth: where the hope of mercy or release can never enter, but the *wrath of God abideth forever and ever!*[197]

FINIS

[196] The first phrase in italics is from 2 Corinthians 4: 4, which speaks of those "that are lost" and "In whom the god of this world hath blinded the minds." The second phrase, which refers to Smith's wife, was a literary construction, common at the turn of the 19th century (Robert Burns, among others, makes use of it). For the meaning of "inmate," see note 184.

[197] In the last lines, Bates inserted a reworking of Matthew 22: 13 and the last words of Revelation 15: 7.

PART II. BEFORE 2 AUGUST 1814

II. 1. Walter Bates, [The Stranger's First Appearance]

[These are the first pages of the third edition, following directly Bates's preface, in which he has announced his decision to retell the story in chronological order. His research into Smith's life before 2 August 1814 has not been very productive, but he does manage to add a few interesting facts about the stranger's criminal life in Nova Scotia, as well as more details about the theft of Knox's horse.]

Henry More Smith, the noted individual who forms the subject of this Narrative, made his first appearance among us in the year 1812. Previous to this, we have no information concerning him. Some time in the month of July, in this year, he appeared at Windsor, in Nova-Scotia, looking for employment, and pretended to have emigrated lately from England. On being asked what his occupation was, he stated that he was a Tailor; but could turn his hand to any kind of mechanical business or country employment. He was decently clothed, genteel in his appearance and prepossessing in his manner, and seemed to understand himself very well.

Although an entire stranger, he seemed to be acquainted with every part of the Province, but studiously avoided to enter into close intimacy with any person, associated with few, and carefully concealed all knowledge of the means by which he came to the country, and also of his origin and connexions, keeping his previous life and history in entire obscurity.

Finding no better employment, he engaged in the service of Mr. Bond, a respectable farmer in the village of Rawden, who agreed with him for a month on trial, during which time he conducted himself with much propriety and honesty; was industrious, careful, and useful, to the entire satisfaction of Mr. Bond, his employer, and even beyond his expectation. He was perfectly inoffensive, gentle, and obliging; used no intoxicating liquors, refrained from idle conversation and all improper language, and was apparently free from every evil habit. Being engaged for some time in working on a new road with a company of men, whose lodging was in a camp; rather than subject himself to the pain of their loose conversation in the camp, he chose to retire to some neighboring barn, as he pretended, to sleep in quiet, and was always early at work in the morning; but as the sequel will discover, he was very differently engaged.

A ready conformity to Mr. Bond's religious principles, who was a very religious man and of the Baptist persuasion, formed an easy yet successful means for further ingratiating himself into the favour of Mr. Bond and his family: his attendance on morning and evening prayers was always marked with regularity and seriousness; and, in the absence of Mr. Bond, he would himself officiate in the most solemn and devout manner. This well directed aim of his hypocrisy secured for him almost all he could wish or expect from this family; he not only obtained the full confidence of Mr. Bond himself, but gained, most effectually, the affections of his favorite daughter, who was unable to conceal the strength of her attachment to him, and formed a resolution to give her hand to him in marriage. Application was made to Mr. Bond for his concurrence, and, although a refusal was the consequence, yet so strong was the attachment, and so firmly were they determined to consummate their wishes, that neither the advice, the entreaties, nor the remonstrances of her friends, were of any avail. She went with him from her father's house to Windsor, and under the name of Frederick Henry More, he there married her on the 12th of March, 1813, her name having been Elizabeth P.

While he remained at Rawden, although he professed to be a Tailor, he did not pursue his business; but was chiefly engaged in farming or country occupations. After his removal to Windsor, and his marriage to Miss Bond, he entered on a new line of business, uniting that of the tailor and pedlar together. In this character he made frequent visits to Halifax, always bringing with him a quantity of goods, of various descriptions. At one time he was known to bring home a considerable sum of money, and upon being asked how he procured it and all those articles and goods he brought home, he replied that a friend by the name of Wilson supplied him with any thing he wanted, as a pedlar and tailor. It is remarkable, however, that in all his trips to Halifax, he uniformly set out in the afternoon and returned next morning. A certain gentleman, speaking of him as a tailor, remarked, that he could cut very well and make up an article of clothing in a superior manner. In fact, his genius was extraordinary, and he could execute any thing well that he turned his attention to. A young man having applied to him for a new coat, he accordingly took his measure, and promised to bring the cloth with him the first time he went to Halifax. Very soon after, he made his journey to Halifax, and on his return, happening to meet with the young man, he shewed him, from his portmanteau, the cloth, which was of a superior quality, and promised to have it made up on a certain day, which he punctually performed to the entire satisfaction of his employer, who paid him his price and carried off the coat.

About this time a number of unaccountable and mysterious thefts were committed in Halifax. Articles of plate were missing from gentlemen's houses; silver watches and many other valuable articles were taken from Silversmith's shops, and all done in so mysterious a manner, that no marks of the robber's hands were to be seen. Three volumes of late acts of Parliament, relating to the court of Admiralty, were missing from the office of Chief Justice Strange about the same time: he offered a reward of three guineas to any person who would restore them, with an assurance that no questions should be asked.[198] In a few days after, Mr. More produced the volumes, which he said he had purchased from a stranger, and received the three guineas reward without having to answer any enquiries. This affair laid the foundation for strong suspicions that Mr. More must have been the individual who committed those secret and mysterious thefts which produced so much astonishment in various quarters; and just at this crisis, these suspicions received not only strong corroboration, but were decidedly confirmed by the following fact. While the young man whom he had furnished with the new coat, as was previously noticed, was passing thro' the streets of Halifax with the coat on his back, he was arrested by a gentleman who claimed the coat as his own, affirming that it had been stolen from him some time since. This singular affair, which to the honest young man was extremely mortifying and afflictive, threw immediate light upon all those secret and unaccountable robberies. A special warrant was immediately issued for the apprehension of More: however, before the Warrant reached Rawden, he had made his escape, and was next

[198] Sir Thomas Andrew Lumisden Strange (1756-1841) had been Chief Justice of Nova Scotia from 1790 and 1796. In 1813, he was in India, as chief justice of the Madras supreme court (1800-1817). However, he had sponsored a law library in Halifax and it is likely the overseer of the library offered the reward.

heard of as travelling on horseback, with a portmanteau well filled with articles which he offered for sale, as he proceeded on his way by the River Philip: and early in the month of July, 1814, he made his appearance in Saint John, New-Brunswick, by the name of Henry More Smith. He did not, however, enter the city with his horse: but put him up, and took lodgings at the house of one Mr. Stackhouse, who resided in a bye-place within a mile of the City, and came into the town upon foot. He found means to become acquainted with the officers of the 99th Regiment, who, finding him something of a military character, and well acquainted with horsemanship, shewed him the stud of horses belonging to the regiment. Smith, perceiving that the pair of horses which the Colonel drove in his carriage did not match, they being of different colours, and one of them black, observed to the Colonel, that he knew of an excellent black horse in Cumberland, that would match his black one perfectly. The Colonel replied, that if he were as good as his own, he would give fifty pounds for him. Smith then proposed, that if he, the Colonel, would advance him fifteen pounds, he would leave his own horse in pledge, and take his passage in a sloop bound for Cumberland, and bring him the black horse. To this the Colonel readily consented, and paid him down the fifteen pounds. This opened the way to Smith for a most flattering speculation: he had observed a valuable mare feeding on the marsh contiguous to the place where he had taken his lodgings, and cast his eye upon a fine saddle and bridle belonging to Major King,[199] which he could put his hand on in the night. With these facilities in view, Smith entered on his scheme: he put himself in possession of the saddle and bridle, determined to steal the mare he saw feeding on the marsh, ride her to Nova-Scotia, and there sell her; then steal the black horse from Cumberland, bring him to the Colonel, receive his two hundred dollars, and without loss of time transport himself within the boundaries of the United States.

This scheme, so deeply laid, and so well concerted, failed, however, in the execution, and proved the means of his future apprehension. Already in possession of the saddle and bridle, he spent most of the night in fruitless efforts to take the mare, which was running at large in the pasture. Abandoning this part of his plan as hopeless, and turning his horse-stealing genius

[199] Major A. S. King appears in the Army List as serving in the 99th Regiment in New Brunswick.

in another direction, he recollected to have seen a fine horse feeding in a field near the high way as he passed through the Parish of Norton, about thirty miles on, on his journey. Upon this fresh scheme, he set off on foot, with the bridle and saddle in the form of a pack on his back, passing along all the succeeding day in the character of a pedlar. Night came on, and put him in possession of a fine black horse, which he mounted and rode on in prosecution of his design, which he looked upon now as already accomplished. But with all this certainty of success, his object proved a failure, and that through means which all his vigilance could neither foresee nor prevent. From the want of sleep the preceding night, and the fatigue of travelling in the day, he became drowsy and exhausted, and stopped in a barn belonging to William Fayerweather,[200] at the bridge that crosses the Mill-stream, to take a short sleep, and start again in the night, so as to pass the village before daylight. But, as fate would have it, he overslept; and his horse was discovered on the barn floor in the morning; and he was seen crossing the bridge by daylight. Had he succeeded in crossing in the night, he would in all probability have carried his design; for it was not till the afternoon of the same day, that Mr. Knox, the owner of the horse, missed him from the pasture. Pursuit was immediately made in quest of the horse, and the circumstance of the robber's having put up at the barn proved the means of restoring the horse to his owner, and committing the robber to custody: for there at Mr. Fayerweather's, information was given which directed the pursuit in the direct track. Mr. Knox, through means of obtaining fresh horses on the way, pursued him, without loss of time, through the Province of Nova Scotia, as far as Pictou, a distance of one hundred and seventy miles, which the thief had performed with the stolen horse in the space of three days. There on the 24th July, the horse having been stolen on the 20th, Mr. Knox had him apprehended by the Deputy Sheriff, John Parsons, Esq.[201] and taken before the County Justices in Court then sitting. Besides the horse, there were a watch and fifteen guineas found with the prisoner; and a warrant was issued by the Court, for his conveyance through the several Counties, to the gaol of King's County, Province of New-Brunswick, there to take his trial.—Mr. Knox states,

[200] William Fairweather (1771-1842) was a settler born in Norwalk, Connecticut who had arrived in 1783 with his father Thomas.

[201] Actually, John Pearson (see note 8).

that he, the prisoner, assumed different names and committed several robberies by the way; that a watch and a piece of India cotton were found with him, and returned to the owners: that on the way to Kingston gaol he had made several attempts to escape from the Sheriff, and that but for his own vigilance they never would have been able to reach the prison with him, observing at the same time, that unless he were well taken care of and secured, he would certainly make his escape. He was received into prison for examination on the warrant of conveyance without a regular commitment.

II. 2. Walter Bates, [A Letter from Mr. Knox]

[This letter was only published in the second edition, from the summer of 1817. It remains a mystery why Bates did not include it in the third edition.]

I have obtained from Mr. Knox for the purpose of these memoirs, the following letter, giving an account of the pursuit and apprehension of the prisoner:

"*Norton, King's County, New-Brunswick,*
October 16th, 1816.

DEAR SIR,

I received your letter yesterday, and shall willingly give you what information I have respecting Henry More Smith, from my pursuit and apprehension of him at Pictou, in Nova-Scotia, to the delivery of him into your custody.

On the afternoon of the 20th of July, 1814, I missed a very fine horse out of my pasture, and from every circumstance had reason to think he had been stolen the night before; I therefore immediately went in pursuit of him, alone, on the Westmoreland road—I was quite a stranger that way, but finding that a man had gone that road on a horse answering exactly the description of mine, with a good saddle and bridle, I travelled all night. The thief having so much the start, with so good a horse, I did not gain much of him, but, procuring fresh horses, kept up the pursuit.

I soon discovered the man who had my horse to be a most artful character—travelling day and night without rest, and not stopping more than an hour at any of the taverns, where he always behaved in the most imperious manner, seldom finding any thing good enough for himself—always taking great care of the horse, and feeding him well—but not paying for what he got, promising to be back in a fortnight, and showing some doubloons[202] which either he did not wish, or they were unable to exchange.

I believed he had accomplices, and detained one person whom I suspected.

I sat out totally unprepared for a long journey, and soon found that it would cost me more than the value of my horse to obtain him, as he would probably be much injured by forcing through so extraordinary a journey, but as this was the first instance of horse-stealing I had heard of in this country, where our property is so much exposed, I deemed it my duty to do my utmost to apprehend the thief, to prevent like depredations in future.

On arriving at Amherst, about 150 miles from home, I learnt that he had told a gentleman who admired the horse, that he was taking him to Halifax, where he could sell him for 50l. Further on, he appeared anxious to know when the tide would be out to enable him to cross the head of the Bay of Fundy for Newport,[203] a different direction. I also found he was exerting his ingenuity to elude a pursuit by changing his name, and he generally went a different direction from what he professed where he stopped. He called his name *Mead*, *Coppigate*, *Mc-Donald*, and *Henry Moon*. I met with a man who saw him on the road, who knew him in Nova-Scotia, and who informed me he had committed several depredations in his neighborhood, but had baffled their exertions to bring him to justice.

Just before my horse was stolen I had him shod by a blacksmith from the U. States, who, by my direction, made the heel of the shoes much broader than common, and I thought by this I should be able to discover whether he had crossed the Bay. I therefore examined the beach, but could not observe the track of my horse. I therefore continued on the road to Truro, a very neat and pleasant village, where the roads cross, leading to Halifax, Pictou, &c. He did not stop there, but went

[202] The doubloon, a Spanish gold coin that was very common in the West Indies, was rated at 4 pounds and became the "dominant coin in Nova Scotia" (McCullough 138) after the War of 1812.

[203] The township of Newport, Nova Scotia, founded in 1761, is now a community called Brooklyn, in Hants County. It is also quite close to Rawdon (see note 148).

by in the night, taking a piece of India cotton, which had been hung out to dry, which was afterwards recovered. I pursued on the road to Halifax, and had proceeded but a few miles when I was overtaken by a boy who had come from Pictou, and met a man driving a horse, both answering the description I had left behind me. I returned to Truro, where I employed Mr. John Pearson, of Pictou, who happened to be there, to pursue the thief, who arrived at Pictou, 40 miles distant, on the 24th, where he apprehended him the day after, as he was bargaining to sell the horse, for which he was to receive 40l. and had him committed to prison.

It appeared he arrived at Pictou on the 23d, a distance of 270 miles from where he took the horse, in little better than three days.

I proceeded to Pictou, and when I arrived there he could hardly believe the owner of the horse was so quick after him. He declared his innocence—said he had purchased the horse, but gave the gaoler 14 guineas to offer me for my trouble if I would take the horse and let him go. He certainly fed the horse well, and I did not find him much injured—Those who accompanied me observed that he appeared to know my voice immediately.

The man was examined, and ordered to be conducted to New-Brunswick for his trial. He now called himself *Henry More Smith*, by which name I shall hereafter call him. He was then remanded to prison and put in irons, when our preparations being made, we sat out on our return. Smith was put on horseback. We had not proceeded far when we discovered his handcuffs to be nearly cut in two, and the crevice filled with black wax.

I found it necessary to exert all my vigilance to keep him, as he induced many people to think he was an innocent man. He frequently pretended to be sick and unable to ride, but when I found I was determined to convey him back, if in a cart, he would go on horseback. He made one attempt to escape, when within about ten miles of Dorchester.[204] In the dusk of the evening, as we were leaving a tavern where we had stopped to refresh, Smith was put on a smart horse, which had been lent me to pursue him, and the sheriff who had him in charge

[204] The shire town of Westmorland County, the first county in New Brunswick the would go through as they were travelling from Nova Scotia (see note 50).

had occasion to step into the house for a moment, when, I suppose, he thought my horse too fatigued to overtake him, he started off on a full gallop till he arrived at a thicket, where he threw himself off, and had nearly succeeded in getting away—I, however, came up with him, and the sheriff was with us in an instant. He had previously used every persuasion to induce me to release him, but I had already found him too dangerous a character to be let loose upon society.

We pursued our journey without any material occurrence until I placed him in your custody.

On getting home, I found that the saddle and bridle which were taken with the horse at Pictou, and which I brought with me, were advertised as stolen from the stables of Major King, of the 99th Regiment, then at St. John, and it appeared Smith had brought them on his back 26 miles for the purpose of taking my horse.

Smith appeared to be a man of good education, and I have learnt married into a respectable family in Nova-Scotia. I have now given you an account of my journey, and remain

Your most obedient humble servant,

WILLS FREDERICK KNOX.

WALTER BATES, Esq."

II. 3. Testimonials

[These three letters, from John W. Harris, Murdoch Stewart, and Abraham Gesner—the first two dated 1857, the third dated 1863—appeared in the presumed Barry edition (see the discussion in the introduction to this volume). They were clearly added no earlier than 1863, even though the rest of the book is a reproduction of George W. Day's edition from 1856. They only appeared in this version, probably printed in Barry's native Nova Scotia, not in Day's Saint John, NB. This would account for the fact that the testimonies are from Nova Scotians and that they offer an unprecedented insight into Henry More Smith's life before and during the time the pursuit and apprehension with which Bates's narrative began in 1817.]

THE FOLLOWING ARE THE ORIGINAL LETTERS NEVER BEFORE PUBLISHED.

When Henry More Smith was arrested in Pictou, by John Pearson, he was committed to the custody of John W. Harris,

Esq. then Deputy Sheriff of the District of Pictou.[205] On his arrival he had taken up quarters in James Patterson's barn;[206] he went to town and in ten minutes returned with curry comb and brush, which he stole from the stables of Alexander Thain,[207] to trim his horse.

On the first day he was examined before George Smith and Dr. Burton, Esqrs., Justices of the Peace,[208] who remanded him till the following day, when he was again examined before Edward Mortimer, Esq., and Colonel Pearson, father of Sheriff Pearson,[209] who granted a warrant for his removal to Cumberland County jail and through to St. John. Whilst he was undergoing his examination in Pictou, Murdoch Stewart of Mount Thom,[210] came to town, and accused him of having stolen two watches.

[205] Both John Pearson (see note 8), who captured Smith, and John Washington Harris (1777-1860), who received the prisoner, appear as deputy sheriffs in Pictou. However, the older Harris was in charge (with Pearson as his deputy), but he could not use the title of High Sheriff before 1837, after Pictou (formerly a district of Halifax County) became an independent county in 1835. A native of Truro (like Pearson), Harris was the second (he followed his cousin in 1811) in a long line of sheriffs from the same family. He held the position until 1857 when he retired.

[206] James Patterson (c.1761-1857), a native of Philadelphia, was the son of Squire Robert Patterson, one of the founders of the town of Pictou.

[207] The Thains were a prominent Pictou family, who had immigrated from Scotland in the 1790s.

[208] Dr. John Burton (not related to the better-known Nova Scotian Baptist minister of the same name), a magistrate and a militia surgeon, who came to Pictou in the early 1800s, remains relatively obscure (he died in 1816). George Smith, a Scottish immigrant who became a successful businessman, served in the province's Legislative Assembly between 1819 and 1836.

[209] Edward Mortimer (1768-1819), born in Scotland, came to Pictou in 1789 and quickly established himself as a businessman, a judge, and a member of the Legislative Assembly (where he was replaced after his death by George Smith, from the note above). His influence was such that he was sometimes called "the king of Pictou." Thomas Pearson, a native of South Carolina, came to Nova Scotia in 1784 and settled first in Rawdon, where he was a neighbour of Smith's father-in-law, John Bond. He later moved to Truro and became county treasurer and a justice of the peace.

[210] Mount Thom is a small community in Pictou County, first occupied by a few newcomers from Philadelphia. It was settled in earnest during the first years of the 19th century by families arrived from Scotland, including that of Murdoch (or Murdock) Stewart.

It appears that Smith, on coming to Pictou, called at Stewart's, and priced them and gone back and stolen them. The prisoner affected great simplicity and innocence, and asked how could he have stolen the watches, as he was at Patterson's barn the evening previous, and also early in the morning? The fact was, he had gone back at night to Mount Thom and stolen them. He was very highly clad in Nankeen,[211] and we searched him minutely in vain, but he had previously offered a watch seal for sale, and it answered Stewart's description, and he had watches in his pocket when he came here, and no trace of them could be found, and he stated that he had sold them to a sailor through the window.

He was confined in the lower room, the floor was of an inch and half thick strongly spiked to the sleepers on the ground, and sometime afterwards there was occasion to remove the floor in order to clear the drain, and George McKenzie, (known as Whistling Geordie), carpenter,[212] then found the two watches and seal on the ground under the floor. Mr. McKenzie and I carefully examined to see how the watches were deposited, but could not contrive how Smith could possibly have done it. The watches were returned to Stewart, and he gave the gold seal a present to Mr. McKenzie.

When the prisoner came to Pictou with the horse, he enquired for Colonel Adamson as he wanted the Colonel to buy the horse,[213] but as the Colonel was in Merigomish,[214] attending a muster of militia, Smith had to wait for his return, and whilst so waiting he was arrested by Mr. Pearson.

The description given by Walter Bates is correct, and I would only add that he affected great innocence and simplicity of demeanor. When first searched, he had fourteen pounds in cash which Mr. Knox took from him. Though thoroughly searched before leaving Pictou, when in Truro on his way to jail,

---

[211] Either a sturdy cotton fabric, of a pale yellow colour, originally made in Nanking (China), or trousers made of that fabric.

[212] There were several McKenzie families in Pictou County, all immigrants from Scotland, though this carpenter's nickname suggests he was born in Yorkshire. He might be the George McKenzie who was reputed as one of the best pipers in Nova Scotia.

[213] This must be Thomas Fenn Addison, of the 100th Regiment of Foot, stationed in Nova Scotia. He was not yet a colonel, but Harris, writing in 1857, might not remember this accurately.

[214] Merigomish is a small community in Pictou County, first settled in 1761 by immigrants from Philadelphia.

he accidentally dropped two guineas on the floor. On his way to Truro, his handcuffs were separated by a bar of iron which appearing to be a little bent, was examined and broke off easily, as it had almost been cut through and the cut filled up, but no one could tell how or when he did it.

One night whilst I was keeping guard over Smith, one Nason, a servant of mine, went to the dungeon window and said in my hearing, "Smith, tell us where the watches are and I will let you out, I have the keys."

Smith said "Can you let me out?" "Yes, I have the keys."

Smith reflected a little and then said, "Ah, you d——d scoundrel, I will have you punished to-morrow." The night was very dark and Smith did not know Nason, nor did he know I was there. Next day at the trial, when Nason came into Court, Smith said to Mr. Mortimer "there is the man who offered to let me out last night."

I cannot imagine how Smith knew Nason.

JOHN W. HARRIS

Witness,

JOHN MCKINLAY.[215]

Pictou, 23rd February, 1857.

When Henry More Smith came over Mount Thom with the horse, he took dinner at my house on a Friday; he saw the watches on a nail near the window and wanted to buy the silver one. He offered me seven pounds, but I wanted eight. On Monday morning I missed the watches, and came to town as I suspected him. I accused him and he denied it. I heard part of the examination of Smith by the Justices, and on Squire Mortimer remarking that he pitied his case. Smith said it was not as bad as that of the man who offered to let him out of the jail if he would give up Stewart's watches. He did not pay his bill, but offered a Doubloon which was clipped, but wanted the full value, but we did not take it. He had a bottle of wine for his dinner. On his return from Pictou in custody, he wished the Sheriff's officers to pay the bill, but it was not paid, and never has been paid. My watches were found under the jail floor about eleven years afterwards. Smith had attached a gold seal to one of them. The seal was not mine and George McKenzie of Pictou got it. McKenzie took up the

[215] John McKinlay was a lawyer from Pictou. He died in 1888.

floor, assisted by a Carriboo man[216] then in jail. It was this man that found the watches when levelling the ground, and I gave him thirty shillings. The steel works of the watches were destroyed by rust, and although I got them repaired they cost more than they were worth. Richard Masters repaired them in Pictou. The horse stolen was a very fine one with a beautiful saddle. I groomed his horse, and all the pay I got was the loss of my watches. I heard afterwards that Smith paid all his bills by offering the clipped Doubloon at full value, and stating he had no change.

MURDOCH STEWART.

Witness,
JOHN MCKINLAY.
Pictou, 10th March, 1857.

DEAR SIR,—In response to your enquiry regarding a person who, some years ago was distinguished in the Province, under the name of Henry More Smith, I may state that some time about the year 1816, (I cannot give the exact date,) while myself and an elder brother were at play in a field, where my father's men were ploughing, at Cornwallis, a handsome well-dressed young man jumped over the fence and accosted us by saying, "Here, my good fellows, I have lately seen your brother at Woodstock." The stranger had a large bundle in his hand, and immediately joined in our sports. In all these he beat us with the greatest ease; and he made us acquainted with several tricks we had not known before. We were so well pleased with him that we invited him home, and he took tea with the family. He conversed with my father in German, and read French rapidly. He played the violin and flute and delighted us lads with his fun and anecdotes. But he did not, it seemed, like my father, and although we offered every kindness and hospitality, he would not be persuaded to remain all night; but went to the house of Thomas Mee and asked for lodgings.[217] He was kindly received, and during the evening he opened his bundle and displayed a number of gold and silver watches, much to the surprise of our kind hearted neighbor. Next morning he called at my father's house to take leave, and from the hour of his departure, my

[216] Caribou is a small community in Pictou County.

[217] Cornwallis Township was one of the first English settlements in Nova Scotia; Thomas Mee was one of its earliest settlers.

mother never could account for the loss of a large silver spoon. We next heard of our visiter at the residence of the late worthy Holmes Chipman,[218] where he had hired as a blacksmith. He gave every satisfaction in the business; he could shoe a horse, or make a fox trap, or anything else; but it was observed that he would work after hours, to make, as he said, some little things for his own private use. Every person was pleased with the stranger, whose manners were very polite and agreeable. After a fortnight of hard labor, he left Mr. Chipman very suddenly in the evening. The night following he stole the best horse from the stable of the late Hon. C. R. Prescott,[219] and not being able to find a saddle, he strapped the gig cushions upon the horse's back and started. He was next heard of at Annapolis;[220] but before his pursuers could overtake him he had sold the horse and departed for New Brunswick. The person gave his name as Henry More Smith. He was a gentleman in his address, he was a scholar and an artist. Now, the rest of the acts of this man, are they not written in a pamphlet published years ago in the Province of New Brunswick, where he performed many extraordinary exploits.

Yours truly,

A. GESNER.[221]

JAMES M. ROSS, ESQ.[222]
Halifax, June 1st, 1863.

---

[218] Holmes Chipman (1778-1844) was the son of Judge Handley Chipman, one of the founders of Cornwallis. Jared Ingersol Chipman (see note 263) was his nephew.

[219] Charles Ramage Prescott (1772-1859), born in Halifax, had settled in Cornwallis in 1812, where he built his residence, the "Acacia Grove" (today the Prescott House Museum). He was member of the Legislative Assembly for Cornwallis (1818-1820).

[220] Annapolis Royal, in Annapolis County, captured from the French in 1710.

[221] Abraham Gesner (1797-1864), born in Cornwallis, Nova Scotia, in a family of German origin, studied medicine in London, where he acquired a passion for geology and mineralogy. In 1838 he moved to Saint John, New Brunswick, where he opened (in 1842) the Gesner Museum. He is known as the discoverer of kerosene.

[222] James Ross (1811-1886) was principal of Dalhousie University, which Gesner joined as professor of natural history in 1863.

Joseph Brown Comingo, *View of Saint John*, c. 1814.

Carleton Martello Tower in Saint John, NB,
built between 1813 and 1815.

APPENDIX I

NEW BRUNSWICK IN THE EARLY 19TH CENTURY

I. 1. [Walter Bates], A Description of New Brunswick, Nova Scotia, &c. &c.

[This brief description of the places mentioned in Bates's narrative was placed at the beginning of the London edition, pp. xiii-xvi. It may have been written by Bates, since it is not claimed, like the preface, the postscript, and some of the footnotes, by the editor. However, some references to the *Colonial Journal* and unusual mispellings place his authorship in doubt.]

For the better elucidation of the facts presented in the Narrative, an introductory description of New Brunswick, the principal scene of their occurrence, and of its position, with respect to those parts of the united States that are also mentioned, is here prefixed.

New Brunswick and Nova Scotia are two of the four provinces, territories, or governments, which have been erected in the eastern part of British America.

New Brunswick and Nova Scotia are comprehended within the country once called *Acadie*, a name bestowed by the French, who were the first to attempt its colonization.[223] The French being expelled, the whole country, bounded on the north by the Gulf of Saint Lawrence, and on the south by the Province of Maine, was granted, in 1621, by King James I, to Sir William Stirling,[224] upon consideration of forming settlements upon it. The country then received the name of Nova Scotia; but the project failed; and nothing was effectually done, till the year 1749, when the town of Halifax was built.

[223] The French began settling Acadie (the Canadian Maritimes and parts of Maine) in the early 17th century.

[224] William Alexander, 1st Earl of Stirling (c.1567-1640) was granted a royal charter to resettle Acadie as Nova Scotia, but the territory was returned to France in 1632.

The division of Nova Scotia into two provinces, of which the largest has received the name of New Brunswick, did not take place till 1784, subsequently to the acknowledgment of the independence of the thirteen revolted colonies, now the United States. New Brunswick comprizes the whole of the country, first called Acadie, and afterwards Nova Scotia, with the exception of the peninsula, formed by the Bay of Fundy, on the south, and by Bay Verte,[225] on the north. That peninsula is the modern Nova Scotia.

New Brunswick is bounded on the west by the British province of Lower Canada; on the east, by the Bay of Fundy, the British province of Nova Scotia, and the Atlantic Ocean; on the north, by the Gulf of Saint Lawrence; and on the south, by Maine, a part of the United States. The river Sainte-Croix, which falls into the Bay of Passamaquady, forms the southern boundary, from its mouth to its source. The chief towns of New Brunswick are, Saint-John, Frederic-town, Saint-Andrew, and Saint-Ann.[226] The principal rivers are, Saint-John, Magedavic, Dicwasset, Sainte-Croix, Miramichi, Grand Codiac, Petit Codiac, and Memramcook,[227] all of which, the three last excepted, empty themselves into the Bay of Fundy. The river Saint-John runs through a fine country of vast extent, being bordered by low grounds, locally called *intervals*, as lying between the river and the mountains, and which are annually enriched by the inundations. The greater part of these lands are settled, and under cultivation. The upland is generally well timbered; the trees are pine and fir, beech, birch, maple, elm, and a small proportion of ash. The pines are the largest to be met with in British America. The rivers which fall into the Bay of Passamaquady (an inlet from the Bay of Fundy) have

[225] Baie Verte is part of the Northumberland Strait, which separates the mainland (New Brunswick and Nova Scotia) from Prince Edward Island.

[226] St Ann's was part of Fredericton, but older settlers still saw them as two different towns.

[227] Saint John, Sainte-Croix, Miramichi, Petitcodiac, and Memramcook are all names still in use today for some of the most important rivers in New Brunswick. "Magedavic" is actually Magaguadavic (pronounced Maga-day-vik); "Dicwasset" must be the Digdeguash River (usually pronounced "di-gi-dee-wash"), which also had the older, native (Passamaquoddy) name Diktequesk; but there is no river called "Grand Codiac" (this is a likely reference to one of the many tributaries of the Petitcodiac River). All these names, correct or not, were later reproduced in some early-19th-century British encyclopaedias (the British edition of Bates's book seems to be their source).

meadows and low-lands along their banks, and, as appears from the remains of large trunks, still to be met with, have formerly been covered with heavy timber. Timber and fish (the latter the produce of the neighbouring seas) have hitherto been the principal exports of New Brunswic; but the gradual clearing of the country, and increase of population, will hereafter render its produce, in cattle, grain, and other agricultural commodities, of equal, if not superior, importance.

The sea-coast of New Brunswic abounds with cod and scale fish, and its rivers are annually visited by immense shoals of herrings, shad, and salmon. The numerous harbours along the coast are most conveniently situated for carrying on the cod-fishery, which may be prosecuted to any extent imaginable. The herrings which frequent its rivers are a species peculiarly adapted for the West India market; being equally nutritious with the common herrings, and possessed of a greater degree of firmness, they are capable of being kept longer in a warm climate. In such abundance are they annually to be found, that the quantity cured can only be limited by the number of hands employed in the business.

The interior of the province, as well as the parts bordering on the sea-coast, is every where intersected by rivers, creeks, and lakes, on the margin of which, or at no great distance from them, the country, for the most part, is covered with inexhaustible forests of pine, spruce, birch, beech, maple, elm, fir, and other timber, proper for masts of any size, lumber, and ship-building. The smaller rivers afford excellent situations for saw-mills, and every stream, by the melting of the snow in the spring, is rendered deep enough to float down the masts and timber of every description, which the inhabitants have cut and brought to its banks, during the long and severe winters of this climate, when their agricultural pursuits are necessarily suspended. The lands in the interior of the province are generally excellent, and, where cleared, have proved very productive.

Great advances have not hitherto been made in agriculture, for want of a sufficient number of inhabitants; yet, within a few years, there has remained, beyond the domestic supply, a considerable surplus, in horses, salted provisions, and butter, for exportation.[228]

[228] A note here in the original edition reads: "See the Quarterly Colonial Journal." The reference is to an account of fish exported from the provinces British North America from 1805 to 1808, published in the *Colonial Journal* 1: 2 (July 1816), 358.

Nova Scotia lies to the eastward of New Brunswick, the Bay of Fundy entering between the two colonies. Its dimensions are much smaller than those of New Brunswick; and, as above intimated, it is, for the most part, surrounded by the sea. Like New Brunswick, its chief riches have hitherto consisted in timber, or lumber, and fish; but its agricultural produce is now increasing, and its climate is found to be very superior to what has been hitherto represented.[229]

Halifax, situate in the Bay of Chebucto,[230] on the Atlantic Ocean, is the capital of Nova Scotia; and Windsor, situate in the Bay of Fundy, is a principal town of the same province.

Maine, a district of the United States, and part of the state of Massachusetts,[231] borders to the southward, on New Brunswick, and like it, is bounded on the west by Lower Canada and New Hampshire. Like Nova Scotia and New Brunswick, its principal exports are lumber and fish, and its agriculture is also advancing. A strong spirit of emigration, however, prevails among its inhabitants, great numbers of whom are leaving it, in order to settle on the Ohio and Mississippi. Portland is its principal town.

Massachusetts Proper, of which the principal town is Boston, lies to the southward of Maine.

Connecticut, of which Newhaven is a principal town, lies to the southward of Massachusetts; and New York is to the southward of Connecticut.

[229] A note in the original edition indicates: "For Meteorological tables, and various exact details concerning the climate of Nova Scotia, and for a view and description of Halifax, see the Quarterly Colonial Journal, No. VI, &c.

[230] Now known as Halifax Harbour. "Situate" is an archaic adjective, later replaced by "situated."

[231] Maine became a state on 15 March 1820. Until then, it was a district within Massachusetts.

I. 2. Joshua Marsden, [New Brunswick in the Early 1800s]

[Joshua Marsden (1777-1837) was an English Methodist missionary who arrived in Halifax in October 1800 and, for the next eight years, preached and converted in Nova Scotia and New Brunswick. In 1808, he took an appointment in Bermuda, where he remained until 1812. His *The Narrative of a Mission to Nova Scotia, New Brunswick, and the Somers Islands* was published in 1816 by J. Johns, in Plymouth-Dock. The following is from the original version, pp. 85-90, the end of the sixth chapter.]

The little society in St. John flourished exceedingly this winter [1804]. We had a number of awakenings, and in the midst of a most severe winter, much harmony and love; the cold was indeed intense, and the snow in general about six feet deep; out hogsheads of rain-water were frozen solid, and all liquids, less strong than ardent spirits, froze, unless kept underground, in what are called frost-proof cellars. I know not the reason why New Brunswick is so much colder than Nova Scotia, unless it is owing to its being less cultivated, and more full of woods, rivers, and lakes, and perhaps its contiguity to Lower Canada may in some measure account for it. As New Brunswick is little known in England, and not unfrequently confounded with Nova Scotia, (although it is a distinct province and separate government), I will detain my readers with a short account of the country and capital.

The city of St. John, is built on the mouth of a river of the same name, at the western side of the bay of Fundy, in latitude 45 degrees north, longitude about 65 degrees and 30 minutes west. It is nearly opposite Digby, in Nova Scotia, and about twenty or thirty miles distant from the bay of Passamaquady. The town or city (for it has a royal charter) is but about thirty years old, and was first settled by royalist emigrants from the United States, after the evacuation of New York, by the king's troops. It contains about 500 houses, and probably 3000 inhabitants. It cannot indeed, boast of many public buildings; if we except the church, the steeple of which, recalls to my memory, the loss of a respected friend, John Venning, a native of Plymouth-Dock.[232] This excellent man and skilful artist,

[232] John Venning (1763-1810) died during the construction of Trinity Church, while Marsden was in Bermuda. Plymouth Dock, which was also Marsden's birthplace, is today known as Devonport and is a district of Plymouth, in South West England.

who usefully filled the offices of steward, trustee, leader, and local preacher, was in a moment precipitated from a scaffold (he was building the steeple) upon the roof of the church, and from thence upon a bed of rock, and was literally dashed to pieces. His death was mysteriously awful; but as he was one of those few who have no cause to fear death in any shape, his mourning friends drew consolation both from the goodness of God and his genuine and unaffected piety. The Methodist chapel, on the foundation stone of which, I had the pleasure to preach, will hold nearly a thousand people, and is one of our best and largest places of worship in all British North America. There is also in the town, a court-house, academy, and barracks. The river is wide, and has a noble fishery for salmon, shad, herrings, and sturgeon, which furnishes employment and wealth to several hundreds of the inhabitants. The tide, in the river, rises nearly forty feet,—a circumstance that renders the bay of Fundy famous through all the world; for perhaps, in no part of the earth does the phenomena [sic] of the tide bear such marked and striking characters as on the shores of this bay, along which, it rolls with a majesty and grandeur I never saw in any other place, making in some places a current of from five to seven miles an hour.

The trade of St. John is chiefly to England and the West Indies; to the former they send masts, spars, and staves, scantling and lumber of all kinds; and to the latter fish, potatoes, pork, butter cheese, oats, staves, &c. &c. In times of peace they have a good trade to the United States of America; to which they carry gypsum (plaister of Paris) and grind stones; but this commerce involves much smuggling, and great quantities of contraband goods are hence brought into the province. Two miles from the city are the falls of the river, which, at ebb tide, are grand and terrific. A body of water nearly a mile wide, and from 20 to 30 feet deep, is all at once compressed betwixt a bed of rocks, through and over which it rushes with such an impetuosity and force as no language can possibly describe. The descent is about 20 feet; the noise is terrible, and gives a tremulous motion to all the surrounding scenery; it covers the whole harbour with foam and froth, and diffuses a hollow roaring noise for several miles round; and yet, when the powerful tides in the bay of Fundy rise to the level of the waters above the cataract, vessels can go through for a few minutes, so that the river is navigable nearly 100 miles above the falls. Round the city for several miles, nothing beautiful or charming attracts the eye; the whole scene is rocky, barren, and hilly; perhaps Faulkland Islands themselves are not more dismal. Whoever travels through the world to behold delightful scenery, clear streams, pleasant valleys and groves, must not go to St. John. The whole landscape (if such it may be called) unites an assemblage of the most forbidding traits of nature that the traveller could select. Here are irregular clumps of stunted spruce growing among the rocks; salt marshes, bounded by jutting and fearful crags; muddy creeks, where swarms of pestiferous musquitos annoy the neighbouring inhabitants; in a word, nature has stamped the impression of barrenness and deformity on all around, as if to serve as a foil to many of her lovely and enchanting departments; hence, the neighbourhood of St. John looks best when a vail[233] of snow has covered its nakedness and concealed its sterility; however, to recompence these defects, all the blessings of life are brought in the greatest abundance down the river, in the summer season by boats, and in the winter by sleds; hence, the market is remarkably cheap; I have bought good beef for two pence per pound, mutton for two pence farthing, and fine fat geese for twenty pence each; for a fine salmon, weighing 12 or 14 pounds, I have given two shillings and sixpence. Roots were equally cheap; potatoes and turnips one shilling a bushel. But what is most singular, amidst this cheapness the wages of mechanics are seldom less than from seven shillings and sixpence to ten shillings per day. In the winter great quantities of frozen pigs, poultry, quarters of mutton, beef, and a variety of other articles are exposed on the sleds for sale. It is on sleds all the inhabitants travel, whether to church, to meeting, a visiting, or to market; they are constructed in various ways, according to the taste of the respective proprietors; some are fanciful and elegant, others are plain and clumsy, but they are all admirably adapted for a journey, for when the snow is well beaten you may travel in these vehicles from six to eight miles an hour with the greatest possible ease. In these I have performed my journies up and down the river, sometimes until as late as the latter end of March or the beginning of April, when the ice has been worn so thin by the action of the current beneath, and the sun above, that myself and those with me, were every moment apprehensive we should plunge into the abyss. Sometimes the melting of the snow in the woods raises the water to so great

[233] Archaic spelling of "veil."

a height that the whole body of ice is loosened from the sides, and often cracked the whole width of the river; in this situation I have travelled many miles, sitting upon the edge of the sled to prepare for a spring, as the awful cracks and wide gaps in the ice rendered the greatest caution necessary; for should you plunge into the abyss, the horses generally sink first, and with a little activity those in the sled may escape. Almost every winter numbers fall a sacrifice to the dangers that attend these ice journies. One of my friend whose name was Watton, a class-leader,[234] rode on a weak part and was seen no more. Another friend, Mr. Wilson, a member of the assembly, riding with some others, the sled and horses plunged in, and went directly under; he was saved by being thrown on the loose ice, but three of his companions never rose. Some are lost through imprudence and rashness; riding upon this fragile bridge after it is worn so thin as to give frequent warnings of the danger. A terrible accident of this kind befell one who had been a serious man, and a member of society, but who gradually declined, until he had lost all his religion, the form as well as the power. Being a taylor by trade, he frequently finished and sent home his work on the Lord's day, and when reproved for thus profaning the sabbath, would, with impious humour, reply "it is no harm to borrow a little from the Lord provided we pay him again." This wicked practice was continued, until riding one sabbath day upon the ice, the horse and sled plunged in, and he was seen no more. How often does Jehovah write our sin by the finger of his justice: it is awful to trifle with the Almighty; he is terrible in wrath, and fearful in majesty.

I. 3. Peter Fisher, [King's County]

[Peter Fisher (1782-1848), often considered New Brunswick's first historian, arrived in New Brunswick in 1783 with his Loyalist parents. He was a lumber merchant for most of his life. He published his *Sketches of New Brunswick* in 1825 anonymously. The following is from pp. 49-50 of his *Sketches* (Saint John: Chubb & Sears, 1825)]

Lies likewise [i.e., like Queen's County] on both sides of the river Saint John, and is bounded on the North by a line running

[234] In early Methodism, class meetings were small groups of 12 to 15 members who met weekly under the guidance of a leader.

South West and North East, from the South point of Spoon Island in the river Saint John. On the East by Northumberland and Westmorland. On the West by Charlotte, and on the South by the County of Saint John. It contains seven thousand nine hundred and thirty inhabitants.

It comprehends the Long Reach, the Kennebeckasis and Belisle, and is divided into the following Parishes—Westfield, Greenwich, Kingston, Springfield, Norton, Sussex, and Hampton. Kingston has a Township regularly laid out, which bears the name of the Parish. It has a neat Church, with a resident Minister, and a number of neat buildings, which make a fine appearance. The Court-House, however, is a considerable distance from the Town. The settlers in most parts of this Parish have the appearance of comfort and affluence, although the land is inferior in fertility to most of the other Parishes. The Parish of Sussex has a Church with a resident Minister, and an Academy for the instruction of the Indians, but little good has accrued to these wanderers from that Institution. A beautiful strip of land lies in this Parish called the Vale of Sussex, which is highly cultivated and covered with excellent houses and barns.—Agriculture is in general well attended to, and its effects are evident in independent farmers, good stocks of cattle and an air of comfort and cheerfulness, the sure returns of industry and husbandry. The roads and bridges are in good order and well attended to. The great road of communication passes through this Vale to Westmorland.

The river Kennebeckasis intersects this County, and falls into the Saint John, near the Boar's Head. This is a considerable stream, and has several Islands scattered through its course. It is navigable upwards of twenty miles for vessels of any burthen, and sixty miles farther for small vessels and boats. It is well adapted for Ship-building, having abundance of excellent timber in its neighborhood, and several vessels are annually built here for the merchants of Saint John.

The Nerepis another considerable stream, falls into the Saint John at the foot of the Long Reach. This river runs a considerable distance into the country and has a settlement along its banks.

There are two quarries of excellent Plaster of Paris on the river Kennebeckasis. There is likewise a salt spring in this part of the country, from which small quantities of salt have been made by the Indians and Inhabitants settled near the place, which has proved of an excellent quality for the table, and their [sic] can be no doubt of its possessing valuable medicinal qualities; but no attention has yet been paid to analyse it. Great quantities of sugar are extracted from the sugar maple in this county, upwards of ten thousand pounds have been made in a year, of that valuable article in one Parish.

Several of the Parishes in this county have Churches, some of which have stated Pastors, and others are supplied occasionally.

I. 4. Emily Elizabeth Beavan, [Moving a House]

[Mrs. Beavan (1818-1897) was born in Belfast as Emily Elizabeth Shaw and came to New Brunswick with her parents in 1836. She lived in Kings County until she returned to England in 1843. She published there her *Sketches and Tales Illustrative of Life in the Backwoods of New Brunswick*, from which the following has been taken.]

Our house was a good one. We did not like to leave it. [. . .] Two stout trees were then felled (the meanest would have graced a lordly park), and hewed with the axe into a pair of gigantic sled runners. The house was raised from its foundation and placed on these. Many hands make light work; but, had those hands been all hired labourers, the expense would have been more than the value of the house, but 'twas done by what is called a "frolic." When people have a particular kind of work requiring to be done quickly, and strength to accomplish it, they invite their neighbours to come, and, if necessary, bring with them their horses and oxen. Frolics are used for building log huts, chopping, piling, ploughing, planting, and hoeing. The ladies also have their particular frolics, such as wool-picking, or cutting out and making the home-spun woollen clothes for winter. The entertainment given on such occasions is such as the house people can afford; for the men, roast mutton, pot pie, pumpkin pie, and rum dough nuts; for the ladies, tea, some scandal, and plenty of "*sweet cake*," with stewed apple and custards. There are, at certain seasons, a great many of these frolics, and the people never grow tired of attending them, knowing that the logs on their own fallows will disappear all the quicker for it. The house being now on the runners, thirty yoke of oxen, four abreast, were fastened to an enormous tongue, or pole, made of an entire tree of ash. No one can form any idea, until they have heard it, of the noise made in driving oxen; and, in such an instance as this, of the skill and tact required in starting them, so that they are all made to pull at once. I have often seen the drivers, who are constantly shouting, completely hoarse; and after a day's work so exhausted that they have been unable to raise the voice. Although the cattle are very docile, and understand well what is said to them, yet from the number of turnings and twistings they require to be continually reminded of their duty. Amid, then, all the noise and bustle made by intimating to such a number whether they were to "haw" or "gee," the shoutings of the younger parties assembled, the straining of chains and the creaking of boards, the ponderous pile was set in motion along the smooth white and marble-like snow road, whose breadth it entirely filled up. It was a sight one cannot well forget—to see it move slowly up the hill, as if unwilling to leave the spot it had been raised on, notwithstanding the merry shouts around, and the flag they had decked it with streaming so gaily through the green trees as they bent over it till it reached the site destined for it, where it looked as much at home as if it were too grave and steady a thing to take the step it had done. This was in March—we had been waiting some time for snow, as to move without it would have been a difficult task; for, plentifully as New Brunswick is supplied with that commodity, at some seasons much delay and loss is experienced for want of it—the sleighing cannot be done, and wheel carriages cannot run, the roads are so rough and broken with the frost—the cold is then more intense, and the cellars, (the sole store-houses and receptacles of the chief comforts) without their deep covering of snow, become penetrated by the frost, and their contents much injured, if not totally destroyed—this is a calamity that to be known must be experienced—the potatoes stored here are the chief produce of the farm, at least the part that is most available for selling, for hay should never go off the land, and grain is as yet so little raised that 'tis but the old farmers can do what is called "*bread themselves*:" thus the innovation of the cellars by the *frost fiend* is a sad and serious occurrence—of course a deep bank of earth is thrown up round the house, beneath which, and generally its whole length and breadth, is the cellar; but the snow over this is an additional and even necessary defence, and its want is much felt in many other ways—in quantity, however, it generally makes up for its temporary absence by being five and six feet deep in April.

APPENDIX II

THE LOYALISTS OF 1783

II. 1. Walter Bates, [Comfort in the Wilderness]

[In 1840, Walter Bates had a "historical sketch" ready for print. It is in no way a tidy narrative like the one he brought out in 1817. It lays out the two centuries of the history of British settlement in North America, before, during, and after the American Revolutionary War, as a conflict between the Puritans and the Anglicans, with the former succeeding in establishing a republic and drawing out the latter, who were forced to seek shelter in the wilderness of New Brunswick, where they rebuilt their churches, found peace and prosperity, but once again had to face the incursions of various dissenters from the south. Parts of it were included in W.O. Raymond's 1889 booklet *Kingston and the Loyalists of 1783*; others were published by D.G. Bell in 1984. The following is from Raymond's transcription of Bates's manuscript. Raymond probably operated the division into paragraphs and made some corrections. Some passages have been left out here and are marked below by ellipses between brackets. Typographical errors have been corrected, but inconsistent spelling and punctuation have been preserved. The narrative begins in 1775 in New York and Connecticut.]

Everything but decency and order overran the colony, and frequent irruption was made in which many loyalists were disarmed, plundered and made prisoners, among whom was the Rev. Dr. Seabury and the mayor of the city of New York.[235] Governor Tryon[236] and others happily escaped their fury through a back window.

Mr. Rivington, the King's printer, was one of the sufferers by loss of property. They plundered his house of all his printing

[235] Samuel Seabury (1729-1796) was arrested in November 1775 and kept in jail for six weeks. Whitehead Hicks (1728-1780), who was mayor of New York at the time, was forced to resign, but his replacement, David Mathews (c. 1739-1800), was arrested in June 1776 and sent to Connecticut, from where he escaped. He remained mayor during the British occupation of New York, after which he immigrated to Nova Scotia.

[236] William Tryon (1729-1788) was governor of New York from 1771 to 1777. He was a given a rank of general and commanded a series of raids in Connecticut. He returned to England in 1780.

materials—since employed in the service of their congress.[237] The King's statue maintained its ground in New York until Washington took possession of the city, when it was indicted for high treason against America, found guilty and received sentence that the lead of it should be run into bullets for the destruction of the English.[238]

Mr. Washington thought proper to notice in his General Order next day he was sorry his soldiers should in a riotous manner pull down the statue of the King, yet he could not but comment them for defaming every monument of British tyranny.

Meanwhile, in Connecticut organized mobs continued their acts of violence and outrage, breaking windows in the houses of loyalists and crying out, "No Bishops, Lords or Tyrants!" The New Englanders felt that the authority of the government in England and the National church must be crushed or their Puritanism be overthrown. It was this spirit largely which originated the late rebellion in America.

Throughout this unhappy war, the Episcopal church, in some places veiled in obscurity, still continued to exist in America, notwithstanding the utmost persecution evil men could bring upon it, and at length I have happily lived to see what so long I vainly hoped for—Dr. Seabury, the persecuted priest from the city of New York, return the first consecrated Diocesan Bishop of Connecticut—my native land.[239]

In July, 1776, Congress declared Independency, and ordered the Commonwealth to be prayed for instead of the King and Royal family. All the loyal churches were thereupon shut up, except one at Newton, Connecticut, of which the Rev. John Beach was rector.[240] His gray hairs adorned with loyal and Christian virtues overcame the madness of his enemies. This faithful disciple entered his church, saying: "If I am to credit the surmises kindly whispered to me, that unless I forbear from

[237] James Rivington (1724-1802) was the publisher of a prominent Loyalist newspaper. His offices were destroyed by Patriots in 1775. He resumed publication in 1777, when the British occupied New York City, but was soon acting as a spy for George Washington. His newspaper finally closed in 1783.

[238] The equestrian statue of George III stood in Bowling Green (a park in Lower Manhattan) from 1770 until 9 July 1776.

[239] In 1784, Seabury (see note 235) was consecrated Bishop of Connecticut. He later became the first bishop of the Episcopal Church.

[240] John Beach (1700-1782) was rector of Newton Parish since its foundation in 1732.

praying for the King I shall never pray or preach more, I can only say, whilst no intimation could well be more distressing, it admits not one moment's delay: with all due respect for my ordination oaths, I am firm in my resolution while I pray at all to conform with the unmutilated liturgy of the church, and pray for the King and all in authority under him."

Upon this the rebels seized him, resolved to cut out his tongue. He said, "If my blood must be shed, let it not be done in the house of God." The pious mob then dragged him out of the church. "Now, you old devil," said they, "say your last prayer!" Whereupon he devoutly kneeled down, saying, "O Lord and Father of mercies, look upon these mine enemies and forgive them. They know not what they do; they are blindly misled; O God, in mercy open their eyes."

By the Providence of God, the council of his enemies was brought to naught and his life spared.

In September, 1776, Washington was compelled to evacuate New York, by General Howe, to the great relief of loyalists in New York.[241] He penetrated into the country as far as White Plains, about twelve miles from Stamford, to the alarm of all the sympathizers with the British cause.[242] In the day of battle we were collected by the mobs and confined, under strong guards, where we could hear the report of guns, hoping soon to be relieved. The British returning shortly after the mobs all dispersed and the "Tories" were set at liberty.

The British fortified Lloyd's Neck with a garrison, opposite the islands and coves lying between the churches of Norwalk and Stamford,[243] whose inhabitants were wealthy farmers—Churchmen and Quakers—all loyalists that afforded a complete asylum and safe passage, by which my three brothers and hundreds of others passed by night almost continually to the British Garrison.

[241] William Howe (1729-1814) was Commander in Chief of the British land forces from September 1775 to May 1778. He occupied New York City in September 1776.

[242] The Battle of White Plains, a British victory, was fought on 28 October 1776.

[243] Lloyd's Neck is a peninsula on the north shore of Long Island. The area is now part of Lloyd Harbor, Huntington, Suffolk County. The distance between Stamford, Connecticut, and Lloyd's Neck is about 11 miles (over the Long Island Sound), easily covered by boat. Norwalk, Connecticut is about 9 miles east of Stamford. Bates was born in today's Darien, halfway between Stamford and Norwalk.

At length the thing I greatly feared came upon me. A small boat was discovered by the American guard, in one of these coves, by night, in which they suspected that one of my brothers, with some others, had come from the British. They supposed them concealed in the neighbourhood and that I must be acquainted with it.

At this time I had just entered my sixteenth year. I was taken and confined in the Guard House; next day examined before a Committee and threatened with sundry deaths if I did not confess what I knew not of. They threatened among other things to confine me at low water and let the tide drown me if I did not expose these honest farmers. At length I was sent back to the Guard House until ten o'clock at night, when I was taken out by an armed mob, conveyed through the field gate one mile from the town to Back Creek, then having been stripped my body was exposed to the mosquitoes, my hands and feet being confined to a tree near the Salt Marsh, in which situation for two hours time every drop of blood would be drawn from my body; when soon after two of the committee said that if I would tell them all I knew, they would release me, if not they would leave me to these men who, perhaps, would kill me.

I told them that I knew nothing that would save my life.

They left me, and the Guard came to me and said they were ordered to give me, if I did not confess, one hundred stripes, and if that did not kill me I would be sentenced to be hanged. Twenty stripes was then executed with severity, after which they sent me again to the Guard House. No "Tory" was allowed to speak to me, but I was insulted and abused by all.

The next day the committee proposed many means to extort a confession from me, the most terrifying was that of confining me to a log on the carriage in the Saw mill and let the saw cut me in two if I did not expose "those Torys." Finally they sentenced me to appear before Col. Davenport,[244] in order that he should send me to head quarters, where all the Torys he sent were surely hanged. Accordingly next day I was brought before Davenport—one of the descendants of the old apostate Davenport, who fled from old England[245]—who, after he had

[244] Abraham Davenport (1715-1789), a Stamford native. He was a judge a member of the Connecticut House of Representatives. During the Revolutionary War, he served as colonel in the Connecticut State Militia.

[245] John Davenport (1597-1670) was a Puritan pastor who co-founded the Colony of New Haven in 1638.

examined me, said with great severity of countenance, "I think you could have exposed those Tories."

I said to him "You might rather think I would have exposed my own father sooner then suffer what I have suffered." Upon which the old judge could not help acknowledging he never knew any one who had withstood more without exposing confederates, and he finally discharged me the third day. It was a grievous misfortune to be in such a situation, but the fear of God animated me not to fear man. My resolution compelled mine enemies to show their pity that I had been so causelessly afflicted, and my life was spared. I was, however, obliged to seek refuge from the malice of my persecutors in the mountains and forests until their frenzy might be somewhat abated.

After two years' absence, on my return home, I found my father down with the small-pox, suspected to be given him by design, consequently the family were all in inoculation, which I also had to endure, after which I could not by any means think of leaving my father until I had assisted him in his wheat harvest.

The first night after I was summoned with a draft for the Continental Service with three days' notice, consequently was compelled to flee for refuge, I knew not where, but providentially found myself next morning in the immediate neighbourhood of a British garrison. Here I was informed I must go through the regular process, be reported, and take the oath of allegiance.

I was provided with the necessary pass from the commanding officer to General DeLancey at Jamaica (Long Island),[246] who furnished me with a pass directed to General Smith at Brooklin,[247] who furnished me with a pass to Colonel Axtell at Flat Bush,[248] who administered the oath and also furnished me with a pass to General DeLancey again at Jamaica.

[246] Jamaica is now a neighbourhood in Queens, New York. General Oliver De Lancey (1718-1785) was the commanding officer of the so-called "De Lancey's Brigade" of the Loyalist forces. Soldiers of this unit who settled in New Brunswick (see notes 80 and 106) were accompanied there by James De Lancey (1746-1804), the general's nephew, who, however, settled in Nova Scotia.

[247] General Francis Smith (1723-1791). He commanded a brigade during the Battle of Long Island.

[248] William Axtell (1720-1795) was a wealthy New York merchant who served as colonel in the loyalist militia. His country home was Melrose Hall in Flatbush, Long Island. He fled to England after the war.

Here not being acquainted with customs of the army exposed me to great inconvenience. I just only prudently *knocked* at the same door where I had received my pass the day before. This I was informed was considered an offence and that the old General was apt to be very severe after drinking wine all night.

At length the old General came down from his chamber, and surely his face looked to me as red as his coat.

"Where is that damned rascal who has disturbed my quarters this morning? Send him to the guard house!" roared he. This subjected me to great difficulties, too unpleasant to mention.

Yet kind providence seemed to prepare ways and means, unforeseen by me, for my escape and preservation amidst all troubles, afflictions and dangers by land and sea, and during that unhappy war there were many instances of God's mercy for which I can never be sufficiently grateful. For example in the case of my eldest brother's sickness, on Long Island, with the fever that few survived at that time, I was providentially in a situation to render him every comfort he could receive while in life, and after his death to attend to his decent burial in the town of Huntington,[249] the 10th day of September, 1781; and soon after I was taken sick with the like fever on Lloyds Neck, where I must soon have died had not I providentially been removed to a friendly house in Huntington, where I received the kind attention of the family. It was feared that I could not survive until morning, a doctor was called late at night who administered medicine which, under providence, gave immediate relief and I was soon restored to my former health.

Shortly after this I commenced teaching a school on Eaton's Neck,[250] where all the people were Loyalists and most part with myself, churchmen from Connecticut.

Here some of the Church clergymen came occasionally to hold divine service on Sundays.

There being none of other religion on the "Neck" we were so united the church at Eaton might be justly styled a church of *Eden*.

The Rev. John Sayre[251] came to attend public worship here in April, 1783, and at the same time to acquaint us that the King

[249] Huntington is a town in Suffolk County, on the north shore of Long Island.

[250] Eatons Neck is a hamlet, today part of the town of Huntington.

[251] John Sayre (1738-1784) was from New York, but had been a missionary in Fairfield County, Connecticut. He arrived in New Brunswick in 1783 and died in his parish at Maugerville.

had granted to all Loyalists who did not incline to return to their homes, and would go to Nova Scotia, two hundred acres of land to each family, and two years provisions: provide ships to convey them as near as can be to a place for settlement where lands would be granted for support of church and school. The next day I obtained the articles for settlement (yet in my possession) from Huntington. A general meeting was held on Eaton's Neck to investigate the same together with our present and future prospects.

After we had discussed the matter it was resolved by all present, and mutually agreed to remove with all their families into the wilderness of Nova Scotia, and settle all together in such situation as we might enjoy the comforts of a church and school in the wilderness, fully relying for future support in the promises of God to His people.

I here introduce the rhymes of a young School master:

Come Loyalists all come
    And listen to my word;
We left our country and our home
    And trusted in the Lord;
Let us not now forsake our trust
    Returning back with sorrow;
I fain would see the Rebels flee
    Like Sodom and Gomorrow,
Yet think these offers very just
    And thank the King sincerely—
Altho' the Rebels gain so much,
    We see not yet quite clearly;
God is too wise to be unjust,
    Too good to be unkind,
While subject to his sovereign will
    Our hearts are well inclined.
God when He gives supremely good,
    Not less when He denies;
Afflictions from His Sovereign hand
    Are blessings in disguise.
For in the wilderness, we're told,
    God's church will comfort give,
And no good thing will He withhold
    From those who justly live.

W. BATES.

It seemed as if heaven smiled upon our undertaking, selecting the best ship in the fleet for our comfort, and by far the best captain. And so, with warm, loyal hearts, we all embarked with one mind on board the good ship *Union*, Captain Wilson,[252] who received us all on board as father on a family.

Nothing was wanting to make us comfortable on board ship, which blessing seemed providentially to attend us throughout.

From Eaton's Neck the ship sailed through East River to New York.

Having a couple on board wishing to be married we called upon Reverend Mr. Leaming[253] who received us with much kindness and affection, most of us having been formerly of his congregation; who after the marriage reverently admonished us with his blessing that in our new home we pay due regard to church and school as means to obtain the blessing of God upon our families and our industry. We re-embarked. Next day the ship joined the fleet and on the 26th day of April, 1783, upwards of twenty sail of ships under convoy left Sandy Hook[254] for Nova Scotia—from *whence* our good ship *Union* had the honor of leading the whole fleet fourteen days and arrived at Partridge Island[255] before the fleet was come within sight.

Next day our ship was safely moored by Capt. Daniel Leavett, the pilot, in the most convenient situation for landing in the harbor of St. John all in good health.

We remained comfortably on board ship till we could explore for a place in the wilderness suitable for our purpose of settlement. Those who came in other ships were in some cases sickly, or precipitated on shore. Here again we were favored.

A boat was procured for the purpose of exploration, and David Pickett, Israel Hait, Silas Raymond and others proceeded

---

[252] Consett Wilson actually had the rank of master, but he was the commanding officer of the *Union*.

[253] Jeremiah Leaming (1717-1804) had been a Church of England minister in Norwalk, Connecticut. Though a Loyalist, he chose to remain in the United States. He was elected the first Bishop of Connecticut, but declined because of old age, and Samuel Seabury (see notes 235 and 239) was selected in his place.

[254] Sandy Hook is a village in Connecticut, founded in 1711, today part of the town of Newtown.

[255] An island in the Bay of Fundy, off the coast of Saint John, New Brunswick.

sixty miles up the River Saint John. On their return they reported that the inhabitants were settled on intervale land by the river—that the high lands had generally been burned by the Indians, and there was no church or church minister in the country.

They were informed of the existence of a tract of timber land that had not been burned on Bellisle Bay, about thirty miles from the harbor of Saint John, which they had visited. They viewed the situation favorable for our purpose of settlement. Whereupon we all agreed to disembark from on board the good ship *Union* and proceed thither. We departed with Captain Wilson's blessing, and embarked on board a small sloop all our baggage.

The next morning with all our effects, women and children, we set sail above the Falls, and arrived at Bellisle Bay before sunset.

Nothing but wilderness before our eyes; the women and children *did not refrain from tears!*

John Marvin, John Lyon and myself went on shore and pitched a tent in the bushes and slept in it all night. Next morning every man came on shore and cleared away and landed all our baggage, women and the children, and the sloop left us alone in the wilderness.

We had been informed the Indians were uneasy at our coming, and that a considerable body had collected at the head of Bellisle. Yet our hope and trust remained firm that God would not forsake us. We set to work with such resolution that before night we had as many tents set as made the women and children comfortable.

Next morning we discovered a fleet of ten Indian canoes slowly moving towards us, which cause considerable alarm with the women. Before they came within gunshot one who could speak English came to let us know, "We all one brother!" They were of the Micmac tribe and became quite friendly, and furnished us plentifully with moose meat.

We soon discovered a situation at the head of Bellisle Creek suitable for our purpose of settlement with Church and school.

[. . .]

Whereupon every man was jointly employed clearing places for building, cutting logs, carrying them together by strength of hands and laying up log houses, by which means seventeen log houses were laid up and covered with bark, so that by the month of November every man in the district found himself and family covered under his own roof and a happier people never lived upon this globe enjoying in unity the blessings which God had provided for us in the country into whose coves and wild woods we were driven through persecution.

[. . .]

The Rev. John Sayre who ministered to us at Eaton's Neck soon after his arrival in the fall fleet removed to Maugerville.

The Rev. John Beardsley officiated for us occasionally, and made some preparation for building in Kingston.

On Thursday, the 7th day of October, 1784, I had the honor of the first marriage by the first minister. On the death of the Rev. John Sayre, in 1786, the Rev. John Beardsley was removed to Maugerville.

The vestry appointed to hold church at the house of Elias Scribner, and Mr. Frederick Dibblee to read the prayers. Public worship was thus attended regularly on Sundays till July, 1787, when Rev. James Scovil came from Connecticut, with the view of removing to this province as a missionary. As an encouragement we voted him the lot reserved for the parsonage, and on the following summer he removed with his family into Kingston, and attended public worship on Sunday in the house of Elias Scribner, where he found, and much to his comfort, a full congregation of church people in the wilderness ready to do everything in God's name the exigencies of the church required.

With the coming of the Rev. James Scovil and the establishment of all the ordinances of religion, our little community was well content.

These homes for weary pilgrims made,
Like happy tents of peace they stand
Amid the dark and silent shade,
The Altar cheers our forest land.

No splendor clothes each humble dome,
No shingled roof or painted shrine,
Yet faith and hope find here a home—
The Christian feels the place divine.

"Yea, the sparrow hath found her an house and the swallow a nest where she may lay her young, even Thy altar, O Lord of Hosts, my King and my God."[256]

[. . .]

In February it was agreed to build the Church 50 feet in length and 38 in breadth under the direction of the vestry, and it was further agreed to allow fifteen shillings a thousand for eighteen inch shingles and three shillings a day for common labour.

On Saturday the 27th day of June, 1789, the frame was raised in perfect harmony and in good order and by united exertion was so far advanced that on the 5th day of November it was dedicated to the service of Almighty God by the Rev. James Scovil by the name of TRINITY CHURCH.

[. . .]

In 1803, the Rev. James Scovil being infirm and unable to hold Divine service on all occasions, it was proposed to employ his son, Elias, who was then ordained, to assist his father, and to secure forty pounds a year, to be paid half-yearly. He to officiate one-half of his time in Kingston, one-fourth in Hampton and one-fourth in Springfield. The former place to raise twenty pounds and the others ten each.

[. . .]

It may be mentioned that on Mr. Frederick Dibblee's removal from Kingston in 1790 to be ordained as the first clergyman at Woodstock, it was voted that some fit person be appointed to read prayers and a sermon in the absence of the Rector. Walter Bates was selected and by this means the Church in Kingston has ever been kept open upon the Lord's Day.

[256] Psalms 84: 3.

II. 2. William Cobbett, [In the House of a Yankee Loyalist]

[William Cobbett (1763-1835), the famous English pamphleteer who had such an impressive career as a journalist on both sides of the Atlantic, joined the 54th Regiment of Foot in 1783 as a private. He was stationed in New Brunswick from 1785 to 1791 and he rose to the rank of sergeant-major. He also fell in love and got engaged to the daughter of an artillery sergeant. His fiancee returned to England and waited four years for his service to end. His account of the loyalists of New Brunswick is more vivid, less sober than those of his contemporaries. This episode is set in 1789,]

Partly from misinformation, and partly from miscalculation, I had lost my way; and, quite alone, but armed with my sword and a brace of pistols, to defend myself against the bears, I arrived at the log-house in the middle of a moonlight night, the hoar frost covering the trees and the grass. A stout and clamorous dog, kept off by the gleaming of my sword, waked the master of the house, who got up, received me with great hospitality, got me something to eat, and put me into a feather-bed, a thing that I had been a stranger to for some years. I, being very tired, had tried to pass the night in the woods, between the trunks of two large trees, which had fallen side by side, and within a yard of each other. I had made a nest for myself of dry fern, and had made a covering by laying boughs of spruce across the trunks of the trees. But unable to sleep on account of the cold; becoming sick from the great quantity of water that I had drank during the heat of the day, and being, moreover, alarmed at the noise of the bears, and lest one of them should find me in a defenceless state, I had roused myself up, and had crept along as well as I could. So that no hero of eastern romance ever experienced a more enchanting change.

I had got into the house of one of those YANKEE LOYALISTS, who, at the close of the revolutionary war (which, until it had succeeded, was called a rebellion) had accepted of grants of land in the King's Province of New Brunswick; and who, to the great honour of England, had been furnished with all the means of making new and comfortable settlements. I was suffered to sleep till breakfast time, when I found a table, the like of which I have since seen so many in the United States, loaded with good things. The master and the mistress of the house, aged about fifty, were like what an English farmer and his wife were half a century ago. There were two sons, tall and stout, who appeared to have come in from work, and the youngest of whom was about my age, then twenty-three. But there was another member of the family, aged nineteen, who (dressed according to the neat and simple fashion of New England, whence she had come with her parents five or six years before) had her long light-brown hair twisted nicely up, and fastened on the top of her head, in which head were a pair of lively blue eyes, associated with features of which that softness and that sweetness, so characteristic of American girls, were the predominant expressions, the whole being set off by a complexion indicative of glowing health, and forming, figure, movements, and all taken together, an assemblage of beauties, far surpassing any that I had ever seen but once in my life. That once was, too, two years agone; and, in such a case and at such an age, two years, two whole years, is a long, long while! It was a space as long as the eleventh part of my then life! Here was the present against the absent: here was the power of the eyes pitted against that of the memory: here were all the senses up in arms to subdue the influence of the thoughts: here was vanity, here was passion, here was the spot of all spots in the world, and here were also the life, and the manners and the habits and the pursuits that I delighted in: here was every thing that imagination can conceive, united in a conspiracy against the poor little brunette in England! What, then, did I fall in love at once with this bouquet of lilies and roses? Oh! by no means. I was, however, so enchanted with the place; I so much enjoyed its tranquillity, the shade of the maple trees, the business of the farm, the sports of the water and of the woods, that I stayed at it to the last possible minute, promising, at my departure, to come again as often as I possibly could; a promise which I most punctually fulfilled.

Winter is the great season for jaunting and dancing (called frolicking) in America. In this Province the river and the creeks were the only roads from settlement to settlement. In summer we travelled in canoes; in winter in sleighs on the ice or snow. During more than two years I spent all the time I could with my Yankee friends: they were all fond of me: I talked to them about country affairs, my evident delight in which they took as a compliment to themselves: the father and mother treated me as one of their children; the sons as a brother; and the daughter, who was as modest and as full of sensibility as she was beautiful, in a way to which a chap much less sanguine than I was would have given the tenderest interpretation; which treatment I, especially in the last-mentioned case, most cordially repaid.

It is when you meet in company with others of your own age that you are, in love matters, put, most frequently, to the test, and exposed to detection. The next door neighbour might, in that country, be ten miles off. We used to have a frolic, sometimes at one house and sometimes at another. Here, where female eyes are very much on the alert, no secret can long be kept; and very soon father, mother, brothers and the whole neighbourhood looked upon the thing as certain, not excepting herself, to whom I, however, had never once even talked of marriage, and had never even told her that I loved her. But I had a thousand times done these by implication, taking into view the interpretation that she would naturally put upon my looks, appellations and acts; and it was of this, that I had to accuse myself. Yet I was not a deceiver; for my affection for her was very great: I spent no really pleasant hours but with her: I was uneasy if she showed the slightest regard for any other young man: I was unhappy if the smallest matter affected her health or spirits: I quitted her in dejection, and returned to her with eager delight: many a time, when I could get leave but for a day, I paddled in a canoe two whole succeeding nights, in order to pass that day with her. If this was not love, it was first cousin to it; for as to any criminal intention I no more thought of it, in her case, than if she had been my sister. Many times I put to myself the questions: "What am I at? Is not this wrong? Why do I go?" But still I went.

[. . .]

The last parting came; and now came my just punishment! The time was known to every body, and was irrevocably fixed; for I had to move with a regiment, and the embarkation of a regiment is an epoch in a thinly settled province. To describe this parting would be too painful even at this distant day, and with this frost of age upon my head. The kind and virtuous father came forty miles to see me just as I was going on board in the river. His looks and words I have never forgotten. As the vessel descended, she passed the mouth of that creek which I had so often entered with delight; and though England, and all that England contained, were before me, I lost sight of this creek with an aching heart.

APPENDIX III:

DANGERS

III. 1. [Walter Bates], [A Plague of Light-Fingered Gentry]

[This is the last footnote of the British edition of *The Mysterious Stranger*. Since it is not one of the many footnotes clearly identified as belonging to the "Editor," it may have been added either by Walter Bates himself or by some other mysterious contributor to this version of the book.]

The European settlements in America appear to be plagued with extraordinary examples of the *light-fingered gentry*. A recent United States' newspaper contains the following paragraphs:—

"Among a number of persons lately tried at Troy, [in the state of New York,][257] for various crimes, there was a man of the name of Haggerty, convicted on two indictments for grand larceny, and one for forgery, and sentenced to the State Prison for 14 years. The Troy 'Post' thus speaks of him:—

'John Haggerty affords a remarkable instance of depravity. He was first committed to gaol for stealing a pocket-book from a gentleman's pocket, while riding in the waggon with him; which was but a few weeks before he was tried. While in prison, he committed a forgery, in counterfeiting a bank bill; and, on the first day of the term in which he was tried, he stole about fifty dollars in money, and sent it to counsel, for a fee to defend him. He was tried on all the above offences, and convicted. When he was on trial in court, he stole, from the pockets of a gentleman who sat in the bar before him, two handkerchiefs, for which, however, it was thought unnecessary to convict him.'—*New York Advertiser*."

From Halifax, under date August 24, 1816, we have the following paragraph, the hero of which has so many points of resemblance to Henry Frederick Moon, that, from the mere

[257] The explanation in the brackets is from the original text.

description, we might easily mistake him for the same identical person. It appears, however, that he is only a second specimen of the kind:—

"CAUTION.

A London Black-leg infesting these Provinces.

A very genteel-looking person, about five feet six or seven inches high, calling himself Alexander Atherton, lately from London, *via* New York, and (to different persons) assuming the characters of Clergyman of the Established Church, Merchant, Lawyer, School-master, &c. visited this city last week, and has swindled persons to a considerable amount: several articles are missing from his lodgings, particularly a black silk waistcoat, and a pair of silver tea spoons, not marked, which no doubt were taken by him. It is ascertained, that he left this on Wednesday morning last, in a schooner belonging to Mr. Appleby, for Moose Island; has a companion with him, who he calls '*Captain*'—endeavoured, while here, to get English stamp Bills of Exchange,[258] and applied at the office of this paper to get envelopes for letters printed, with '*On His Majesty's Service*' upon them; these circumstances, together with his having swindled several persons here, fully corroborate the opinion, that he is a professed swindler; he has a large quarto Bible with him, a suit of plain naval uniform, which he has swindled persons out of here, and carries with him a quantity of United States Bank paper, and of the Steam Boat Company; occasionally exhibits a certificate signed '*John W. Croker, Esq. Secretary of the Admiralty*,' certifying his having served as Chaplain in one of his Majesty's ships. He wore a black coat, blue pantaloons, and black bound waistcoat, with glass buttons; he is a smart good-looking man, and his affability will enable him to pass unsuspected in any company.

A reward of five pounds will be given to any person apprehending the above named Alexander Atherton, and lodging him in any of the gaols within this province, &c."

---

[258] A bill of exchange is a written agreement between a buyer and a seller. Those drawn in England had to carry an English stamp. The term "blackleg" used in the headline usually referred to a card sharp and cheater, but here it clearly refers to a forger (and confidence man).

III. 2. George Patterson, [The First Murder in Pictou]

[Rev. George Patterson (1824-1897) was the grandson of one of the founders of the town of Pictou. The following is from his *A History of the County of Pictou, Nova Scotia* (Montreal: Dawson Brothers, 1877), 218-220. The story he recounts occurred only a couple of years before Smith first arrived in Pictou and at least one of the people mentioned below met Smith in 1814.]

Thomas Harris, Sr., was deputy sheriff till 1811, when he was succeeded by the late John W. Harris, who continued in office till the county was divided in 1836, when the Government appointed J. J. Sawyer, who had been High Sheriff of the united county of Halifax, to be High Sheriff of the three counties of Halifax, Colchester and Pictou, and Mr. Harris was appointed his Deputy. But when the Legislature met, the House of Assembly set their faces against this plurality system, and in the following year, he was appointed High Sheriff, which office he continued to hold till 1857, when his son, Wm. H. Harris, succeeded him.

In connexion with this, we may here notice the first trial for murder in this county. The crime was committed on the 26th May, 1811, by a man named McIntosh. He had been originally a tradesman, but took up the idea of going into business. He went to Halifax and obtained a supply of goods, which he put on board a schooner to bring around to Pictou, but was detained all winter in Guysborough.[259] Giving himself out as a person of some importance, he succeeded in marrying there a lady, renowned for her beauty. Arriving in Pictou in spring, he commenced merchandizing, and flourished while the goods lasted; but when they were done he found himself in debt. His creditors had him arrested, when a friend, named Dougald McDonald, obtained his release by becoming security for his appearance in court. When the time arrived, however, he failed to appear. The judge told his bailsman to take him wherever he could find him. The latter accordingly went with the sheriff to try to seize him. McIntosh shut himself in his house, which stood on the east side of Yorstons wharf, a little below where Hamilton's bakery now stands. McDonald took a crowbar and

[259] A township (and county) on the eastern shore of Nova Scotia. The name of the merchant was Alexander McIntosh.

commenced prying open the door. As soon as he had it partially open, McIntosh fired a blunderbuss at him, the contents of which lodged in his body, so that he bled to death in an hour or two.

The magistrates met and immediately issued a warrant for the arrest of McIntosh. But he armed himself and defied any one to arrest him, threatening death to every person who should touch him. Leaving his house, he crept under the wharf, and perching upon some of the logs, it was no easy matter to dislodge him, and almost every person was afraid to venture near. At length, John Sylvester, of Middle River,[260] a fearless old man-of-war man, undertook, with another, to make him prisoner. Taking a pistol, he went under the wharf, and, immediately presenting it, ordered McIntosh to come down, threatening to fire if he did not do so at once. Seeing his determination, the latter surrendered.

McIntosh was arraigned for murder at the Supreme Court, on the 3rd of August, 1811, and his trial came on in due course on the 5th, before Judge Monk.[261] There being then no proper court house, the trial took place in the old Presbyterian church. As this was the first case of the kind in Pictou, great interest was excited, and the house was crowded. Trials were not conducted in so tedious a manner as they are now, but this was prolonged well into the night, so that the closing address was delivered by candlelight. R. J. Uniacke, the Attorney-General,[262] conducted the case for the Crown, and the prisoner was defended by Halliburton and Chipman,[263] who set up as a defence that an Englishman's house was his castle, and that he had a right to defend it against any person breaking in. the Attorney-General closed the case in a manner that excited general admiration. He had taken no notes either of the evidence or the addresses of the opposing counsel. But with his marvellous memory, he omitted no fact bearing on the case, and no point in the

[260] A small community on the banks of the river of the same name, in Pictou County.

[261] George Henry Monk (1748-1823), at the time puisne judge of the Supreme Court of Nova Scotia (1801-1816).

[262] Richard John Uniacke (1753-1830), an abolitionist, was attorney general of Nova Scotia from 1797 until his death.

[263] William Hersey Otis Haliburton (1767-1829), a lawyer and judge (Thomas Chandler Haliburton was his son); and Jared Ingersol Chipman (1788-1832), who had studied in New Brunswick with Ward Chipman (see note 69), his cousin once removed.

objections of the defense, disposing of all opposition with consummate ability. McIntosh was accordingly condemned, and on the 7th sentenced to be executed. But while he lay in prison, the jubilee of George III. was proclaimed, and he was pardoned. During his imprisonment, he seemed affected by his situation, and every Sabbath sent a request for the prayers of the church. But on obtaining his freedom all his concern vanished. He afterward went to St. John, where he was drowned. His widow married in the United States a very wealthy man, and was living till recently.

Works cited in the footnotes

Acheson, T[homas] W[illiam]. *Saint John: The Making of a Colonial Urban Community.* Toronto: University of Toronto Press, 1985.

Baxter, John B.M. *Simon Baxter.* Sackville: The New Brunswick Museum, 1943.

[Beckford, William Hale]. *Leading Business Men of New Haven County.* Boston: Mercantile Publishing, 1887.

Bunting, William Franklin. *History of St. John's Lodge, F. & A. M. of Saint John, New Brunswick.* Saint John, N.B.: J.&A. McMillan, 1895.

Davidson, Stephen. *Black Loyalists in New Brunswick.* Halifax: Formac, 2020.

Elliot, Samuel Hayes. *The Attractions of New Haven, Connecticut: A Guide to the City.* New York: N. Tibbals, 1869.

Ganong, William F[rancis]. "A Monograph of Historic Sites in the Province of New Brunswick." *Transactions of the Royal Society of Canada.* Second Series. Volume V. Section II. Ottawa: J. Hope & Sons; Toronto: Copp-Clark, 1899. 213-357.

Ganong, William F[rancis]. "A Monograph of the Place-Nomenclature of the Province of New Brunswick." *Transactions of the Royal Society of Canada.* Second Series. Volume II. Section II. Ottawa: J. Durie & Son; Toronto: Copp-Clark, 1896. 175-288.

Gilman, George H. [An Old Pioneer]. *History of the Town of Houlton, Maine, from 1804 to 1883.* Haverhill, Mass.: C.C. Morse & Son, 1884.

Hale, Nathan. *Chronicle of Events, Discoveries, and Improvements, for the Popular Diffusion of Useful Knowledge.* Boston: S.N. Dickinson, 1840.

Hodges, Graham Russell Gao, and Alan Edward Brown, Eds. *The Book of Negroes: African Americans in Exile after the American Revolution.* New York: Fordham University Press, 2021.

Holmes, Oliver W. "Stagecoach Travel and Some Aspects of the Staging Business in New England, 1800-1850." *Proceedings of the Massachusetts Historical Society*, third series, 85 (1973), 36-57.

Hoyt, Azor. *"Ice Out Past My House:" The Diary of Azor Hoyt, a King's County Loyalist.* Eds. Jack Edwin Hoyt and Sandra Keirstead. Elora, Ont.: s.e., 1993.

McCullough, A[lan]. B[ruce]. *Money and Exchange in Canada to 1900.* Toronto: Dundurn Press, 1984.

Patterson, George. *A History of the County of Pictou, Nova Scotia.* Montreal: Dawson Brothers, 1877.

Thomas, Earle. *Greener Pastures: The Loyalist Experience of Benjamin Ingraham.* Belleville, Ont.: Mika, 1983.

Troxler, Carole W. "A Loyalist Life: John Bond of South Carolina and Nova Scotia." *Acadiensis* 19: 2 (Spring 1990), 72-91.

1760

14 March, birth of Walter Bates, in the eastern part of Stamford, Connecticut.
8 July: British naval victory agasint the French at Restigouche.
8 September: with the surrender of Montreal, all French possessions in North America are de facto British.

1762

The first English settlement on the Saint John River area begins with Massachusetts settlers led by Francis Peabody. They move downriver to establish Maugerville.

1763

10 February: The Seven Years' War ends with the Treaty of Paris.

1764

The area at the mouth of the Saint John has about 400 inhabitants.
1 March: trading enterprise for the mouth of the Saint John is established at Portland Point (Saint John).

1765

Sunbury County is established as the northernmost county of Nova Scotia (it includes most of future NB).

1770

3 February: The *Betsy*, the first schooner built on the river Saint John (by the firm of Simonds and White at Portland Point), sails for Newburyport, Massachusetts, under Captain Jonathan Leavitt.

1774

15 June: Reverend Seth Noble becomes resident pastor in Maugerville (the first on the river Saint John).

1775

There are between 1,200 and 1,500 inhabitants along the Saint John valley. About 30 families are at Passamaquoddy.
Young Loyalist Walter Bates is arrested and tortured.

1776

A Court of Common Pleas is held for the first time at Saint John.
4 July: American Declaration of Independence.
12 November: the Eddy Rebellion: Jonathan Eddy attacks Fort Cumberland (Aulac) in support of the American Revolution, but fails.

1777

Fort Howe is built within the territory of today's city of Saint John.

1780

King George III approves plans for the establishment of a new province between the St Croix and Penobscot (Maine), to be called New Ireland.

1782

30 November: Paris agreement. Britain recognises the independence of the thirteen colonies. Preparations to evacuate loyalist refugees.

1783

18 May: Loyalists begin landing (the spring fleet, with c. 3,000) on the site that will become St John, NB. By the time the final fleet arrives on 17 October, about 7,000 new settlers had come to NB in one year.
Bates appears in the ship's manifest as single, occupation farmer, from Stamford.
18 December: At Carleton (Saint John), Loyalists William Lewis and John Ryan publish NB's first newspaper, *The Royal Gazette and Nova-Scotia Intelligencer.*

1784

NB portioned off NS (c. 17,000 Loyalists form the population of NB; 14,000 new arrivals) under Governor Carleton, who arrives from London. Ward Chipman arrives as Solicitor General. NB divided into seven counties; "parishes" created where settlement had occurred.

10 September: the Privy Council of Great Britain approves an official Great Seal of New Brunswick.

6 October: The first murder, reported by Dr. Samuel Moore of Saint John. John Mosley, a black man, was killed with a pitchfork by his wife Nancy. She is found guilty (3 February 1785) and sentenced to branding with the letter M on her thumbs.

1785

Parrtown and Carleton are amalgamated by Royal Charter and St John is thereby incorporated as a city (Canada's first city) and shire town of the newly created Saint John County.

22 February: Governor Carleton orders the survey of a town at St Anne's Point, to be called "Frederick's Town" after the king's second son, the Duke of York. King's County is created on 4 July.

October: First provincial election in NB; riot at Mallard's Tavern (troops from rt Howe intervene).

1786

irst sitting of the NB legislature is held in Saint John

: David Nelson and William Harboard shoot and kill Pierre Bonwah, a unty Maliseet in his canoe on the river St. John (over a dispute about ogs). At the trial in June in Fredericton, they are found guilty of lson is hanged.

, "An Act for preventing idleness and disorders, and for punishing nds, and other idle and disorderly persons."

e invited to make assessments for the building of public gaol house.

1788

of Assembly meets in Fredericton for the first time, in the House; some members are unable to attend because of

1789

tic performances in NB: *The Busy Body* and *Who's the* ohn (in the Long Room of the Mallard House on

1792

ips carrying 1,180 freed slaves sails from Halifax

1794

the Duke of Kent (son of George III) the Chipman House) and Fredericton (at

800

1809

New regulations regarding the import of timber for the British market come into effect, with the government guaranteeing the safety of imports from British North America.

1811

Jonathan Odell, "Song for the 104th"

2 May: Henry Chubb begins the *New Brunswick Courier* in Saint John.

1812

Jonathan Odell, "The Battle of Queens Town, Upper Canada"

12 June: The US Congress declares war on Great Britain, citing especially naval blockades and seizure of American sailors at sea.

27 June: At Saint John, owners of the sloop *General Smyth* apply for a letter of marque to cruise against American ships. They do not receive it, but they will engage in privateering during the War of 1812.

1813

16 February: First company of NB's 104th Regiment of Foot leaves Fredericton for Kingston, Ontario. 600 men march 1,100 km on snowshoes, in 52 days.

1814

Henry More Smith is brought to Kingston Gaol.

1815

1 March: End of the War of 1812. No more privateering.

12 July: Ward Chipman is appointed agent for Great Britain in the boundary dispute with the US over the Fundy Islands. Chipman succeeds in defending the British claim over the Grand Manan Island.

1816

Walter Bates and four other citizens of Kingston join the Society for Promoting Christian Knowledge in London.

20 May: NB's first steamboat (launched on 11 April), the *General Smyth* sails from Saint John to Fredericton, with a stop in Maugerville.

1817

Walter Bates, The Mysterious Stranger, *first and second edition in New Haven; a Halifax edition; two London editions.*

The population of NB is about 35,000.

1818

27 May: Saint John and Halifax are declared free ports, in order to avoid trac restrictions with the US.

1821

2 October: Duel between George Ludlow Wetmore and George Frede Street. Wetmore dies and Street flees to Maine, though he is later acquitte murder.

1824

Fist census in NB: 74,176 inhabitants. St John County has 12,907 (c.12, the city itself). Fredericton, maybe 1,200 or less. 1,403 people of colo population of Kings' County is 7,930.

Julia Beckwith Hart, *St Ursula's Convent; or, The Nun in Canada.*

1825

Oliver Goldsmith, *The Rising Village*

Peter Fisher, *Sketches of New Brunswick*

Anthony Lockwood, *Map of New Brunswick*

The Great Miramichi Fire, largest ever recorded in the Maritimes. One fifth of NB burns. Fire ends on 7 October; 15,000 left homeless.

1827

28 July: The steamer *Saint John* begins service between Saint John and Eastport, Maine.

1829

1 January: Kings College (UNB) and the Old Arts Building (Sir Howard Douglas Hall) officially opened by Sir Howard Douglas, lieutenant-governor.

1830

23 June: A "pest-house" is established on Partridge Island after smallpox and typhus are reported on immigrant ships.

1833

Peter Fisher, *The Lay of the Wilderness*

20 June: The *Maid of the Mist*, a steamboat running regularly between Saint John and Windsor, Nova Scotia, has its 20-hour maiden voyage.

1834

The population of New Brunswick is 119,457. In Saint John County live 20,668 people. In King's County, 12,195.

Oliver Goldsmith, *The Rising Village* (revised)

1835

14 November: First lunatic asylum in NB opens in Saint John under Dr. George Peters (he had led the movement to segregate the insane from criminals).

1836

8 March: The Saint Andrews and Quebec Rail Road Company is incorporated.

1837

Third edition of The Mysterious Stranger *published by Cunnabell in Halifax.*

1838

Peter Fisher, *Notitia of New Brunswick*

14 August: New city water works, including fire hydrants, in Saint John.

1839

8 February: Aroostook War breaks out in Madawaska.

16 September: George Fenety founds the first penny newspaper in the Maritimes, in Saint John: *The Commercial News and General Advertiser* (later called the *Morning News*).

1840

Another third edition of The Mysterious Stranger *is published by Avery in Saint John.*

The population of New Brunswick is 156,162.

10 August: First balloon ascension in Canada by Monsieur L.A. Lauriat, from Barrack Square in Saint John.

1841

The Amaranth; a Monthly Magazine begins publication in Saint John.

1842

11 February: Walter Bates dies in Kingston, New Brunswick.

5 April: First museum in Canada opens in Saint John at the Mechanics Institute: the Gesner Museum.

9 August: The Webster-Ashburton Treaty defines the Maine-New Brunswick border.

CPSIA information can be obtained
at www.ICGtesting.com
Printed in the USA
BVHW050746240223
659125BV00006B/114